Restore the Respect

Restore the Respect
How to Mediate School Conflicts and Keep Students Learning

by

Ondine Gross

Nationally Certified School Psychologist
Champaign, Illinois

Baltimore • London • Sydney

Paul H. Brookes Publishing Co.
Post Office Box 10624
Baltimore, Maryland 21285-0624
USA

www.brookespublishing.com

Typeset by Progressive Publishing Services, Emigsville, Pennsylvania.
Manufactured in the United States of America by
Sheridan Books, Chelsea, Michigan.

Case stories and mediation examples are composites based on the author's experiences or were
created for instructional purposes. Real stories and actual names and identifying details are used
by permission. All interviews held with administrators and personnel at Centennial High School
have been edited and condensed for narrative purposes.

Author photograph © Jon Dessen, Illini Studio.

Library of Congress Cataloging-in-Publication Data

The Library of Congress has cataloged the print edition as follows:

Names: Gross, Ondine, author.
Title: Restore the respect : how to mediate school conflicts and keep students learning / by Ondine
    Gross, School Psychologist and Student Services Department Chair, Centennial High School,
    Champaign, Illinois.
Description: Baltimore, Maryland : Paul H. Brookes Publishing Co., 2016. | Includes bibliographical
    references and index.
Identifiers: LCCN 2015043863 (print) | LCCN 2016004235 (ebook) | ISBN 9781598579420
    (paperback) | ISBN 9781598579727 (pdf) | ISBN 9781598579734 (epub)
Subjects: LCSH: Teacher–student relationships. | Mediation. | Conflict management. |
    Behavior modification. | Student suspension—Prevention. | BISAC: EDUCATION /
    Classroom Management | EDUCATION / Teacher & Student Mentoring | EDUCATION /
    Decision-Making & Problem Solving | EDUCATION / Behavioral Management |
    EDUCATION / Counseling/General.
Classification: LCC LB1033 .G765 2016 (print) | LCC LB1033 (ebook) | DDC 371.102/3—dc23
LC record available at http://lccn.loc.gov/2015043863

British Library Cataloguing in Publication data are available from the British Library.

2020   2019   2018   2017   2016

10   9   8   7   6   5   4   3   2   1

Contents

About the Forms

Purchasers of this book may download the filled-in forms found in this book (Figure 2.4, Figure 4.2, Figure 4.3, Figure 4.4, Figure 7.12, Figure 9.1, Figure 9.3, Figure 9.4, Figure 9.5, and Figure 10.10), and may download, print, and/or photocopy the blank forms in Appendix A: Your Mediation Toolbox and Appendix B: Tier II Intervention Guide for educational or professional use. These materials are included with the print book and are also available at **www.brookespublishing .com/gross/materials** for both print and e-book buyers.

About the Author

Ondine Gross, M.S., Ed.M., is a nationally certified school psychologist who has worked in public school settings for more than 30 years. She began her career in diverse California public school districts, and the California Association of School Psychologists named her an "Outstanding School Psychologist." While in California, Ondine earned licenses as a marriage and family therapist and as a licensed educational psychologist.

In Champaign, Illinois, Ondine has worked as the school psychologist at Centennial High School. In Illinois, she became a licensed clinical professional counselor and a mediator. She earned a master's degree in educational policy, organization, and leadership from the University of Illinois at Urbana-Champaign as well as certification to be a school administrator. In addition to her school psychology duties, Ondine is Centennial High School's student services department chair.

Ondine speaks publicly on a wide range of topics related to students and families. She has appeared on TV and radio and has presented to national professional conferences, school districts, and parent and community groups. Ondine and her husband live in Champaign and Chicago and are the proud parents of twin daughters.

Foreword

Ondine Gross shows her wisdom and years of school experience in this important book. Having worked in numerous school settings with challenging discipline problems, she offers us something quite different from the same old reactive discipline approach. Though consistent with the proactive approach of positive behavior supports (PBS), she goes well beyond PBS to get to real solutions to daily classroom management challenges, disrespect, and never-ending power struggles. In schools where children come from challenging home environments, and teachers feel overwhelmed and underappreciated, Ondine hones in on the true prerequisite to better behavior, establishing trust, caring, and mutual respect between teachers and students.

As Ondine points out, disciplinary actions are reactive and do not typically solve chronic disobedience in the classroom. They often worsen situations by breaking down trust and escalating power struggles. Both teachers and students need to learn more effective ways to relate to each other rather than being punished. Through teacher–student mediation, Ondine helps us find a better way to increase mutual understanding, get to the bottom of conflicts, and improve behavior. The proof is in the positive outcome data she reports.

The mediation strategies she provides are extended to student to student conflicts as well as conflicts between adults. In a clear, concise way, Ondine explains the rationale for mediation and the strategies to implement mediations and provides all the tools and forms necessary to succeed. Every school should adopt *Restore the Respect* as a key resource to improving relationships in school settings! Having spent my entire career in school settings, first in inner-city schools and then in suburban schools supporting students with special needs, I often found that the largest focus of my work was helping teachers and students better understand each other. Only with greater understanding would teachers be willing to entertain suggested supports. I wish I had *Restore the Respect* earlier in my career so I could have had such a clear framework for improving these crucial relationships.

Jed Baker, Ph.D.
Director of the Social Skills Training Project
Author of No More Meltdowns

Preface

I've learned that people will forget what you said, people will
forget what you did, but people will never forget how you
made them feel.

—Maya Angelou

Students about teachers: "My teacher hates me"…"Everybody was talking but he sent me out!"…"If she doesn't show me respect, why should I show her respect?"…"Mr. Jones plays favorites!"

Teachers about students: "I used to get along great with Brittany, but now she's rude to me and I don't know why"…"Joe will not put away his phone and stop talking, no matter how many times I ask"…"Rosie comes to class and puts her head down. This never used to happen before"…"Between you and me, Willy will not shut up!"

Students about students: "If I see Mark walking down the hall, I'm going to kick his @$%!" "Mary keeps staring at me!" "Kim is saying %@#$ about me on _____ [Facebook, Instagram, Twitter—fill in blank depending on year]."

Teachers about teachers: "Linda and I will never agree on how to teach reading!"…"Alan has his own way of doing things"…"Tammy and I grade our students very differently, and I'm tired of talking about this!"

Teachers about administrators: "When will Mr. Chase realize that I just want to be left alone to teach my class?"…"What now!? Another 'flavor of the month' program? Great!"…"I sent Ricky out of my class for rude behavior, and all he got was 'a talk' from the administrator."

In my more than 30 years of frontline experience as a school psychologist in large, busy, and diverse public schools, I have often wondered how schools can function amidst the number of unresolved conflicts in the air:

- A high school sophomore curses at a teacher, gets suspended, and then a few hours or days later returns to class as though nothing happened.

- A seventh-grade teacher writes up dozens of disciplinary referrals sending a misbehaving student to the office. The receiving school administrator has already issued countless consequences from the code of conduct, including detention minutes, time in the in-school suspension room, a call home, parent conferences, and a 3-day out-of-school suspension—and there is no improvement.

- A high school freshman fights and risks getting suspended or possibly arrested because of a "he said–she said" rumor blown out of proportion by peers.

- A third-grade teacher is professional and polite but refrains from engaging in earnest dialogue with colleagues or administrators, misses meetings, and does not respond to emails. This behavior lasts for years.

- A parent of a fifth grader misses work in order to pick up her son from school because he was disobedient—again. On the way home, he says he hates school and never wants to go back. But he returns the next day, and 3 days later the parent gets another call to pick him up. There is no improvement in his attitude and behavior.

While rocky roads and challenges are an inevitable part of the life of any family or organization, unresolved conflicts can lead to high frustration, low motivation, and a downtrodden environment. Successfully educating the nation's children is everybody's business; yet with all the money that is poured into education to overhaul everything from the curriculum, to assessment practices, to the use of technology, one can forget that schools are made up of people, and how people treat each other makes all the difference. Relationships matter!

Students perform best when they believe their teachers care about them (Hughes, 2011). If students feel that a teacher dislikes them, they may refuse to come to school. Or, if they attend school, they may withdraw, underperform, or become disruptive. Then they will miss instruction due to disciplinary consequences involving removal from the classroom. This quickly affects attendance, academic achievement, and graduation rates. Teenagers may be experiencing hormonal swings, ups and downs in their peer relationships, distractions by cell phones and technology, and real-life hardships. If students' conflicts are with other students, their behavior and performance are also affected, and learning is compromised.

I have tremendous respect for instructors who teach a room full of children with vastly different learning styles, personalities, and emotional needs. Teachers are also a product of their own backgrounds, training, and belief systems. They can be stressed out and burned out, particularly by students who do not behave as they should, and those "shoulds" can differ from teacher to teacher, and classroom to classroom—hence the conflicts and confusion. Many teachers are frustrated because they are responsible for effectively teaching all students yet do not always have the opportunity or skill set to repair relationships that go awry. Teachers benefit from positive collaboration with other adults, but when those relationships are stressful, avoidance and isolation result, thereby decreasing the opportunities for professional growth. Improved relationships bring back the joy of teaching.

What are the costs of unresolved conflicts for school administrators? Administrators must constantly put out fires to keep schools safe. Rule-breaking students are sent to them, but the code of conduct book does not have all the answers. Assigning 200 detention minutes will not have an impact on a student who has already had 3,700 minutes. Removing a student from the classroom will not improve that student's learning. But what is the alternative when the student's ongoing disruptions have an impact on other learners and the teacher's ability to teach? And what about adult conflicts? An administrator's duty to provide leadership and promote positive collaboration is undermined when staff members are disgruntled. Administrators also supervise employees who assist with clerical tasks, food, and the cleanliness and operation of the facility. What if those staff members avoid each other, and it has an impact on the smooth operation of the school? Lastly, administrators must exhibit a respectful and productive partnership with parents. (In this book, the word *parents* includes guardians, grandparents, foster parents, or other adults in supportive roles with children.) If parents and teachers are in conflict, this may adversely affect a child, and parents may avoid coming to school altogether if they are only hearing about their children's misbehavior.

To make matters worse, many school conflicts cross racial lines. National data show that black males are disproportionately removed from educational settings for infractions. African-American males and students with disabilities are the most heavily affected by discipline policies that exclude them from their education (Klotz, 2014). There is an urgent need for continuing dialogue and solutions to address these disparities.

As a school psychologist, I felt like a plumber who heard the same dripping faucets for decades, and I even had a decent set of wrenches. I was eager to jump in to do what I could to help. But as any plumber knows, you fix one faucet and sooner or later, another faucet springs a leak. While I have kept quite busy repairing one faucet at a time, I needed some fresh ideas. This book is about that quest, and it started when my twin daughters left home for college.

As an empty nester with time on my hands, I sought to learn new skills and a way to volunteer in the community. I heard about an organization called Prairie Land Conflict Mediation Center that provided a standard 40-hour mediation training in return for donating mediation services in the community. I signed up immediately. I also decided to go back to school.

I enrolled at the College of Education at the University of Illinois at Urbana-Champaign to obtain administrative certification and a master's degree in educational policy, organization, and leadership. Not many school psychologists become school administrators because we love the work we do with students and families. However, I knew that such an education could broaden my skills, knowledge, and practice, and I was right. I learned about the impact of poverty on learning, the achievement gap among different racial and socioeconomic groups, and that trends in education were moving away from zero tolerance disciplinary procedures toward more humanistic interventions designed to keep students in school. I also learned about the importance of visionary, courageous leadership.

My new knowledge of mediation and school leadership started to percolate. One summer day in 2011, I visited Centennial High School, my workplace since 1993, in order to clock administrative internship hours for my diploma. Centennial High School is a socioeconomically and ethnically diverse public high school with close to 1,400 students in the college town of Champaign, Illinois. On that day, I was supposed to help our associate principal plan the master schedule for the upcoming school year. Lucky for me, serendipity played a hand. I came upon two talented administrators standing at a white board listing new ways to intervene with students who had multiple disciplinary infractions. They were in the beginning stages of using positive behavioral interventions and supports (PBIS) principles to construct a response to intervention (RTI) multi-tiered system of schoolwide positive behavior support (SWPBS). They sought to improve student behavior and better address disciplinary problems. The board had Tier I, Tier II, and Tier III sectioned off. As an uninvited, "passing through" person who had not been there all day with them, somehow I found the courage to blurt out, "Hey, can I start doing teacher–student mediations?" They said, "Okay," and added Teacher–Student Mediation under the Tier II heading. This book tells the story of what happened next.

While I had experience in hundreds of meetings helping parents and children work through conflict and improve communication, it was less common to meet with teachers and students. But how many times did a minor teacher–student conflict snowball into something bigger and embed itself into daily life, affecting the climate of the classroom and other learners? How hard would it be to provide a safe, structured way for teachers and students to hear one another's perspectives, clear up a misunderstanding, and develop a plan to move forward? I was curious to see if the structure and principles of mediation could be used to resolve conflicts and improve relationships among teachers and students. I had many questions: Would mediation even work? Would teachers be resistant? How would we measure effectiveness? Would students like it? Would it have a positive impact on school climate? Would parents appreciate it? As a parent of public school students, I knew the sinking feeling of hearing your child come home to say, "My teacher hates me."

I began conducting teacher–student mediations at Centennial High School in the 2011–2012 school year and observed something extraordinary: Away from the hubbub of the classroom and all the other students, away from grade books and discussions of missing assignments, the structure of mediation provided a teacher and student with the opportunity to speak with a different voice, hear with different ears, and see with a different perspective. I was touched as I saw teachers lean in and show care, compassion, and a sincere desire to help their students. I was moved to see students rise to the occasion and respectfully, honestly, and appropriately express themselves to an adult. People were real in these meetings, speaking about hopes, goals, and frustrations. Sometimes there were tears. Sometimes there were hugs. Teachers and students relaxed and beamed when positive statements were made: "I like Ms. Reynolds because she cares"…"Martin makes really insightful comments."

The universal human need to be understood and validated cannot be underestimated, and the structure of the mediation facilitated these game-changing moments. People could tell their full stories without interruption; they were heard nonjudgmentally; and they were given a safe space to address concerns, make amends, and move forward. Mediation allowed teachers and students alike to move away from "the danger of a single story" (so beautifully described in the 2009 TED talk by Chimamanda Ngozi Adichie) to a more nuanced, multifaceted understanding of one another. Adichie said, "The single story creates stereotypes, and the problem with stereotypes is not that they are untrue, but that they are incomplete. They make one story become the only story." The mediation revealed that the "student who doesn't care" in fact does care, and the "unfair teacher" in fact is struggling to be fair.

Because the introduction of teacher–student mediations occurred simultaneously with the implementation of a multi-tiered system of SWPBS at Centennial High School, I wasn't the only one who saw positive outcomes. There were the data to prove it. For 3 years straight, approximately 80% of the time, there were no further office disciplinary referrals from a teacher to a student who participated in a mediation. A survey conducted at Centennial High School asked teachers who had participated in mediations to rate the following statement as true or false: "The addition of teacher–student mediations to Centennial Tier II interventions is a positive step toward improving student behavior and learning." Eighty-seven percent of the teachers picked "True." Mediation as a Tier II intervention was here to stay. It made sense to focus attention on ways to reduce conflict and improve understanding between the two most important individuals in a school: a teacher and a student. What took us so long?

After personally conducting more than 200 teacher–student mediations, I am writing this book to share this easy, common-sense intervention as well as tips and insights I've obtained as a public school insider. Filled with humor and real-life examples, this book is for anyone who is eager to learn a new way to resolve conflicts, improve relationships, and build trust.

This teacher–student mediation technique restores the respect so that teachers can teach and students can learn. The minute a student walks into the school building and a teacher walks into a classroom, there is an investment of time, hope, and expectations. The mediation techniques introduced in this book were simplified from my own training and adapted for use in schools by busy people like me. They are quick, easy, efficient, and doable in a typical 50-minute class period. While this technique employs mediation principles, it is not to be confused with the more complex negotiation work outlined in outstanding books such as *Getting to Yes* (Fisher, Ury, & Patton, 2011) or used by professional mediators in divorces, property disputes, and so forth.

This book begins with a description of traditional disciplinary policies and why a school's code of conduct alone is inadequate. I cite the 2014 U.S. Department of Education pleas to come up with better solutions. There is a national call to action to move away from zero tolerance policies toward interventions that promote mental health and social-emotional learning and that teach appropriate behaviors: prosocial communication, anger management, and conflict resolution skills. I also discuss the need to bridge racial and cultural divides, to foster trust, and to move toward greater teacher reflection and courageous leadership.

For those readers, particularly school administrators, who wish to understand RTI, PBIS, and SWPBS, Chapter 2 provides an overview of those initiatives, discusses the challenges and benefits of organizing a multi-tiered system of supports (MTSS) to address student needs, and explains how and why Centennial High School adopted an MTSS. (I use MTSS as an umbrella term for these initiatives.) I present compelling before and after data that the implementation of a system of MTSS significantly reduced the number of student disciplinary referrals and suspensions across all student demographics.

For readers wishing to learn how to conduct teacher–student mediations, Chapter 3 provides a thorough explanation of what mediation is and why it is important to mediate with teachers and students. In Chapter 4, I provide comprehensive training on how to conduct effective teacher–student mediations using dialogues and examples. The mediation technique can be used at the secondary level (Grades 6–12) and may also be modified for use with younger children.

In Chapter 5, I discuss the skills necessary to conduct mediations, with special emphasis on the importance of identifying one's own biases and beliefs in order to be more open and nonjudgmental. I present a communications skills refresher, including a reflective listening pop quiz.

In Chapter 6, I discuss many root causes of stressors that have an impact on teachers and students. Sometimes the reason for a student's acting-out behavior or need for mediation is a manifestation of a deeper problem, and I provide guidance for how to respond. I also share examples of mediations and problem-solving strategies and discuss how mediations are effective with students who receive general and special education.

Many wonder if teachers are resistant to mediation with students, and in Chapter 7, I discuss how to address possible teacher resistance and/or the perception that mediation might represent a shift in power. I additionally show feedback from surveys and discuss how to make adjustments based on the feedback. In Chapter 8, I present 3 years' worth of data-based evidence showing the utilization, growth, and success rates of teacher–student mediation as a Tier II intervention at Centennial High School. The majority of student participants in teacher–student mediation at Centennial High School are African-American; hence, mediation is a positive way to boost understanding and rapport across racial lines and promote learning.

In Chapter 9, I present the mediation technique for use with students and an adult mediator, which may be used to address student conflicts and bullying and to prevent fights. I share the step-by-step mediation technique, problem-solving strategies, and examples of student contracts, reporting how Centennial High School added student mediation to its Tier II supports and that 88% of the students who participated had no further disciplinary action due to conflicts with their mediation partner.

Finally, in Chapter 10, I advocate for adult mediation to be used in schools among staff and between parents and staff to encourage more respectful, honest, and productive practices. Appendix A in this book contains printable mediation referral forms, teacher and student feedback forms, and a sample follow-up letter. Also included are three samples of student contracts. Appendix B contains specific descriptions of Centennial High School's Tier II supports and a sample data collection chart.

Throughout the book, I have inserted voices from students, teachers, and administrators and use composites of realistic dialogues and examples. The book is intended to provide comprehensive training on mediation in schools and introduce a fresh, practical intervention to restore the respect, reduce suspensions, improve social skills, and keep students learning.

Here is an added bonus: Many people I have trained to mediate in schools have happily shared with me that they used the same techniques at home with family members with great success! Mediation provides a safe structure for sharing, listening, understanding, and even empathizing with another person, and these are the foundations for any healthy relationship.

Acknowledgments

This book would not be written were it not for the following organizations and individuals:

Prairie Land Conflict Resolution and Mediation Center, in Champaign, Illinois—a grassroots, community-based nonprofit organization promoting peace.

Centennial High School's visionary administrators: Principal Greg Johnson and Administrators Ryan Cowell, Tony Maltbia, Charles Neitzel, and Angela Schoonover. Their humanity, excellence, and dedication allowed the mediation program to flourish. You are my dream team. I also thank our superintendent, Judy Wiegand.

The inspiring and richly diverse students, teachers, and families I have been privileged to work with throughout my career, and most recently at Centennial High School: Thank you for trusting me with your personal stories and struggles.

My University of Illinois at Urbana-Champaign College of Education professors: Kern Alexander, Carolyn Little, Linda Sloat, and Laura Taylor. I also thank Shirlee Davis, Jerome Glover, and Herschel Swinger, former California State University, Los Angeles professors, for their humor, wisdom, and guidance on my path toward school psychology.

The National Association of School Psychologists, for encouraging practitioners to "shine a light" on effective school-based practices by presenting at national conventions. I also thank the many school psychologists, counselors, social workers and school nurses I have been blessed to work with and learn from.

Gratitude to Rebecca Lazo of Brookes Publishing Co. for her openness, enthusiasm, and editing expertise. Thank you for championing this book and being a steadfast ally throughout the process. I also thank Kimberly Beauchamp for outstanding editing assistance, and Cathy Jewell and the entire Brookes staff for their talent and many contributions to this book.

My first readers, who gave me their frank reactions and insightful suggestions: Margareth Etienne, Meghan Gentry, Arielle Gross, George Gross, Gianna Gross, and Krystyna Newman. It takes a village to write a book; however, all errors are my own, and I take full responsibility for them.

My "tribe"—the people that have graced my life with their wisdom, humor, and love: Magalie Austin, Marianne Carter, Frankie Conner, Margareth Etienne, Terence Fitzgerald, John Greer, Linda Greenberg, Elizabeth Hogan, Jacqueline Jochims, Joseph LiVecchi, Krystyna Newman, Lisa Quateman, and Susan Schneider.

My loving parents and extended family for showing me that humor, patience, and ongoing communication help us through any challenge.

And lastly, this book would not be written were it not for the love and unflagging support of my husband, George, and daughters, Arielle and Gianna. I am grateful for you, I am proud of you, and I love you dearly.

For children…
and those who care for them

A Call to Action

Reforming Discipline, Improving Relationships, and Building Better Schools

If you do what you always did, you will get what you always got.

—Anonymous

Scruffy-haired, baby-faced Johnny said, "Shut your face!" to his fifth-grade teacher. Shy, 12-year-old Hannah suddenly threw books off the shelf in her classroom. Feisty 16-year-olds Louie and Ethan shoved each other in the cafeteria. For decades, the only reaction to these kinds of misbehaviors was to discipline the students. The problem is that discipline, whose root is the Latin word *disciplina*—meaning "to teach"—is typically delivered as a punishment. Usually, an administrator calls home, a parent or guardian has to come to the school, and the school penalizes the student. At no point in such a situation is the *teaching* part of the school's disciplinary consequence addressed, nor do the administrators fully examine the underlying causes of the behavior. If there are counselors, social workers, or school psychologists (i.e., student services staff) in the building, they might never be consulted about a student's misbehavior. Student services staff are expected to promote children's social-emotional development and provide guidance and support, but due to time and logistical or even philosophical constraints, they are not always consulted when it comes to the delivery of disciplinary consequences.

THE PROBLEMS WITH TRADITIONAL DISCIPLINE POLICIES

What are traditional discipline policies? They can be found in most schools' codes of conduct, where each infraction and consequence is listed. Take, for example, consequences for disruptive behavior and disobedience. For a first offense, detention may be given. This generally means that the student must sit in a designated spot for a period of time before or after school or during a lunch period. For a second offense, the student's parent or guardian might be asked to come to the school for a conference, and the student may be given a one-day (in-school or out-of-school) suspension. What if the infraction involves a student expressing profanity to a staff member? The first offense could mean a parent conference and up to a 3-day out-of-school suspension. If there is a second offense, the suspension could last up to 5 days. Repeated offenses could bring other 5-day suspensions, reassignment to an alternative school, or expulsion. All of these compounding consequences remove the student from the learning environment and can create a harmful cycle for the student.

Consider the following example: Mark, a high-energy ninth grader with a bushel of red hair, disobeys his algebra teacher, Ms. Colton, by refusing to stop talking and disrupting other learners. Mark is generally a good student, but algebra is his least favorite subject, and he often struggles to understand new concepts. This algebra class meets directly after lunch, and Mark is playfully bantering with three other students. Ms. Colton, who sees that Mark is the instigator of all the chatter, issues three warnings, and finally, in exasperation, sends Mark to the office with a disciplinary referral (DR). It is Mark's first DR of the school year, so the administrator, Ms. Reese, has a talk with Mark. She attempts to get to know him, build a rapport, and explain to Mark the reasons why talking in class is disruptive. Ms. Reese assigns detention minutes that Mark may serve after school or during lunch. Mark fails to show up at the assigned time and is observed by a hall monitor to be with his friends instead. This situation compounds his punishment, so the next day, Mark has to serve a full school day of detention. This time, he shows up to the detention room, but it had not been possible for the school staff to gather all of his relevant classroom assignments in time to coincide with his detention. The reading, puzzles, and other busywork Mark is given does not hold his interest, and Mark finds it impossible to sit quietly. Soon, he becomes disruptive. The detention supervisor reprimands and redirects him, but this turns into a shouting match in which Mark uses profanity. Mark again compounds his punishment; he has to return to the administrator and gets sent home for a 3-day suspension period.

Upon Mark's reentry into the classroom after serving his suspension, there is no discussion with his teacher, Ms. Colton, about what occurred. Mark has been simmering about the original DR that Ms. Colton wrote because he thought it was wrong that he was punished when others were talking just as much. Mark must simply return to the class and pick up where he left off. But rejoining a class is like entering a movie theater 70 minutes after the show starts. Mark does not understand the lesson, assignments, discussions, and activities. Because this is an algebra class, Mark has lost critical instruction on early building block skills due to his time away from the classroom. He feels confused and overwhelmed when he attempts to reintegrate himself to the lesson, and he raises his hand in order to get help from the teacher. Ms. Colton cannot help Mark right away because the class has to review for an upcoming unit exam. Mark thinks, "Doesn't she see my hand?" He becomes angry that Ms. Colton is ignoring him. Mark erupts with another verbal outburst, and the cycle starts again. What if this continues to happen to Mark on a frequent basis? What if he repeatedly cycles through these consequences?

Too often, the same sequences of traditional disciplinary practices are enacted over and over in the classroom without causing behavior to change. There is a long-standing consensus in educational research that the typical punishments are not effective and do not improve student behavior (Gottfredson, 1997; Loosen & Skiba, 2010; Maag, 2001; Skiba, 2000) and that such punishments only provide short-term solutions—they have no long-term effects on student behavior (Carr et al., 1999; Skiba & Peterson, 1999) and are reactive rather than proactive.

As illustrated in Mark's case, traditional disciplinary measures do not allow for examining the root cause of problematic behavior or provide an organized system for teaching students better ways to behave. Mark may have told his version of events to the administrator or his parents, but the discussion ended there, and no provisions were made for Mark's transition back to the class. Though Ms. Colton is an excellent teacher who runs a lively class and often interjects humor in the lesson, Mark now has no sense of belonging; he feels misunderstood and believes that nobody cares about or supports him even when he is trying (his hand was up!). Ms. Colton tries to develop a better relationship with Mark, but mutual suspicion and mistrust have set in after the first time Mark misbehaved. There is not enough time or a safe means to rebuild the trust and respect that is necessary in a teacher–student relationship, so the cycle of misbehavior, futile consequences, and negative feelings continues. Everyone loses:

- The administrator becomes frustrated because no other disciplinary options besides removal and detention are available.

- Mark's parents become upset about getting so many calls from the school and the need to miss work. They are angry with the school for not doing more to help their child. They worry about Mark's grades.

- Mark's teacher struggles to teach a child who has such sporadic attendance, with one day present and two days absent.

- The school counselor who is involved with and cares about Mark is discouraged because his efforts to promote Mark's participation in positive, supervised, and healthy extracurricular activities are thwarted. Mark's large number of detentions makes him ineligible for team sports and dances.

- The detention room supervisor is hurt and insulted by Mark's behavior in her room. She thought they had a good relationship.

- Mark feels hopeless because he is in a hole and has no clue how to dig himself out. He feels isolated from his peer group, and he remains angry because he believes he is treated unfairly. With his parents forced to leave him at home unsupervised because of repeated suspensions, Mark could, for example, potentially turn to loitering, vandalism, drinking, drug use, drug dealing, or theft as he loses faith in school.

The 2014 U.S. Department of Education report titled *Guiding Principles: A Resource Guide for Improving School Climate and Discipline* noted the various costs of suspension and expulsion as consequences for student misbehavior. For example, students who are suspended and expelled miss out on positive teaching, peer interactions, and adult mentorship within the school environment. They lose out on developing skills that would allow them to improve their behavior and avoid future problems. They also struggle academically; these students typically score lower on standardized tests and have poorer academic achievement. Students who are suspended likely are unsupervised during the day and are at risk for future suspensions, repeating a grade, dropping out, and getting involved in the juvenile justice system. Ultimately, society pays direct and indirect costs. Undereducated people are more likely to be unemployed, earn less when employed, be saddled with greater poverty-related health problems, or be incarcerated.

Although suspensions and expulsions can have detrimental effects, a 2011 study by Boccanfuso and Kuhfeld found that 95% of out-of-school suspensions were for seemingly minor disruptions such as disrespect or tardiness. How is student disrespect defined? Is Kevin disrespectful because he did not open a book? Is Olga disrespectful because she rolled her eyes? It depends on who you ask. Tardiness is not straightforward either. Is Manny tardy if he is not seated when the bell rings? Is Kiki tardy if she is at the classroom entrance when the bell rings? Is Sue tardy if she sets her books down and dashes to the restroom, returning just after the bell rings? Determining misbehavior is a subjective process that can change based on circumstance or the interpretation of those in authority.

Also troubling about today's common school discipline practices is the unfortunate but well-documented phenomenon that discipline policies that exclude students from their education have the most impact on black males and students with disabilities (Klotz, 2014). Skiba, Michael, Nardo, and Peterson (2002) cited findings from 25 years of research that "consistently found evidence of socioeconomic and racial disproportionality in the administration of school discipline" (p. 318). Studies have shown that race matters more than socioeconomic class and that black students are more likely to be sent to the office for infractions that could be interpreted subjectively (Skiba et al., 2002). Should sandy-haired Kevin, a jovial athlete who wears designer polo shirts and is the son of a school board member, receive a lighter disciplinary consequence for "horseplay" (because "boys will be boys") than Jamar, an African-American 15-year-old residing in the "bad neighborhood" whose single mother works the night shift at the local factory? If Jenny, a blonde cheerleader, disrupts class by teasing and joking with her fellow students, will she receive as harsh a reprimand as Shymira, an African-American volleyball player who is also laughing and trading insults with her classmates? Many educators might answer by proclaiming, "I don't see color!" Yet it is important to acknowledge that the way we see others can be affected by their race, gender, sexuality, (dis)ability, religion, ethnicity, appearance, neighborhood, family background, and socioeconomic status so that we can challenge any assumptions or stereotypes that might be influencing disciplinary practices and the way school staff relate to students. It is also important to consider how school staff are seen by their diverse students. Age, ethnicity, style, warmth, and the formality or informality of communication styles may have an impact on a student's reactions, comfort level, and motivation.

With regard to students with disabilities, a 2015 study by Miller and Meyers noted that male and female students with disabilities were more likely to receive in-school suspensions than students without disabilities. They also found significant differences in the rates of suspensions and drop-out rates across types of disabilities. Students with emotional disabilities had a higher dropout rate, followed by students with learning disabilities, and then students with autism. Students with individualized education programs (IEPs) are entitled to protections if their disciplinary infractions are found to be a manifestation of their disability. Consider the following example.

Roland, a seventh grader with autism spectrum disorder (ASD), performs well with his daily routine. His IEP documents that when there are unexpected changes in his routine, he becomes agitated and shouts profanities. Roland's IEP goals and objectives are to improve his emotional regulation and social skills so that he can better cope with transitions and unexpected circumstances.

One day, Roland's teacher is out sick, and a substitute teacher, Ms. Finkel, is assigned to Roland's morning homeroom class. Roland has a field trip that day and panics because he fears that Ms. Finkel will not know about the field trip. Roland shouts profanities and gets in Ms. Finkel's face, yelling, "I am going to hurt you, you stupid lady!" but does not touch her. Ms. Finkel feels threatened and calls the administrator.

The administrator, who has a positive relationship with Roland, calms him down, contacts Roland's parent, and sends him home for the rest of the day. The school staff follow the code of conduct, and Roland is given a disciplinary consequence. Threatening a teacher is an expellable offense under some circumstances. Roland's IEP team holds a manifestation determination meeting, following proper procedures and protocols, to determine whether Roland's problem behavior was a result of his disability. Because Roland's IEP and school evaluation documented that he becomes agitated and shouts profanities with unexpected transitions, the IEP team determines that Roland's behavior toward Ms. Finkel was a manifestation of his disability, and he is not expelled. Roland's IEP team is instructed, however, to modify Roland's IEP and write goals to specifically teach alternative behaviors to making verbal threats.

When disciplining students, school staff should take care to analyze how they approach, think about, and label each child. As crass as it sounds, there is still a tendency to refer to students as *good* or *bad*. If Steven is a *good kid*, will he be smiled at and given greater leeway for his misbehavior? If Steven is a *bad kid*, will he be treated in a cold, gruff manner? Are good kids entitled to greater sensitivity and understanding, whereas bad kids are not worthy? What does it take for a good kid to be perceived as a bad kid? Could one misunderstanding do the trick? Is there unconscious bias related to racial, class, and ability differences in who is being sent out of the classroom? It is important to ask these tough questions in order to remedy inconsistencies and inequalities in the way staff members handle behavioral issues in schools.

For some schools, the response to inconsistencies and questions of subjectivity in discipline results in the implementation of a *zero tolerance* policy. A zero tolerance policy, as defined by the American Psychological Association Zero Tolerance Task Force in 2008, "mandates the application of predetermined consequences, most often severe and punitive in nature, that are intended to be applied regardless of the gravity of behavior, mitigating circumstances, or situational context" (p. 856). Yet the difficulties faced by students across America—poverty, disability, mental health challenges, a lack of environmental support systems, or a lack of suitable medical care—make zero tolerance policies inhumane as well as ineffective. The 2014 U.S. Department of Education task force reported that zero tolerance policies resulting in the removal of disruptive students through suspension and expulsion were not effective in improving student behavior, school climate, or school safety.

Behavioral infractions that might carry a zero tolerance policy include possessing or selling drugs, bringing a weapon to school, or having a physical confrontation with an adult. The following is an example of an inhumane zero tolerance policy.

It is the first week of high school. Sheila, a quiet, high-achieving 14-year-old freshman, whispers to her friend on the bus that she has a way to protect herself from Hally, a sophomore known to bully other students who has been threatening to fight Sheila. A student overhears the conversation and reports it to Mr. Garcia, a school administrator, when the bus arrives at school. Mr. Garcia calls Sheila into the office and asks her about the conversation on the bus. Mr. Garcia hears about Hally's bullying and how terrified Sheila is. He knows Hally sometimes picks on freshmen and will investigate further. Sheila admits that the way she intended to protect herself was to tell Hally to back off because she had a knife. Sheila has no history of violent behavior and has no intention of using the knife; however, when Mr. Garcia checks Sheila's backpack, he finds a butter knife. Under zero tolerance policy, Sheila is expelled from high school for bringing a weapon to school.

As Sheila's circumstance illustrates, more nuanced, graduated consequences are required for students, but more important, students need to be explicitly instructed on behavioral expectations and given appropriate supports to help improve their behavior. Consider another example.

It is 1:30 p.m. on a Thursday. Ms. Jarvis, single mom to Jason, a bright and popular African-American middle school student, is working at a beauty salon. Today, the afternoon is booked. Her cell phone rings. It is her son's school—she needs to pick up Jason immediately. Jason's father, Mr. Jarvis, is a professional truck driver and is required to be away from home several days each week. On this day, he is out of the state, so the burden to pick up Jason lies with Ms. Jarvis. This is the fourth time this year that Ms. Jarvis has been called.

Ms. Jarvis scrambles to find someone to cover her appointments. She worries about her business and about the clients who might stop coming to her because of this inconvenience. She does not own a car, so she will have to borrow one or take public transportation. Costs are involved before she has even entered the school.

Ms. Jarvis knows the routine for picking Jason up. She goes into the office and spots Jason cowering in a chair with his head down. Mr. Thomas, the principal, tells Ms. Jarvis what Jason did this time. She signs an official letter and is required to take Jason home for the rest of the day and 2 additional days. The letter details Jason's infraction: disobeying a teacher for not sitting in his assigned seat in the class and exiting the class without permission, verbally abusing staff for using profanity toward the teacher, and having a physical confrontation with the teacher. When Jason tried to leave the class, the teacher, Mr. Runyon, blocked the doorway and told Jason he was not permitted to leave. Jason lightly pushed Mr. Runyon's arm off the door handle so that he could leave. Under zero tolerance policy, Jason's physical contact with Mr. Runyon could be grounds for expulsion, but the principal, Mr. Thomas, has already spoken with Mr. Runyon, and expulsion will not be pursued. Mr. Runyon feels he bears some responsibility because he should not have tried to block Jason from exiting the class.

Ms. Jarvis's mind is reeling. She has no child care arrangements. She wonders how the letter she signed will have an impact on Jason's permanent record. What will this mean for his future or how others see him? She has already taken away Jason's favorite electronic devices. She has already grounded him. She has no idea why Jason keeps misbehaving. On the drive home, Jason wants to tell his mother his version of the events, but a frustrated Ms. Jarvis says, "I don't even want to hear you right now. You are grounded."

What is wrong with this scenario?

- Mr. Thomas, the administrator, is continually issuing the same harsh consequence even though there is no improvement in Jason's behavior. Jason is repeatedly removed from the learning environment.

- Ms. Jarvis, Jason's mother, does not know how to stop her son's misbehavior. As a working mother, she struggles to be able to pick up Jason when he is suspended and care for him during the day, which causes her great stress and puts a strain on the family's finances. She has reached her frustration limit and has run out of ideas on how to help her son improve his classroom behavior.

- A school psychologist has an office at the school; however, it does not occur to either Mr. Thomas or Ms. Jarvis to consult with the psychologist. What do school staff know about Jason? What is going on in his life? Is the class too hard or too easy? Is he struggling with personal, learning, or health issues? There is no system of supports to identify reasons for Jason's patterns of misbehavior or to use existing staff members to provide comprehensive, evidence-based interventions that teach him better ways to act.

As a school psychologist who has worked in diverse public school settings for more than 3 decades, I have encountered many students who repeatedly get into trouble. Similar to many other school psychologists, counselors, and social workers, I made it a point to develop a collaborative, trusting relationship with my school administrators and worked to publicize all of the support services offered in the school so staff, students, and families knew we were available to help them. Many administrators were pleased to team up with me or another staff member in student services, but there was no systematic means of communicating about student needs. Administrators are tasked with numerous job responsibilities, including maintaining an effective and orderly learning environment. They have a high-stress job and are on the go throughout the day. Sometimes the physical layout of a school is such that administrators and support staff have little face time. In larger schools, there is insufficient opportunity to collaborate with student services staff every time a student misbehaves.

With no formal system in place, how is it determined which students require only a disciplinary response and which ones might be referred for additional supports, counseling, or an evaluation for special education services? I might be working with Tony, Lyla, and Dan, but why not with Julie and Paul? Our counselor was working with Joaquin and Marcie, but why not Zander, Lisa, and Jordan? We were all very busy, but how effective were our efforts?

CASE STUDY: CENTENNIAL HIGH SCHOOL

My place of employment, Centennial High School, is one of two public high schools in Champaign, Illinois. School demographics regularly shift, with families moving in and out of a district. According to the 2013–2014 Illinois Report Card (Illinois State Board of Education, n.d.), Centennial High School had approximately 1,425 students: 45% White students, 34% Black students, 10% Asian students, 7% Hispanic students, and 4% Multiracial students. Approximately 51% of the students were reported as low income (this number is derived from the number of students who apply for and are granted free and reduced lunches). Centennial High School had experienced rapidly shifting demographics over the 2002 to 2014 school years (see Table 1.1).

In 2002, the Champaign Unit 4 School Board signed a consent decree, a binding agreement imposed by the U.S. District Court for Central Illinois. It required the district to reduce the disparities in academic achievement, discipline, and graduation rates among white and minority students. Over a period of 7 years, administrators spent thousands of hours collaborating with the community and on teacher and staff professional development activities. Policies were reviewed and changed so that school practices would be more equitable. Centennial High School also had frequent changes in leadership. From 1972 to 2004, there were two principals, while between 2004 and 2010, there were four different principals.

In 2010, Centennial High School was required by federal and state regulators to submit a restructuring plan because the school failed to make adequate yearly progress (AYP) for 5 years in a row under the No Child Left Behind Act of 2001 (PL 107-110; NCLB). Under NCLB, Congress reauthorized the Elementary and Secondary Education Act of 1965 (PL 89-10; ESEA). The ESEA was passed to provide states with grants to improve the quality of elementary and secondary schools, and specifically sought to improve the educational opportunities for low-income students and special needs students. Among other sweeping reforms under NCLB, schools that did not show significant student growth (i.e., AYP) in reading and math test scores were restructured. Restructuring at Centennial High School entailed monitoring by the state, specific meetings to examine and revise practices, and the removal of several certified staff members.

In 2010, the school board approved a new team of administrators for Centennial High School, including the principal, Greg Johnson, and an administrator, Angela Schoonover. They walked into a building with extremely low faculty and staff morale, high suspension and office discipline referral rates, and a disproportionate representation of African-American students with disciplinary consequences. One of the first things the new principal said was that the building had no "systems" in place. What did he mean by that? Were we not all doing our jobs and working hard?

Table 1.1. Demographics at Centennial High School

Demographics	2002	2014	Difference
Low socioeconomic status	15.9%	51%	+35.1%
White	75.8%	45%	-30.8%
Black	18.4%	34%	+15.6%
Hispanic	0.8%	7%	+6.2%
Asian/Pacific Islander	4.9%	10%	+5.1%
Two or more races	0.1	4%	+3.9%

Sources: Illinois State Board of Education (n.d.); Illinois State Board of Education (2002).

Principal Greg Johnson: There were no series of interventions....If kids got help from a social worker or if they saw a counselor, or if they got referred to somebody in the community, it was just because there happened to be a conversation that led to that. So the building seemed to be a collection of individual teachers and professionals doing their things, but there was no organized pattern to it.

The new administrator also described the challenges from not having a clear system for intervening with students.

Administrator Angela Schoonover: At Centennial, we didn't have a systematic way of intervening with students. At first, we kind of went with the flow. We referred to it as throwing darts at a dartboard. You never knew what you were going to get. It was a long, tough year.

It was time for some much needed reform that would include a formalized system of supports and interventions. There were several problems with the discipline process in place at Centennial:

- Many students with repeated misbehavior received the same ineffective consequences over and over. Educators did not understand the root cause of the students' misbehavior or explicitly teach students how to meet behavioral expectations. There was no rhyme or reason as to why some students received social-emotional support and others did not. And racial and socioeconomic disparities persisted.

- Parents were frustrated and discouraged. They were not consistently given specific help or appropriate resources to address their children's misbehavior.

- If a child's misbehavior seemed sufficiently severe, the solution might be to test the student for placement into a special education program for students with behavioral and/or emotional disabilities. There was an insufficient system in place prior to the evaluation, however, to apply evidence-based interventions and see whether the student's behavior would improve—thereby negating the need for testing.

- Inadequate steps were taken to explore the overall school climate to see whether it was a supportive environment—particularly for diverse student populations and their families.

- Not enough data were being collected or analyzed to identify patterns and trends on how best to allocate resources to those most in need of interventions and whether the interventions that were being applied were effective.

- Staff and teachers did not deliver interventions consistently.

Centennial High School was steeped in the challenges facing high schools across the nation: to end inequities in disciplinary procedures, to provide more social-emotional supports, and to increase interventions to teach and reinforce appropriate behaviors. A call to action rang out from educational researchers; the U.S. Department of Education; and professional teacher, administrator, social worker, counselor, and school psychologist associations.

Educators needed to respond to the call to action, but how?

RESPONDING TO THE CALL TO ACTION

All children need to be taught that certain behaviors are unacceptable, and penalties can sometimes help maintain order and compliance. However, there is a movement away from zero tolerance and other traditional disciplinary policies toward interventions that promote social-emotional learning (SEL) and that teach appropriate behaviors such as prosocial communication, anger management, and conflict resolution skills. This trend was solidified at a national level when, in January 2014, the U.S. Department of Education released for the very first time a comprehensive School Discipline Guidance Package that provided clear guidelines and action steps for improving school discipline. State, district, and school leaders were asked to use the following three guiding principles when examining current school discipline policies:

> Guiding Principle 1: Climate and Prevention—Take deliberate steps to create the positive school climates that can help prevent and change inappropriate behaviors. Train staff, engage families and community partners, and deploy resources to help students develop the social, emotional and conflict resolution skills needed to avoid and de-escalate the problems. Targeting student supports also helps students address the underlying causes of misbehavior, such as trauma, substance abuse, and mental health issues. (U.S. Department of Education, 2014, pp. 5–11)

> Guiding Principle 2: Clear, Appropriate and Consistent Expectations and Consequences—Ensure that clear, appropriate and consistent expectations and consequences are in place to prevent and address misbehavior. Hold students accountable for their actions in developmentally appropriate ways so that students learn responsibility, respect, and the bounds of acceptable behavior in our schools and society. Rely on suspension and expulsion only as a last resort for serious infractions, and equip staff with alternative strategies to address the problem behaviors while keeping all students engaged in instruction to the greatest extent possible. (U.S. Department of Education, 2014, pp. 11–16)

> Guiding Principle 3: Equity and Continuous Improvement—Schools must understand their civil rights obligations and strive to ensure fairness and equity for all students. Continuously evaluate the impact of disciplinary policies and practices on all students using data and analysis. (U.S. Department of Education, 2014, pp. 16–18)

Teachers also sought an expansion of traditional disciplinary practices. The American Federation of Teachers held a symposium in 2014 that called for

> Thoughtful prevention and intervention practices to make schools safer and more productive…All school staff should receive ongoing professional development and training with a focus on evidence-based positive school discipline, conflict resolution, cultural relevancy and responsiveness, behavior management, social justice and equity.

In Illinois and other states, schools were called upon to develop a framework to use and promote SEL. The Illinois Children's Mental Health Act of

2003 (Public Act 93-0495) specified that by 2004, every school district should develop and submit a policy for "teaching and assessing social emotional skills," among other recommendations (Illinois Department of Healthcare and Family Services, 2003).

Merrell and Gueldner (2010) explained that the term *social-emotional learning* was first coined in 1994 and was influenced by Daniel Goleman's 1995 book *Emotional Intelligence.* Researchers have since found benefits of building SEL programming in schools: "Through developmentally and culturally appropriate classroom instruction and application of learning to everyday situations, SEL programming builds children's skills to recognize and manage their emotions, appreciate the perspectives of others, establish positive goals, make responsible decisions, and handle interpersonal situations" (Greenberg et al., 2003, p. 468). A 2011 meta-analysis of 213 universal K–12 school-based SEL programs taught by classroom teachers reported improvements in academic performance as well as improved social-emotional skills, behaviors, and attitudes (Durlak, Weissberg, Dymnicki, Taylor, & Schellinger, 2011). This study used a model of having the teacher embed SEL lessons into the classroom routine. SEL curriculum may also be taught in individual and/or small group lessons by trained staff.

School support professionals are increasingly tasked with ensuring each student's safe and optimal growth in his or her learning environment. For example, in their 2010 "Model for Comprehensive and Integrated School Psychological Services," the National Association of School Psychologists (NASP) listed many recommendations, including school psychologists' duty to help students succeed academically, socially, behaviorally, and emotionally and to participate in the creation of environments for children that support social and learning activities. Another goal was to help "increase the amount of time students are engaged in learning" (NASP, p. 5). NASP also called for practitioners to provide more comprehensive intervention and mental health services (p. 6). Merrell and Gueldner (2010) cited reports that an estimated 20% of school-age children exhibit mental health problems in any given year (Coie, Miller-Johnson, & Bagwell, 2000; Greenberg et al., 2003).

Educators: We have our marching orders. Across America, our students face difficulties caused by poverty, disability, mental health challenges, a lack of home-based supports, or a lack of suitable medical care. We know that we must all work together and infuse our academic institutions with interventions that promote and teach appropriate behaviors and problem-solving skills. We need to bridge racial and cultural divides, use fair and equitable practices, and offer more mental health supports in schools. How do we accomplish this?

I'm sure that many educators, at some point in their career, were told the starfish parable. This story depicts a child tossing starfish into the ocean that have washed up onto the beach. An adult stops the child and asks what he is doing. The child replies that he is saving the starfish. The adult tells the child that he cannot possibly make a difference—there are hundreds of starfish onshore. But the child plucks up another starfish and gently tosses it back into the ocean, stating, "I made a difference for that one."

I have heard many educators say, "If I can help just one kid, I'll know I've done my job." Many of us work in our "spheres of influence," whether it is a classroom, gym, hallway, cafeteria, or counseling office. It is very fulfilling to teach and assist students and families during their time in our schools. Anybody whose life has been touched by a caring teacher, coach, aide, secretary, counselor, or custodian will vouch for the positive value of these relationships. Although the starfish parable reminds us to care for and help each child and to do the best we can, it is important to go a step further. In the parable, we assume that some starfish remain stranded on the beach—one person cannot help them all. It is unacceptable, though, to leave any child stranded, and so it is essential to make necessary organizational changes and to collaborate so that nobody is left behind.

So what is the best way to enact these kinds of schoolwide changes? When will social-skill lessons occur given the limited time available to teach academics? Who will teach the curriculum, and will staff have adequate training? How will training be funded and sustained over time? Will students apply what they learn to novel situations they may encounter? How will data be collected to show effectiveness? What could I do to improve my own effectiveness?

In addition to my regular duties as a school psychologist (counseling, assessment, and consultation), I have also involved myself in attempting to improve school climate and social justice practices in our district. When I started to hear about "best practices" in education, I became eager to learn more about these. I decided to pursue school administrator certification, and on my first day of class at the University of Illinois at Urbana-Champaign College of Education, I sheepishly (because I was the oldest student in the class) raised my hand and asked, "Will we be learning about the current best practices in education?" The professor gave me a withering glance and replied dryly, "There are no such things as best practices." This is because though people have lots of ideas on how to best deliver education, there is no one-size-fits-all approach. Over the course of my education, I was taught to be skeptical. Those who called their practices "best" were possibly making false claims. What makes a practice best? Best for whom? Who is left behind?

Despite my professor's proclamation, educational research is replete with claims of best practices, effective teaching practices, and leadership practices that work. Translating theory into practice is challenging, yet educators are earnest and motivated. They attend professional conferences and apply for grants to share and learn about new techniques and strategies. There is a website maintained by the U.S. Department of Education that culls all the latest research and is called the What Works Clearinghouse (http://ies.ed.gov/ncee/wwc/). Tremendous resources are available on every subject related to teaching and learning and social-emotional development. We have studied "what works."

So what is the problem? In all of our busy activities, educators neglect to acknowledge that "schools are social institutions that depend daily on the quality of the interpersonal relations with which they are imbued" (Goddard, Salloum, & Berebitsky, 2009). Simply put, it's all about the relationships. Trust, strong leadership, and reflection all form the essential foundation for quality relationships and thus facilitate improvements in our schools.

TRUST—AN IMPORTANT FACTOR IN STUDENT SUCCESS

In a 2014 article titled "Teaching Is Not a Business" that appeared in *The New York Times,* author David L. Kirp, a University of California, Berkeley professor, talked about the latest attempts to improve schools using business models that promoted competition and innovation and that required the investment of billions of dollars in technology. He said the business model had not worked because "teaching and learning is an intimate act that neither computers nor markets can hope to replicate" (p. 1). Citing an extensive study of Chicago's public schools, Kirp reported that "Organizing Schools for Improvement identified 100 elementary schools that had substantially improved and 100 that had not. The presence or absence of social trust among students, teachers, parents and school leaders was a key explanation" (p. 1).

Bryk and Schneider (2002) had similar findings: "The quality of social relations in diverse institutional contexts makes a difference in how they function" (p. xiv). The authors spoke of statistical evidence showing that the presence or lack of "relational trust" had an impact on how schools would be able to institute reforms and progress. They discussed, for example, the interactions among four relationship sets: teachers with students, teachers with other teachers, teachers with parents, and teachers with the principal. All parties presumably understand the obligations that come with their roles and have expectations about the roles of others. They noted that "synchrony" is achieved when everyone fulfills those expectations. However, "individuals typically withdraw their trust when expectations are not met, leading to a weakening of relationships, and, in more extreme instances, a severing of ties" (p. 21). The authors reported that school community members view one another through four lenses: respect, competence, regard for others, and integrity. A lack of any one of the four will undermine the development of trust (p. 23). How does relational trust improve school environments? Bryk and Schneider (2002) cited four benefits:

- "When trust is strong, individual engagement with reform does not feel like a call for heroic action. In this sense, relational trust is a catalyst for innovation" (p. 33).

- Relational trust facilitates public problem solving. School principals are afforded a "wider zone of discretionary authority" (p. 33).

- Individuals understand what is expected of them, their obligations, and the consequences if expectations are not met. "Meaningful collective action" is coordinated (p. 34).

- An "ethical imperative" to "advance the best interest of children" is sustained, despite the presence of misunderstandings and conflict. Relational trust provides the "moral resource" for school improvement (p. 34).

Trust is paramount, but how is it earned? Imani Bazzell, an outstanding community educator and organizer, has consulted with the Champaign, Illinois, school district staff for years. Among her efforts was to help educators learn how to build trust with African-American community stakeholders. I am paraphrasing a story she told a group of social workers and school psychologists.

Social workers often go to the homes of mothers whose children were removed from the home because of abuse or neglect. Here are two versions of how those meetings can go:

1. "Hello, Ms. Green. I'm Octavia Jones from the Department of Children's Services. As you know, your children were removed from your home because of abuse and neglect. You are required to attend a 6-week parenting course. You will also be drug tested to make sure you maintain sobriety. When you fulfill these requirements, a hearing will be held to determine your suitability to have the children returned. Do you have any questions?"

2. "Hello Ms. Woods. I'm Sonia Newman from the Department of Children's Services. I'm here to help you get your kids back."

Ms. Newman, in one simple statement, gives this mother her dignity back by presuming she wants to be reunified with her children as soon as possible. Hence, trust is built because Ms. Newman conveys respect and high expectations. Each social worker will do the exact same job to make sure the mothers fulfill their responsibilities. The other social worker, Octavia Jones, does nothing wrong. She reviews all necessary information, yet she is formal and matter of fact. The difference is that most mothers would see Sonia Newman as a supportive ally and be more likely to trust her.

How do we cultivate trust in schools? Think of the perspective of the students: Children directly observe the looks on the faces of teachers and their tones of voice. Behavior that lacks a sincere base rings hollow, and even young children know when an adult's behavior feels disingenuous. Students feel cared for when teachers individually greet them; smile; listen attentively to their questions and concerns; provide reliable, consistent instruction; celebrate their accomplishments; and show interest in their lives outside of the classroom. Goddard and colleagues (2009) reported that children learn best in school environments where social interactions demonstrate

- Benevolence: placing the needs of others before one's own

- Honesty: engaging others with sincerity

- Openness: fully exposing one's actions and intentions in social exchanges

- Reliability: dependability to perform agreed upon responsibilities
- Competence: possessing the skills needed to perform necessary tasks capably

Educators also benefit from school environments that foster trust. Citing trust as necessary for better schools and quality teaching, American Federation of Teachers President Randi Weingarten (2010) said, "Trust isn't something that you can write into a contract, or lobby into law. Trust is the natural outgrowth of collaboration and communication, and it's the common denominator among schools, districts and cities that have achieved success" (p. 6).

STRONG LEADERSHIP

The presence of strong leadership is also important in improving schools and determining the quality of interpersonal relationships. Ideally, administrators embrace the core belief that all children can learn. This is an excellent goal, but what should students be learning? What is the curriculum, and who gets to choose? Administrators need to have an understanding of how students learn and keep track of who is actually learning in their school building—with well-documented achievement gaps, the school leader must have a role in ensuring equitable educational opportunities for all. Lastly, a leader must understand why students learn and have a solid understanding of the purpose of K–12 education within society. What are we really trying to accomplish with our students? A good administrator must address all of the above questions and concerns.

In the classic 2005 book *School Leadership that Works: From Research to Results,* Marzano, Waters and McNulty made a comprehensive list of "Twenty-One Responsibilities" of school leaders. These responsibilities included the need for involvement in and knowledge of the curriculum, instruction, and assessment; visibility; communication; order; and clear focus. The authors also acknowledged the importance of relationships in schools and that a leader should show care and awareness for the personal lives of teachers and staff. We can assume that adults who are respected and affirmed are happier in their workplace and will be more inclined to interact more positively with students.

An effective administrator must promote a safe, respectful climate for students to learn about one another and the world. There must be room for dialogue and reflection. Social-emotional support must be woven into daily interactions, whether that administrator is speaking with a student, parent, or teacher. Disciplinary practices must be humane and educational. Wellness must be promoted in the food that is served and the health services provided. The administrator must foster the sense in all stakeholders that the school is a community for everyone and that everyone's contributions matter: the custodians, the food service staff, the bus drivers, the secretaries, the parents, the teachers, the coaches, the counselors, and the aides. The administrator articulates and reinforces the importance of the work and celebrates all contributors.

Good school leaders model how to treat people with respect and dignity and maintain transparency so that one group is not favored over another (e.g., in decisions about who will be sent to a workshop, funded for field trips, given additional duties). A leader must be present in a positive and affirming way, yet "call out" when there is a lack of equity or some members of the population are not accessing a quality education.

REFLECTION

Reflecting on one's actions and how they impact others is an important task for anyone. Personal reflection is challenging: What did I do? How could I have done it better? Because reliving something can be painful and anxiety provoking, many people choose to put their heads down and keep moving forward. They do not stop to think about how their behavior affects others. The other extreme is people who think too much about their actions. They become riddled with fear, regret their mistakes, and constantly worry about what people will think of them. Despite these challenges, personal relationships are strengthened if we own and take responsibility for our actions and behaviors. The next step is to communicate frankly with others and attempt improvement. Nobody is perfect, but sincere effort matters. How do we improve if we do not stop and reflect?

The first time I heard the word *reflection* used in an educational setting was from the work of Danielson and McGreal (2002), who encouraged "reflection on practice" with regard to teaching and learning (p. 24). In a school setting, where educators interact with hundreds of people with vastly different life circumstances and stories, we are more likely to be reflective when it is encouraged by others and we feel safe.

Trust, sound leadership, and reflection clearly have an impact on the relationships within a school. The greater the trust, the more likely that educators will reflect on their strengths and weaknesses and seek to enhance their practice. Trust is maintained and enhanced by a school administrator who articulates the need for reflection, leads by example, offers emotional support, and brings vision for growth.

MEDIATION: AN INTERVENTION FOR IMPROVING RELATIONSHIPS

As reviewed in this chapter, the current movement in education is to depart from traditional discipline practices toward more restorative practices that maintain quality relationships in schools and to create a more coherent, common sense system for delivering the appropriate intervention to students based on their levels of need. It is also "a move away from piecemeal and fragmented approaches and toward comprehensiveness and greater coordination in planning and implementation" (Greenberg et al., 2003, p. 471).

This book demonstrates how to improve relationships in schools through mediation, an intervention that involves a voluntary meeting with two parties and a trained mediator in which the participants present their full story and work to resolve conflicts and misunderstandings. Mediation is but one of many interventions that can be used to respond to the call to action to improve school climate, strengthen relationships, and better behavior. Readers will learn why mediation works and how to successfully develop and perform mediations in schools. This intervention falls well within the scope of duties for counselors, social workers, and school psychologists, and other trained school or community staff can also perform mediation. Mediations can be done as a stand-alone intervention or can be embedded within a multi-tiered system of schoolwide positive behavior support (SWPBS).

Before discussing the specifics of mediation, I review response to intervention (RTI) and present promising, systematic solutions for coordinating interventions for students using a multi-tiered system of supports (MTSS). Woven throughout the book are real-life examples and candid observations from Centennial High School Principal, Greg Johnson, and administrators, Ryan Cowell, Tony Maltbia, Charles Neitzel, and Angela Schoonover.

2

Systems to Help Students

How Response to Intervention and Multi-tiered Positive Behavior Supports Transform a School

> If the wind will not serve, take to the oars.
>
> —Latin proverb

Administrator Angela Schoonover: Response to intervention has been a major driving force in our educational system. From my experience, educators and administrators are looking for research-based practices to help improve the climate of a building and to decrease the number of discipline referrals, suspensions, and expulsions from school.

Educators are extremely resourceful at identifying students in need, offering support, and referring students for additional help. These activities go on every day across the nation, but some critical questions often go unanswered:

- Who will receive the intervention? Do all students, some, or a few?

- What intervention should be offered? Is there research or evidence that the interventions will work?

- When should the interventions be offered? Time is always limited, so how should that time be prioritized?

- Where will the intervention be provided? Classroom and office space is limited in many schools.

- How will the intervention be provided, and by whom? Is ongoing training required, or do materials need to be purchased? Are there funds?

- How will the intervention be monitored to make sure it is delivered correctly and consistently?

- How will student outcomes be measured to see if the interventions are effective? When should additional support be provided?

Response to intervention (RTI) is a process used to ask and answer these questions. RTI was designed to provide a tiered approach to monitor and assess a student's performance, to systematically intervene (using a scientific, research-based, and/or evidence-based intervention), and then to monitor the child's growth (or response) to the intervention. Cates, Blum, and Swerdlik (2011) identified eight key concepts that contribute to a successful RTI program:

1. RTI focuses on the educational needs of all students.

2. RTI is prevention-oriented as opposed to reaction-oriented.

3. RTI relies on empirical data for decision making.

4. RTI focuses on implementation of empirically supported, scientifically based instruction and intervention.

5. RTI utilizes only those instruction approaches that have proven effectiveness.

6. RTI emphasizes that tiers are not places.

7. RTI services are dynamic and adjusted according to student progress.

8. RTI acknowledges that intra-individual differences in instructional support are likely (i.e., it is possible for a student to need Tier II support for reading, Tier II support for mathematics, and Tier I support for behavior). (p. 12)

The concept that *tiers are not places* is important because tiers are not fixed locations where students are placed; rather, they are levels of support that fluctuate based on student need. The pyramid model shown in Figure 2.1 illustrates the concept of RTI.

Tier I applies to all students in all settings. In Tier I, goals are to prevent academic or behavior problems by clearly defining and teaching expectations and to recognize those students who demonstrate expected behaviors. It can be expected that 80%–90% of students will respond to Tier I interventions. Tier II is aimed at the 5%–10% of students who have not responded to Tier I interventions and supports and may be considered at risk for underachievement. Tier II involves teaching prevention and intervention strategies to smaller groups of students. Goals are to provide research-based interventions that are specific to the student's problematic behavior and to monitor behavioral and academic progress. Finally, Tier III applies to the 1%–5% of students who have

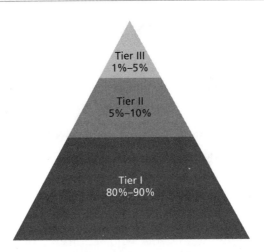

Figure 2.1. Pyramid model of three tiers.

not responded to Tier I or Tier II interventions and supports and may be considered at high risk for school failure. The goal is to provide intensive and individualized interventions to these students. The RTI model also encourages the flexible use of school personnel and collaborative problem solving among staff and parents to improve student performance.

Consider the following hypothetical example of how RTI may be applied to reading instruction. Fig Tree Elementary School wants to know how the fifth graders are performing in reading. The school will administer a universal screening test. This is considered a Tier I activity because all students in the fifth grade are assessed. (Some schools may opt to universally screen their entire student body to identify students who may require additional support.) Janey scores below the 10th percentile on the screening, which is well below average, and her score flags the need for remediation. Under an RTI process, Janey may be invited to receive small group reading instruction on a weekly or biweekly basis, which would be considered a Tier II support. The additional instruction is not in lieu of her regularly scheduled classroom reading period but is added to enrich her reading instruction. During the small group reading session, Janey will be "progress monitored" to assess her growth in reading and so that her teachers may adjust the reading curriculum or the frequency of instruction as needed. If Janey does not make progress in reading after 6 weeks, she may be referred for more individualized, frequent, and intensive reading instruction over a longer duration. This would be considered Tier III support. It is possible that concurrent with the Tier III support, Janey may be evaluated for special education eligibility if the data continue to indicate that her response to the interventions shows inadequate growth in reading.

Prior to the implementation of RTI, a variety of interventions may still have been used to help Janey improve her reading. However, the RTI process is more systematic about identifying student needs, uses research-based supports, measures progress, and is more efficient. Also, RTI aims to reduce the number of students referred for special education while increasing the number of students who succeed in general education (Klotz & Canter, 2006). But what interventions might be used if Janey also has behavior problems in addition to academic concerns?

POSITIVE BEHAVIORAL INTERVENTIONS AND SUPPORTS AND SCHOOLWIDE POSITIVE BEHAVIOR SUPPORT

Administrator Tony Maltbia: These systems are to provide layers to not let students slip through the cracks and to give a team of people a way to brainstorm around helping those students.

Many schools have expanded the use of RTI to identify and more systematically intervene with students who require additional behavioral and social-emotional support. Such expanded use was in response to federal laws, including the No Child Left Behind Act of 2001 (PL 107-110) and the Individuals with Disabilities Education Improvement Act (IDEA) of 2004 (PL 108-446). Included in these federal laws was the stated need to address students' serious behavioral challenges using scientifically based behavioral interventions and supports. In 1997, the U.S. Department of Education began to address the needs of children with serious behavioral challenges by funding the formation of the National Technical Assistance Center on Positive Behavioral Interventions and Supports (PBIS). There have been many versions of what PBIS is and is not. Sugai and Simonsen (2012) provided the following definition:

> PBIS is an implementation framework that is designed to enhance academic and social behavior outcomes for all students by (a) emphasizing the use of data for informing decisions about the selection, implementation, and progress monitoring of evidence based behavioral practices; and (b) organizing resources and systems to improve durable implementation fidelity. (p. 1)

Because schools play a major role in providing positive behavioral supports, the term *schoolwide positive behavior support* (SWPBS) was coined (Sugai & Horner, 2009). The PBIS website states "PBIS is used interchangeably with SWPBS" (Positive Behavioral Interventions & Supports, n.d.). The guidelines for SWPBS are to (Sugai & Horner, 2009)

- Use data to narrow identification of desired goals, expectations, and outcomes

- Establish goals, objectives, and outcomes that are based on local data, described in measurable terms, and are realistically achievable with available resources

- Consider and adapt interventions and practices that have empirical and applied evidence of achieving expected goals, objectives, and outcomes

- Organize resources and systems so that implementers have the opportunities, capacities, and resources to implement the practice with accuracy and fluency over time

Under a system of SWPBS, educators are not handed a one-size-fits-all manual that says, "you must do it this way," but instead are asked to collaborate and analyze data from their own school populations, to thoughtfully identify goals and select interventions based on research or empirical evidence, and to adapt or eliminate interventions based on what the data show.

Let us return to the example of our fifth-grade student, Janey. Janey yells, "No way!" when her teacher, Ms. Vecchio, asks her to do something, and she sometimes refuses to open her book. One day, Ms. Vecchio was passing out construction paper for an art project, and Janey tore up the paper. Although Janey's reading difficulties have been monitored and are more fully understood and addressed, her behavior has not improved. If Fig Tree Elementary educators implement SWPBS, they will begin to ask and answer the following questions:

- How can we expect students to follow a rule when we do not know if they have ever explicitly been taught how to follow that rule?

- If students are not following behavioral expectations, why?

- What is the function or purpose of students' misbehavior? What do they gain from it?

- How are we rewarding students who do follow the rules?

A Tier I team at Fig Tree will develop three positively worded schoolwide expectations and values (i.e., stating what to do, not what not to do). These are referred to as *target behaviors*. Soon Fig Tree Elementary has colorful posters hanging in the lunchroom, hallways, and classrooms that say "Be Responsible, Be Respectful, and Be Safe!" Lesson plans are developed so that teachers can teach, reteach, and have students continually practice what responsible, respectful, and safe behavior looks like. A newsletter is also sent home that describes the target behaviors. All adults at the school continually model and reinforce the target behaviors for students, and those students who perform the target behaviors earn points. Fig Tree Elementary holds daily, weekly, and quarterly drawings for students who have earned points, and Janey is excited because she has earned a few. Meanwhile the Tier I team monitors disciplinary data to see if overall student behavior is improving at Fig Tree Elementary and discusses any needed modifications.

When the data are examined, Janey is still shown to have a higher than average number of disciplinary referrals from Ms. Vecchio. The team suggests that Janey receive Tier II supports. A counselor at Fig Tree enrolls Janey in a small SEL group aimed at teaching appropriate communication and anger management skills. The group meets weekly, and Janey reports that she enjoys attending this activity. This group also gives the counselor the opportunity to get to know Janey better. Janey now knows she has someone in the school she can talk to if she is upset about something. Although Janey has positive experiences in her small group and individual counseling sessions, those positive feelings and behaviors do not always generalize to the regular classroom setting. In fact, Ms. Vecchio has not seen much improvement in Janey's attitude and behavior. If Fig Tree Elementary provided teacher–student mediation as a Tier II intervention, this would be the perfect time for a mediator to set up a meeting with Janey and Ms. Vecchio. The opportunity to focus on Janey and Ms. Vecchio's relationship may provide a key link toward improved classroom behavior. Janey has acknowledged in her SEL group that she has "anger issues" and has been given vocabulary and strategies to cope better with what triggers her anger. She is eager to share her newfound knowledge with Ms. Vecchio, and even to make amends because she knows her behavior has been "bad." Mediation will be restorative, as it will bring Ms. Vecchio and Janey closer as they gain understanding about each other's feelings, perspectives, and needs.

Janey's parents are delighted with the Tier II supports provided by the school and have reported improvements at home. Following the interventions, including the teacher–student mediation, the data finally show a decrease in Janey's disciplinary referrals. All agree that Janey has responded positively to the Tier II supports offered at Fig Tree Elementary, and she does not require more intensive Tier III interventions. At Fig Tree, those interventions might have included weekly individual sessions with a counselor and continued participation in a longer, more intensive SEL group. Parent meetings and suggestions to seek counseling from a community mental health agency would also have been discussed. At some point, the team may have also considered an evaluation to see if Janey required an IEP. The assessment to determine a student's eligibility for special education services might be conducted by the school's multidisciplinary team (school psychologist, social worker, speech-language pathologist, teacher, and/or nurse) in order to assess Janey's cognitive, social-emotional, speech-language, academic, motor, health, hearing, and vision functioning. Fortunately, Janey's academic and behavioral issues were effectively addressed at the Tier II level, and she is experiencing more success and happiness at school.

IMPLEMENTATION OF SYSTEM CHANGE IN SCHOOLS

The implementation of MTSS in schools can move very slowly, especially those supports focused on SEL and on understanding and improving student behavior. Schools are academic institutions, and the task at hand is to improve skills in reading, writing, math, science, and other subjects. Counselors, social workers, and school psychologists spend considerable time intervening to improve students' social-emotional and academic adjustment, but teaching social, problem-solving, and conflict resolution skills are not typically embedded in the day-to-day practices of other school staff. Teachers teach academic curriculum, most administrators are former teachers, and very few people are eager to dive into the "touchy-feely stuff." High school teachers, in particular, may be reluctant to teach social skills because many assume that, by high school, students should understand what behaviors are expected of them and how to behave appropriately in the classroom.

To introduce a multi-tiered system of SWPBS is to restructure the business-as-usual operation of a school. All change brings stress, particularly among busy people who are putting out fires on a daily basis. Is there agreement from the stakeholders: parents, staff, the community, and students? Is there time within the day to schedule team meetings and interventions? Are evidenced-based interventions available, and are people available to deliver those interventions? Is there funding for ongoing professional development? Is there a computer application in place to monitor data and evaluate programs? Lastly, are leaders available who will bring the vision, courage, and persistence necessary to provide continuous support?

For implementation to be successful, "systemic district supports in the form of active leadership participation, coaching and facilitation, localized training expertise, ongoing evaluation, political support, implementation visibility, and recurring institutional funding" (Sugai & Horner, 2009, p. 234) are necessary. Studies also show that the implementation of SWPBS does not occur in 1 year, but is gradual and comes in phases. The usual phases of implementation (Fixsen, Naoom, Blasé, Friedman & Wallace, 2005; McIntosh, Horner & Sugai, 2009; Sugai, Horner & McIntosh, 2008) are as follows:

- Phase 1: Initial adoption and trial implementation with fidelity (1 year)

- Phase 2: Full implementation commitment (1–2 years)

- Phase 3: Self-sustaining and continuously regenerating (2–4 years)

So, it takes from 4 to 7 years to fully implement SWPBS. Success comes with "buy in" from district leadership, ongoing training from outside experts and those working within the district, funding, ongoing evaluation, transparent practices, and support from stakeholders.

We have examined the hypothetical example of fifth grader Janey at Fig Tree Elementary School. Now let us consider the real-life example of Centennial High School.

CENTENNIAL HIGH SCHOOL: INTRODUCING SCHOOLWIDE POSITIVE BEHAVIOR SUPPORT

Administrator Tony Maltbia: Our school, Centennial, made a drastic change towards the better when tiered systems of support were put in place. They support a lot of struggling students socially and academically. That level of support is necessary when you have big schools because it gives a safety net to catch people before they get too far discouraged or behind.

Prior to the implementation of MTSS at Centennial High School, there was one multidisciplinary intervention team that included an administrator, myself as the school psychologist, a general education teacher, a special education teacher, a social worker, a counselor, and a truancy interventionist. A teacher, administrator, or parent could refer a student of concern to the team. The team met weekly and invited the parent to discuss the student's academic history and current needs and challenges. The problem was that this was the only team that met at the school to discuss students who were struggling in academic or social-emotional areas. In a school with more than 1,400 students, the meeting might have helped the students and families that met with us, but one intervention team could not adequately address the volume of student needs at the school. We needed a larger, more comprehensive way to serve the needs of our students.

Over the 2010–2014 school years, a group of administrators I call the "dream team" worked at Centennial High School. Many were enrolled in graduate programs at the University of Illinois at Urbana-Champaign College of Education and/or had familiarity with SWPBS. They were intelligent, compassionate, and good-hearted individuals who shared core beliefs in equity and social justice. They were also professional, hard working, and collaborative. All were resourceful and sought to make research-based decisions and then to evaluate their decisions using academic and disciplinary data. They were the kind of administrators who answered email questions promptly and followed through on what they said they were going to do. They were talented administrators who could move things from talk to action.

As I stated in the Preface, in the summer prior to the 2011–2012 school year, I encountered two Centennial High School administrators, Angela Schoonover and Charles Neitzel, writing on a white board to map out a tiered system of supports. They tapped into current research, looked at other schools, and met with a PBIS consultant to help design the formation of Tier I and Tier II committees. They started to identify what interventions to use, the entrance and the exit criteria for who would receive interventions, and how to collect and track data in order to monitor progress.

Administrator Angela Schoonover: Honestly, the reason we [the administrative team] started tiered systems of supports is that we were really worn out. We were frustrated. We had a terrible month in May. We sat down at the end of the school year and said, "What do we do?" We had heard talk about one of the middle schools in the district doing skill building, and we took that idea and modified it for our needs at Centennial. We looked at our highest number of discipline referrals for infractions. Of course we saw disruptive behavior, disobedience, and verbal abuse to staff, so we created a way to provide interventions based on those. We sat down as an administrative team and just brainstormed all of these ideas that we had. We knew we had to create a system to do it. We had to create a formal way for up to 300 kids to get the interventions, for us to be able to track data, and we had kind of seen that through PBIS, so that's why we chose that.

Administrator Charles Neitzel: We didn't know what it [MTSS] was going to look like, and we borrowed ideas from a lot of different sources. We also monitored our data both before and after putting these [MTSS] in place to make sure we were focusing on the behaviors we wanted to influence. Having all of the interventions under one umbrella and being able to track their effectiveness allowed us to narrow our focus and apply our resources consistently.

So, how to start? Schoonover described important first steps in getting SWPBS off the ground.

Administrator Angela Schoonover: I think you have to look at what supports staff are currently doing...looking at the type of data that can be collected, and identifying a clear way for that data to be consistently collected. You have to look at the resources available to you: the time, the staff, and if you need money...and then kind of go with that. I think that is a big part of the role of an administrator: what is available, what kind of time do we have to do this, and who can do it?

Tier I, Tier II, and Tier III interventions were initially conceptualized as shown in Figure 2.2. Tiered behavioral supports were added to tiered academic supports, as shown in the pyramid depicted in Figure 2.2. For this discussion of SWPBS, I focus on the behavioral side of the pyramid.

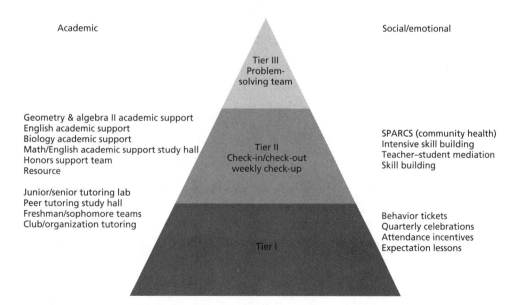

Figure 2.2. Centennial High School pyramid of supports. (*Source:* Schoonover, 2014. *Key:* SPARCS: Structured Psychotherapy for Adolescents Responding to Chronic Stress.)

Administrator Charles Neitzel: When we first started our tiered interventions, I was meeting with a parent and a student who had been involved in an incident at school. It was great to be able to tell them both, "These are the interventions that a student participates in when these incidents happen, to ensure that they don't happen again." It really helped the parent and student feel supported.

Tier I

As noted previously, the goal of Tier I intervention is to provide behavioral supports that allow 80%–90% of the student population to meet schoolwide behavioral expectations. Centennial High School adopted the Tier I ideas of implementing universal or whole-school interventions, which included identifying and teaching expectations and rewarding students for following them. An administrator leads the Tier I committee and shares the committee's activities with the principal, other administrators, and the school community. Also, the Tier I administrator sends home a parent newsletter to describe universal behavioral goals and upcoming celebrations.

Since the implementation of Tier I intervention in the 2011–2012 school year, the committee has met monthly to accomplish three tasks: 1) monitor schoolwide student disciplinary data in order to identify the most problematic behavior, 2) develop a schoolwide intervention that teaches a positive replacement behavior, and 3) reward and celebrate students who meet behavioral expectations.

In order to effectively monitor student data, the Tier I committee asks the following five questions:

1. What was the problematic behavior?

2. Where did it occur (location)?

3. When did it occur?

4. How often does the problematic behavior occur?

5. How many disciplinary referrals have been given to students for this problem?

Administrator Ryan Cowell: When we first formed the [Tier I] committee, I would bring discipline data, usually by infraction type, from the previous month...[and] I'd bring a comparison: September of this year compared with September of last year, just to check ourselves and see how we were doing. My first year we had this rash of fights and we needed to attack that.

After reviewing the student disciplinary data and identifying the most problematic behavior, the Tier I committee identifies a positive replacement behavior, and this information is shared at a faculty meeting. Teachers are asked to instruct students on the replacement behavior through brief "expectation lessons" that are developed by the Tier I committee. These lessons occur schoolwide on the same day and at the same time. At Centennial High School, the most engaging expectation lessons are brief videos created collaboratively with students. The videos feature students who discuss and model the appropriate replacement behavior for their peers. Finally, the Tier I committee celebrates the students who meet behavioral expectations. Parents and community members are invited to attend and help with these recognitions.

Table 2.1 displays a sample behavioral data report taken at Centennial High School for the month of February 2014. The Tier I committee reviewed and analyzed February data and determined that disobedience was the most frequently occurring source of disciplinary referrals.

As shown in Table 2.1, disobedience had the highest frequency (71) and greatest proportion of referrals (48.97%) compared with other infractions. Thus, disobedience was targeted for improvement. A Tier I committee member presented the data at a faculty meeting and in an expectation lesson that teachers could present to the students in their second period classes on a designated day. The Tier I committee members also reinforced the behavioral expectation lesson by creating and displaying posters throughout the school that identified the expected behavior. Teachers and staff members were to hand out "behavior tickets" as a reward to students who exhibited the appropriate behavior.

Administrator Ryan Cowell: The instructional lesson has been useful. We would pick a behavior and do some sort of lesson around it. That's what we did from the beginning and that, I think, is a fine model.

Asking teachers to reward the appropriate replacement behavior was somewhat more challenging.

Table 2.1.   Sample Tier 1 committee data for February 2014

Problem behavior	Frequency	Proportion
Use/possession of drugs	1	.69%
Physical aggression	1	.69%
Forgery/theft	4	2.76%
Fighting	8	5.52%
Other behavior	11	7.59%
Abusive/inappropriate language	17	11.72%
Disruption	32	22.07%
Disobedience	71	48.97%
Total referrals	145	

Source: Cowell (2014).

Administrator Ryan Cowell: We asked faculty to look for those behaviors and give positive behavior tickets when they saw [them]. But what became unrealistic about that, almost immediately, is that a lot of times the behaviors were difficult to see...so these tickets weren't being used as often as we'd like.

One of the benefits of working with committees within SWPBS is the flexibility. By monitoring the effectiveness of initiatives, the team could be nimble, creative, and free to improve upon or even discard ideas:

Administrator Ryan Cowell: At some point in the first year, we started pushing out the idea that behavior tickets can be used for anything you are seeing related to our behavior matrix [the behavior matrix is a list and explanation of three positive behavioral expectations posted in the school: respect, responsibility, integrity]. I think that works better.

Thus, behavior tickets were also to be given out for any and all appropriate behavior. Ticket holders and their families were invited to celebrations, such as a breakfast or an evening dessert. There were also behavior ticket raffles and drawings for prizes:

Administrator Ryan Cowell: I liked that the celebration brought parents in the building.

I asked Cowell about the biggest challenges for Tier I.

Administrator Ryan Cowell: The biggest challenge of Tier I is time [to implement all of the steps]. I think this committee needs an administrator to push it. It's just hard sometimes to pull it all together. Going after something universally requires a lot of moving parts.

Centennial's principal also spoke of the challenges of Tier I.

Principal Greg Johnson: Honestly, Tier I is tough in a high school. I find that it's hard to get a whole bunch of high school students who are at such various stages of emotional and physical development, [in grades] 9–12, to buy into a common approach to expected behaviors, and so I struggle with that as a principal.

However, Cowell also commented on the greatest success he has experienced with Tier I interventions.

Administrator Ryan Cowell: We had a problem with fighting, and we went aggressively after it and it [fighting] just fizzled. We addressed it through a letter, video, and a principal assembly in the auditorium. Our goal in the video was to frame fighting as an antisocial behavior. It does prove that when you go after something universally in the building, you can change the culture.

In this case, a replacement behavior was offered for fighting:

Administrator Ryan Cowell: If you know of a conflict between you and another student or between other students, talk to an adult.

As shown in Figure 2.3, the yearly number of fights at Centennial High School showed a steady decrease since the introduction of SWPBS in the 2011–2012 school year.

Tier II

The Tier II committee includes those individuals who implement the Tier II interventions. At Centennial High School, the Tier II committee members include four school counselors, two social workers, one school psychologist, three assistant principals, one supervised study room supervisor, and one truancy intervention specialist. Representatives of community outreach organizations may also be invited to attend the Tier II committee meetings. For example, in the first 2 years, the school had a collaborative relationship with a nonprofit mental health agency, and two therapists from that organization (who participated in school interventions) regularly attended. Having community members attend Tier II meetings did not breach confidentiality rules because Tier II meetings were to discuss systems and not individual students. These meetings last for 1 hour and are held before school two times per month.

A PBIS consultant provided support during the first 2 years, including valuable input on selecting computer and data systems that could provide the most useful information. The consultant also attended some of the initial Tier II committee meetings.

Centennial High School's administrators and PBIS consultant encouraged the creation of Tier II interventions that would tap into the school's existing resources and strengths. We were told to be flexible and to modify, add, or delete interventions whenever the data did not indicate effectiveness. I very

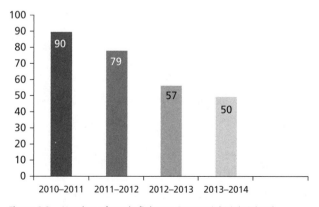

Figure 2.3. Number of yearly fights at Centennial High School.

much appreciated that I could introduce teacher–student mediation—an intervention that had never before been systematically instituted at Centennial High School. (For a full list of Tier II interventions implemented at Centennial over the 2011–2014 school years, see Appendix B: Tier II Intervention Guide at the back of this book.)

When SWPBS is being implemented, school staff often ask themselves, "Are we doing it right?" Our PBIS consultant was able to guide and refocus us while always reminding us that the system was ours: generated within our school, with the resources and people in our school, to fit the needs of our school. She also spoke of "exception rules" because not every student progresses along a tiered system of supports in the same way. For example, we did not get bogged down on whether all students had to move through interventions at the Tier I level to get to the Tier II level to get to the Tier III level of supports, because for some children, exceptions had to be made based on their individual needs. The exception rule allowed us to be flexible in the best interests of students.

Administrator Angela Schoonover: We kept many ideas from PBIS but also went away from what PBIS said we needed to do for the interventions, only because we had to create a contextual fit to the high school. I feel okay about the modifications because there really isn't strong research that shows, 'this is how you do it at the high school level.' A lot of the research is geared towards elementary, some middle school, but not a lot towards high school."

Tier II meetings at Centennial High School always start with the reading of meeting norms. Meeting norms are a collaboratively agreed upon list of behavioral expectations for the meeting. For some, developing and reading norms might seem superfluous or appear to be stating the obvious because it is assumed that everyone will act professionally. However, the contrary is true. Norms restate the expectation of professional conduct, and nobody is immune from needing that gentle reminder. Norms that are developed by the members of a committee protect the integrity of a meeting so that it does not become a complaint session or an arena for multitasking (including cell phone use). The meeting norms used by Centennial High School's Tier II committee are as follows:

- The meeting will always have a set agenda.
- We will remain focused on the topic(s) being discussed.
- We will remain respectful of others by speaking and sharing one at a time.
- We will remain focused on the meeting and not engage in multitasking during the meeting time.
- We will keep our discussions positive and focus on suggestions for improvement.

Meeting agendas are developed by the Tier II committee administrator and generally include one or more of the following tasks:

- Reading norms

- Reviewing current intervention systems. Each interventionist reviews the most recently posted data on the Tier II intervention tracking tool.

- Discussing strengths and concerns with current interventions and sharing ideas to make improvements

- Reviewing modifications to interventions and the possible addition or replacement of supports based on the data

- Proposing various evaluations and surveys to gain additional feedback

Figure 2.4 provides an example of a data spreadsheet compiled and distributed at a Tier II meeting so that all interventions could be discussed. A blank Tier II Intervention Tracking Tool, as well as a list of Centennial High School's Tier II interventions, are located in Appendix B.

Administrator Angela Schoonover: We actually look at data to see, "is this working or not working?" You may hear that a group intervention went really well because it's reported that "the kids had a great conversation." Maybe it felt good in that moment, but when you look at the data and see that there's been a 40% response rate, it might have felt good in the group, but are kids generalizing what they are supposed to be learning?

Tier III

The Tier III committee is the longest-standing committee for student intervention at Centennial High School. During my years at Centennial, the name of this group has changed many times, from "Student Support Team" to "Building Support Team" to "Building Intervention Team" to "Response to Intervention Team" to "Problem-Solving Team."

The purpose of the Problem-Solving Team is to offer a coordinated linkage of supports within and outside of the school system. The team is led by an administrator and includes the school psychologist, a social worker, a general education teacher, a special education teacher, and a truancy intervention specialist. The team meets weekly, but meeting times vary, year to year, depending on team members' and/or parents' schedules. The team receives referrals from the Tier II committee, an administrator, a staff member, or a parent. The team sends an invitation letter to parents, with a follow-up telephone call, inviting them to join the meeting. The team asks teachers to complete checklists to identify the student's current classroom behavior and work habits, and then they review the compiled information at the meeting. Also, a team member reviews the student's record and presents the student's grades, attendance record, test scores, and other relevant information from the student's file at the meeting. Another team member interviews the student prior

School name: Centennial High School   Total school population as of October 1: 1,357

Interventions	Skill-building group		Intensive skill-building group		Check-in/check-out		Teacher-student mediation		Student-student mediation		SPARCS		Total	Total responding
	Number of students participating	Number of students responding	Number of students participating	Number of students responding	Number of students participating	Number of students responding	Number of students participating	Number of students responding	Number of students participating	Number of students responding	Number of students participating	Number of students responding	Total	Total responding
August	0	0	0	0	0	0	2	2	0	0	0	0	2	2
September	2	1	0	0	8	6	2	1	8	8	4	4	24	20
October	10	5	2	0	10	7	13	8	16	16	4	4	55	40
November	15	11	4	0	9	6	10	9	15	15	4	4	57	45
December	4	2	3	1	7	4	7	7	9	9	4	4	34	27
January	5	3	2	1	9	7	0	0	4	4	0	0	20	15
February	2	1	5	2	6	3	9	8	39	31	0	0	61	45
March	4	2	6	5	6	5	8	8	16	12	10	10	50	42
April	3	1	3	3	3	3	3	3	4	2	10	7	26	19
May	4	3	0	0	7	5	3	3	6	6	10	7	30	24
June	0	0	0	0	0	0	0	0	0	0	0	0	0	0
Total	49	29	25	12	65	46	57	49	117	103	14	11	359	279
	59% (+1%)		48% (+4%)		71% (+4%)		86% (+1%)		88%		79%			78%

Responding to skill building group: No discipline referrals/minor infraction referral for the same infraction for 4 weeks after group date

Responding to intensive skill building group: No discipline referrals/minor infraction referrals for 4 weeks after the last group date

Responding to check-in/check-out (CICO): Does not hit the same criteria that caused student to be referred

Responding to teacher-student mediation: Individual student does not receive another discipline referral from the same teacher after teacher-student mediation

Figure 2.4. Tier II tracking tool for Centennial High School. (From Schoonover, A. [2014]. Tier 2 tracking tool for Centennial High School. Unpublished form; reprinted by permission. *Key:* SPARCS: Structured Psychotherapy for Adolescents Responding to Chronic Stress.)

to the meeting. This interview is designed to build rapport, acquaint students with the purpose of the meeting, and to provide students with the opportunity to identify their needs and goals. Once at the meeting, the student is asked to share these thoughts, or else the staff member who interviewed the student will do so.

The Problem-Solving Team suggests appropriate in-school and out-of-school resources for the student and family. The team also reviews student data and discusses whether the student might need to be evaluated for special education eligibility or a 504 accommodation plan or be suitable for an alternative school placement. After the meeting, one member of the team is assigned as the case manager for the student. This team member's job is to ensure that the agreed upon interventions are delivered and to monitor the student's response to the interventions. The team monitors all students referred for intervention on an ongoing basis. But is it enough? High schools, in particular, can always benefit from more support staff to do higher level interventions, particularly for chronically failing or truant students. Sometimes there is insufficient time or training to provide the intensity of mental health services that would benefit the students at the Tier III level, and community linkages do not always come together.

Administrator Charles Neitzel: The biggest challenge is that we have a system and people go into it; [however], we don't have what they need in some cases. The [needs] for each student are so different that it is hard to have consistent interventions that would cover all issues....The connections to outside agencies is great...we talk about outside counseling...but this really relies on the parents/guardians following up on this.

My wish list for every school includes an onsite wellness clinic with nurses, doctors, and therapists that is accessible to the entire school community. Unfortunately, this is not a reality in our school systems, so it is important for school staff to provide as much linkage and support as possible.

Evaluating the Effectiveness of Schoolwide Positive Behavior Support at Centennial High School

Given the challenges and ongoing need for monitoring and modifications, were our supports effective? Figures 2.5 and 2.6 indicate improvements in suspension and disciplinary referrals over time. The 2010–2011 school year represents the "Before," and 2011–2014 represents the "After."

The suspension data in Figure 2.5 and the disciplinary referral data in Figure 2.6 indicate that by the end of the 2013–2014 school year, Centennial High School could document substantial improvements in the reduction of disciplinary referrals and suspensions among all major student groups.

Administrator Angela Schoonover: So I guess over the last three years, we have continuously looked at the data: What's working, what's not working.

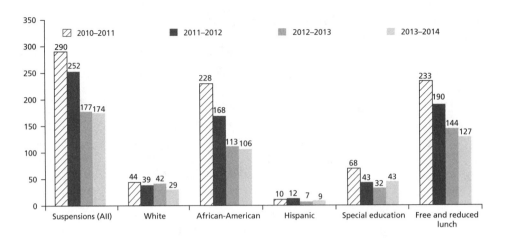

Suspensions	Before 2010–2011	After 2013–2014	Difference
All students	290	174	−40%
White	44	29	−34%
African-American	228	106	−53%
Hispanic	10	9	−10%
Special education	68	43	−37%
Free and reduced lunch	233	127	−45%

Figure 2.5. Suspensions from 2010–2014 at Centennial High School.

We make modifications if we need to add things or if something is really not worth doing because we don't see any results. The first year I was here, 2010–2011, we had 2,406 DRs over all. We decreased that by about 600 the year we started implementing this. The second year in it, we had 1,152. That's an almost 1,300 difference in DRs from the year I started. We are a lot more proactive with things.

Overall strengths in Centennial High School's SWPBS included

- Administrative support from the principal

- Active participation from the administrators who led the committees

- Consistency, accountability, and visibility

- Data-driven decision making

- The flexibility of the system to allow modifications of existing interventions

From my perspective, being a part of a well-run tiered system of supports was collaborative and professionally fulfilling. It brought colleagues together in an organized way, and it kept us productive thanks to the team norms and ongoing review of data. It was satisfying for me to see the social-emotional and behavioral adjustment of students become a schoolwide focus.

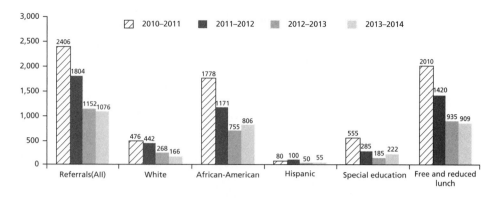

Disciplinary referrals	Before 2010–2011	After 2013–2014	Difference
All students	2,406	1,076	–55%
White	476	166	–65%
African-American	1,778	806	–55%
Hispanic	80	55	–31%
Special education	555	222	–60%
Free and reduced lunch	2,010	909	–55%

Figure 2.6. Disciplinary referrals from 2010–2014 at Centennial High School.

The challenges continue, however: Closing gaps among student groups has been difficult for school districts across the country, and Centennial is no exception.

Administrator Angela Schoonover: We've done a good job at decreasing [disciplinary referrals] but now we need to close the gaps.

Also, despite our systematic efforts, we do not identify all of the students who could use extra help.

Administrator Tony Maltbia: There are kids the system does not catch. This system does not catch the kids who took a dip—the grades are going low, the attendance is getting bad—but they are not at the F range. The system really concentrates on the bottom [lowest performers], but there are still other kids that slip through and need support as well.

Additional challenges in our SWPBS included

- Time: How do we balance the delivery of interventions with other job responsibilities?

- Are the problems of students greater than what the school can solve? Did we do enough? What more can we do?

- Do students learn from our interventions and apply them to real-life situations?

- How do we get parents more involved?

- Sustainability: How do we maintain the fidelity of our systems when there is staff or administrator turnover?

  To continually improve, our work is ongoing. We must

- Follow the team norms that we created in order to keep meetings positive and productive

- Continue to track data and obtain meaningful feedback in regard to student progress

- Hone follow-up systems after interventions

- Strengthen communication with parents, staff, and students, including exit interviews and/or follow-up where appropriate

- Expand upon the Tier II system to include more systematic academic and attendance interventions that close the achievement gaps among student groups

- Create better linkage between Tier II and Tier III

- Create opportunities for ongoing training, particularly for new staff and administrators

SUMMARY AND NEXT TOPIC

This chapter illustrated the nuts and bolts of how visionary administrators, caring teachers, and dedicated support staff can bring about systemic change to a large, diverse school by implementing MTSS. For Centennial High School, there is no finish line, and the administrators provided honest assessments of strengths, weaknesses, and challenges. I am not a university researcher and do not purport to suggest that what happened at Centennial High School can happen in any setting. I will humbly propose, however, that after more than 30 years working in public schools, I know that when there are coordinated efforts among committed individuals, and when there is visibility, accountability, high expectations, strong leadership, trust, and respect, positive transformation will happen.

For the remainder of the book, I return to the topic of mediation. At Centennial High School, data showed that the concurrent implementation of teacher–student mediation and MTSS significantly reduced the number of student disciplinary referrals and suspensions across student demographics. However, while MTSS is an effective means to organize and optimize student supports, as stated throughout this book, mediation can also be introduced as a stand-alone intervention.

In Chapter 3, I provide a thorough explanation of what mediation is and why it is important to mediate with teachers and students. Subsequent chapters provide comprehensive training on how to conduct mediation, discuss the skills necessary for an effective mediator, and explore root causes of teacher and student difficulties, offering guidance on how to respond to common challenges. I also reveal how teachers and students react to the practice of mediation and detail how to use feedback to improve a school mediation program. In addition to discussing teacher–student mediations, this book also presents techniques for mediating with students to address student conflicts, fights, and bullying. Lastly, I endorse and illustrate the practice of using mediation among adults in schools.

3

What Is Teacher–
Student Mediation?

Understanding is another name for love; love is another name
for understanding.

—Thich Nhat Hanh

Teacher Susan Schneider: As a teacher for 37 years, the single most important
factor in the classroom is a positive and mutually respectful relationship
between the student and teacher. When this is compromised, it is essential
to get that back on track...but that is not always an easy process. Teachers
and students deserve skill building in understanding and insight into each
other's worlds. It sounds simple, but it's not always the case. Mediation is a
way to foster empathy, understanding, and a humanization between each
member—student and teacher—for one another.

WHAT IS MEDIATION?

The Latin root for the word *mediation* means "middle carrier." Mediation is an
intervention to help people in conflict reconcile differences, settle a dispute,
or reach a compromise. Many people practice mediation all over the world.
Mediation often refers to the complex dispute resolution process performed by
lawyers or professional mediators in divorce, labor and contract negotiations, or
property or other complex legal disputes. The outstanding *Getting to Yes* books
of Fisher, Ury, and Patton (now in the third edition—2011) are a classic example of how to understand and conduct such negotiations. In a school context,

the Center for Appropriate Dispute Resolution in Special Education (CADRE; see www.directionservice.org/cadre) provides families with an excellent free resource on steps to resolve complex educational disputes with their child's school district. However, not all mediations are complex. In fact, this book promotes the use of a voluntary and efficient mediation technique that can be used among teachers and students, students and other students, and even adults.

The use of mediation is continually expanding within educational, community, and youth settings. Although there is little to no research on the use of mediation as a Tier II intervention to specifically restore and improve teacher–student relationships, since the early 2000s, the use of mediation has been promoted within the context of restorative practices. In 2014, the U.S. Department of Education's *Guiding Principles* defined restorative justice practices as "nonpunitive disciplinary responses that focus on repairing harm done to relationships and people, developing solutions by engaging all persons affected by a harm, and accountability" (p. 24). The goals of restorative justice intervention in schools are "to address the harm committed and enhance responsibility and accountability, build relationships and community, and teach students empathy and problem solving skills that can help prevent the occurrence of inappropriate behavior in the future" (p. 24).

Children make mistakes, and it makes sense to provide venues for them to understand their actions and how those actions affect others and to make amends. Oakland School District has been widely praised for the implementation of restorative justice principles and practices in order to "build community and respond to student misconduct, with the goals of repairing harm and restoring relationships between those impacted" (Oakland Unified School District). Using a tiered system of supports, Oakland's use of restorative justice involves "creating space for dialogue" via mediation, restorative conversations, circles, family group conferences, and community conferences. Citing the positive impact of restorative justice approaches, Ralphe Bunch High School, a continuation school for 250 students in Oakland Unified School District, reported a reduction in suspensions by half (Khadaroo, 2013).

Upon completing a standard 40-hour mediation training in 2009, my new knowledge percolated in my mind for more than a year, and then I saw an opportunity. School discipline was transforming to include a tiered system of SWPBS that recognized the importance of teaching social, communication, and conflict-resolution skills rather than just being a system of punitive consequences. I knew that counselors, social workers, and school psychologists intervened frequently with teachers and students, but why not apply the structure and principles of mediation to teacher–student meetings?

I asked three questions: 1) Would conducting teacher–student mediations be feasible given my busy schedule? 2) Would teachers accept the idea? 3) Would mediations be effective? In the spirit of "action research," which I interpret as permission to try something new and collect data to measure effectiveness, I began to search for answers. Fortunately for me, the formation of Tier II meetings was concurrently being rolled out at Centennial High School. While teacher–student mediation can operate as a stand-alone intervention using existing trained school staff member(s) as the mediators, teacher–student mediation can also be used as a Tier II intervention embedded into MTSS.

Although I was the only practitioner of teacher–student mediations, I had assistance in data collection and analysis at our Tier II meetings. To my surprise, the answers to my initial questions were

Yes: Teacher–student mediations were doable given my busy schedule.

Yes: Teachers can accept the idea.

Yes: According to our data, mediations were effective.

In this chapter, I describe the "what" and the "why" of teacher–student mediation. In Chapter 4, I discuss the "how" in detail. In Chapter 5, I detail the qualities of a skilled mediator. Then, in Chapter 6, I examine the root causes of teacher–student conflicts and provide examples of problem-solving strategies.

WHAT IS TEACHER–STUDENT MEDIATION?

Teacher Beth Hogan: I had the opportunity to participate in a teacher–student mediation that restored the peace in our classroom and healed a fraught teacher–student relationship. The key to this mediation was that the student and I were temporarily asked to step out of our prescribed roles and artificial hierarchy to express concerns and to collaborate toward a resolution. This was a deeply humanizing process for both my student and me, one that prevented a possible suspension for my student, but also increased my joy and effectiveness in the classroom.

Mediation is not simply getting people in a room to talk. Teacher–student mediation takes place in a voluntary meeting with a teacher, student, and trained mediator, usually in a private office during a 50-minute period. Mediation is structured so that the mediator sets the tone and is "in charge." All parties must follow the mediator's directions. Mediation provides the means for people to tell their full story. It is dignifying and healing for people to be heard, understood, and affirmed. Mediation strives to improve the self-esteem and effectiveness of the teacher and student. Mediation also aims to bridge racial and cultural divides and to help build trust. *The goal of teacher–student mediation is to restore respect and improve relationships so that teachers can teach and students can learn.*

The meeting opens with a review of the rules of mediation. The teacher and student are asked to speak only to the mediator and to answer the question: "What brought us here today?" The mediator takes notes and asks clarifying questions during the first part of the 50-minute mediation. Then, the teacher and student are invited to speak directly to each other and to develop a plan to move forward. Mediations are simple and easy. However, there are dynamics that the mediator must be aware of, which are examined in more depth in Chapter 6.

The following four principles, adapted for school use from the 2005 Model Standards of Conduct for Mediators (American Arbitration Association, American Bar Association, & the Association for Conflict Resolution), are useful in school settings:

1. Impartiality: Mediators do not take sides. They are there to listen—not to solve problems, evaluate solutions, or provide options. Mediators are to even-handedly facilitate communication because it is critical for all parties to be perceived as having equal rights and dignity (p. 4).

2. Confidentiality: Within the parameters of mandated public school reporting (i.e., child abuse), a mediation is a private meeting. Knowing the mediation is confidential gives people confidence in the process (p. 6).

3. Self-determination: The two participants choose to talk about whatever topics they wish. The mediation simply provides the structure and safe opportunity to do so. Self-determination empowers the participants and helps them feel more effective (pp. 3–4).

4. Voluntariness: Participants come to mediation voluntarily and stay voluntarily (p. 2).

WHY MEDIATE WITH TEACHERS AND STUDENTS?

Principal Greg Johnson: It's [teacher–student mediation] consistently our highest performing intervention, and of course, it makes sense. You have interpersonal conflict, you resolve that interpersonally. It's clear.

Teacher–student mediation is a common-sense solution that improves student learning and teacher morale, fosters an environment of caring and respect, improves racial understanding, and models conflict resolution skills.

Why Is Mediation Helpful for Teachers?

Teachers are trained and certified professionals. Unfortunately, no training program adequately prepares a teacher for the wide and varied behavioral challenges that students present—a teacher's first years are often "baptism by fire." I often joke that I couldn't last a day in the classroom; the physical, emotional, and organizational demands of the job are nonstop. It is stating the obvious, but teachers are only human and are not immune from adult pressures and bad days. Most can recount a time when a situation with a child could have been handled better. Mediation can help teachers rebuild their relationships with their students and gain additional ways of responding to challenges that students may pose. Even the most experienced teachers ask for assistance in working with some students. Many teachers who come to mediation are highly skilled, sensitive, and have excellent classroom management techniques, but those techniques may not be effective with a particular student. I have deep respect for teachers who walk into a mediation. They are stepping out of their comfort zone in order to improve their effectiveness with a student.

Why Is Mediation Helpful for Students?

Students can benefit from mediation by learning about a teacher's perspective and possibly obtaining a more sympathetic understanding of the teacher's responsibilities. Also, students can benefit from learning how to appropriately express their feelings and discovering how dignifying it feels when those feelings are heard and validated. In addition, a mediation meeting provides outreach and care and models appropriate problem-solving behavior for students. Students come to school with a variety of social, educational, behavioral, and medical challenges. Many are affected by poverty, abuse, neglect, loss, substance abuse, and inadequate exposure to appropriate social and cultural experiences. Mediation gives these students a voice and can provide an outlet for them to discuss some of their life challenges. Anyone referring a student to teacher–student mediation will assess the suitability of this intervention on a case-by-case basis. It has been my experience, however, that students of diverse backgrounds rate their teacher–student mediation experience as a positive one (see Chapter 8).

Why Is Mediation Helpful for Both Teachers and Students?

Teachers and students see each other every school day. Consider the implications of an ongoing interpersonal problem:

- The conflict produces stress and tension. It saps the joy out of teaching and learning.

- Even "planned ignoring" (i.e., consciously avoiding the situation or avoiding communication) requires mental and emotional energy.

- The discomfort reduces the effectiveness of the teacher and student in their activities.

- The negativity permeates the classroom climate and affects other learners.

- The academic achievement of the student is affected, possibly leading to increased truancy, behavioral problems, and disciplinary consequences.

- The ongoing difficulty may reduce the overall success of the teacher in promoting student learning.

- The conflict may be rooted in racial bias or misunderstanding.

- Unresolved conflicts can linger and even snowball. Students and teachers can get into a rut without the tools to form new patterns of behavior.

- Both parties have a stake in improving the relationship: The student wishes to earn a passing grade (and hopefully excel in the class), and the teacher wishes to create an effective, positive, affirming learning environment.

Regardless of the student's age, mediation may provide the first safe venue for the student to problem-solve in an appropriate manner with a teacher. It can also be the first time that a teacher has had an opportunity to have an extended, frank, problem-solving conversation with a student. In many communities in the country, mediation may also provide the first opportunity for a more in-depth cross-cultural dialogue as teachers and students alike are exposed to people of different backgrounds. Mediation provides an excellent opportunity to foster respect and promote cultural awareness for all parties. Consider the following scenario: Sammy, a shy high school freshman, is falling behind in biology. His mother told him to go talk to his teacher about raising his grade. He approaches Mr. Perkins during a 4-minute passing period.

Sammy: Uh, Mr. Perkins, can I talk to you about raising my grade?

Mr. Perkins: OK. Give me a minute to look up what you're missing. It looks like you have three tests to make up, the leaf project, and the homework from Chapters 9, 11, and 14. I'm here most days after school if you need some help and you can do your make-up tests at that time.

Sammy: OK, thanks. Bye.

Sammy now has a pile of homework and make-up tests to do. He may not know how to get started on the work and is too embarrassed to ask for help. Mr. Perkins said to come after school, but Sammy knows he will never do that. He has to catch a bus and get home to help care for his siblings. Mr. Perkins sees that Sammy is a no-show after school and interprets this as Sammy not caring about his grade.

As the weeks pass, Sammy's grade gets lower and lower. His mother is upset. Sammy never turned in the missing homework, and the pile grows. As each day passes, Sammy's rut deepens. His mother grounds him because of his low grades. Soon he has outbursts at home because he is overwhelmed and frustrated.

Maybe all along, all Sammy needed was the time and opportunity to discuss his areas of need with his teacher to help jumpstart him on the right path. What Mr. Perkins sees, however, is a student who does not do his work and does not show up for help—and that does not make a great impression. Though Mr. Perkins did initially invite Sammy to come for help, such brief conversations do not always result in improved student work habits. Mr. Perkins provided the information about make-up work to Sammy and directed him to come after school, yet he did not show a more personal interest in Sammy, identify what had caused him to fall behind in the first place, or provide encouragement. This is not because Mr. Perkins did not care. There simply was not time. When the bell rings, Mr. Perkins must change classrooms and has only 4 minutes to travel to his next destination before the next bell. Such a hectic pace is not conducive to an in-depth conversation.

Mediation provides the means for a completely different interaction. Because the meeting opens with the teacher and student only speaking with the mediator, the tone of voice is different. With all due respect to teachers, I have observed that some tend to use a "teacher voice" when speaking with students who have misbehaved or fallen behind. This voice is slightly stern, always serious, and is not accompanied by smiles. Some students, particularly teenagers, also have a voice they use with teachers. It may be sassy or sarcastic and include a dose of eye rolling. This tone, too, is absent from mediation meetings. In fact, I am continually amazed at the level of kindness and understanding that is expressed by both parties in mediations. This drives my enthusiasm and desire to share this easy, quick, game-changing intervention with others.

Not all teachers will require the use of a mediator in resolving conflicts or improving relationships with students. Many are very adept and comfortable with difficult conversations that root out the problem and develop solutions. Despite the demands of teaching their subject area curriculum, these teachers recognize the importance of building a positive culture in their classrooms and have developed the skills to do so. Such teachers have also examined their own backgrounds and biases and attended to issues of respect, equity, and fairness in their practices.

Administrator Angela Schoonover: As a teacher, I always encouraged students to come to me if they felt as if I was disrespecting them. I had gone to and taught at a camp in California 5 years ago, and there were really good things that came out of it. One of the things was accepting and being able to work through conflict with people. Part of it is acknowledging this is what happened, acknowledging how the other person felt about it, and then moving forward...what do we do to make this better? And so I took that and I actually incorporated it in my classroom. I always encouraged students to come if they felt at any point in my class I disrespected them or treated them unfairly...to please come and talk to me about it. We talked about good times to do that. And I did have students who felt empowered to do that.

AREN'T TEACHERS RESISTANT TO MEDIATION?

Principal Greg Johnson: Strategies about how to get teacher buy in and deal with teacher resistance aren't necessarily needed if the thing you are doing has a chance to breathe and then is obviously and undeniably successful. And so I think what happens with teacher–student mediations is they become their own best advertising tool. They're just working. I've never, ever, heard a teacher complain about it.

Administrator Ryan Cowell: I have seen very little negative response from teachers or students regarding mediation, and I have seen it do tremendous good in many cases. I do a significant portion of the referring for teacher–student mediations, and I rarely run into teachers that do not want to take part in a mediation.

I was surprised and grateful that teachers were not more resistant to the idea of a teacher–student mediation meeting. After the idea of mediation was rolled out at the beginning-of-the-year faculty meeting, I fully expected to get called into the principal's office with the news that many had complained. That never happened. Many teachers appreciated the idea of mediation because they had run out of ideas on how to resolve problems with certain students. They had already written disciplinary referrals, tried reasoning with the student in a hallway chat, sent the student out of class, and even called home. They had not seen improvements and were open to trying something new.

Chapter 7 describes teacher and student reactions to mediation in greater detail; however, I believe there were other significant reasons why there was not more teacher resistance. In 2010, there was a seismic shift and sweeping reforms in the way educators were going to be evaluated throughout the country. In a January 12, 2010, speech, Randi Weingarten, president of the American Federation of Teachers, presented a "serious and comprehensive reform plan to ensure great teaching, taking on systems that have been ingrained in public education for more than a century" (Bass, 2010, p.1). Illinois provides a specific example: The Illinois General Assembly and Governor signed into law the Performance Evaluation Reform Act (PERA), and on June 13, 2011, Senate Bill 7 (see www.isbe.net/PERA/). These laws called for significant reforms to business as usual, including a change in the system for dismissing a tenured educator. School districts were required to develop new teacher evaluation systems, and in the fall of 2012, after much collaboration among administrators, educators, and union representatives, Champaign Schools introduced a teaching evaluation instrument adapted from Charlotte Danielson's popular Framework for Teaching (see www.danielsongroup.org/framework).

Perhaps the greatest strength of the Danielson evaluation instrument is how it spells out, in explicit detail, a description of expectations, including what constitutes *ineffective* to *highly effective* practices. There can no longer be any doubt as to what "good" teaching looks like (or good work for any other certified employee, such as a guidance counselor, psychologist, or social worker).

This is relevant to teacher–student mediation because some components of the Danielson model pertain to the relationship between teachers and students. For example, for New York public schools, the Danielson evaluation instrument spells out how creating an "environment of respect and rapport" looks and provides examples. The following guidelines and rating system, pulled from the *Danielson 2013 Rubric—Adapted to New York Department of Education Framework for Teaching Components*, are used to determine if a teacher has achieved this goal:

Highly effective:

> Classroom interactions between the teacher and students and among students are highly respectful, reflecting genuine warmth, caring, and sensitivity to students as individuals. Students exhibit respect for the teacher and contribute to high levels of civility among all members of the class. The net result is an environment where all students feel valued and are comfortable taking intellectual risks. (p. 21)

Effective:

> Teacher–student interactions are friendly and demonstrate general caring and respect. Such interactions are appropriate to the ages, cultures, and developmental levels of the students. Interactions among students are generally polite and respectful, and students exhibit respect for the teacher. The teacher responds successfully to disrespectful behavior among students. The net result of the interactions is polite, respectful, and business-like, though students may be somewhat cautious about taking intellectual risks. (p. 21)

Developing:

> Patterns of classroom interactions, both between teacher and students and among students, are generally appropriate but may reflect occasional inconsistencies, favoritism, and disregard for students' ages, cultures, and developmental levels. Students rarely demonstrate disrespect for one another. The teacher attempts to respond to disrespectful behavior, with uneven results. The net result of the interactions is neutral, conveying neither warmth nor conflict. (p. 21)

Ineffective:

> Patterns of classroom interactions, both between teacher and students and among students, are mostly negative, inappropriate, or insensitive to students' ages, cultural backgrounds, and developmental levels. Student interactions are characterized by sarcasm, put-downs, or conflict. The teacher does not deal with disrespectful behavior. (p. 21)

Teachers may therefore be incentivized to use teacher–student mediation to improve a difficult relationship. Even if the mediation does not work miracles, teachers will show good-faith effort and an openness to use a novel way to improve communication with a student.

Adminstrator Tony Maltbia: The by-product of mediations is that it improves student behavior. It also improves teacher behavior. It forces both teachers and students to hear and understand the other person's perspective.

There will always be some teachers who view mediation as undermining their authority. These teachers believe that they have clearly spelled out the rules. They have also sent the rules home for parents to review and sign, and any student who violates the rules should expect the consequences. There is generally nothing wrong with this way of thinking, because for 80% of the students (i.e., students in Tier I), this technique works. Mediation is considered a Tier II intervention because the traditional methods to correct student performance were not effective; thus, teacher–student mediation is often for the 20% of students who did not respond at the Tier I level. Perhaps the student needed more from the teacher: more attention, more care, more concern, or more structure. We do not know what the student requires until we ask, and teacher–student mediation provides a safe, structured way to ask and answer important questions.

Other teachers may have concerns that mediation "levels the playing field" and reduces their power. They feel that to be effective, they need to remain in charge. As the adults in the room, teachers do need to be in charge to run an effective classroom. The teacher is the authority figure and has the power to pass or fail a student and send a student out of class. The teacher has the power to decide how to use the time allotted for group work and time allotted for conversations with individual students. The teacher also has the power to greet students with a smile and to use strategies and techniques that provide structure and engaging learning activities. However, there is no one teaching style or classroom management technique that is 100% effective or foolproof in the classroom or guaranteed to build positive relationships with students. Ivana may say that she hates Mr. P., the English teacher, and her classmate Marcus says he loves Mr. P. It is important to remember that both teachers and students exercise power within the classroom on a daily basis—sometimes with positive and sometimes with negative results. Students exercise power in their level of cooperation. Students also exert power by being distracting and disruptive.

Teacher–student mediation is not designed to shift the power dynamics in a class. What may seem initially like a teacher relinquishing power by being on a more equal playing field for the 50 minutes of the mediation can actually restore the teacher–student dynamic to its more traditional place. Replacing anger or resistance with understanding and rapport allows the teacher to teach and the student to learn.

Another area of teacher resistance may fall into the "It's not me, it's him!" category. I cannot overemphasize the following point: *Mediation is not a blame game*, or an investigation into "what really happened." Mediation is not to determine "the truth" or "who was in the right and who was in the wrong."

People cannot possibly "get it right" during each and every interaction. Human imperfection gets in the way. It is precisely those interpersonal relationship glitches—the misread or misunderstood statement, the wrong tone of voice, the lack of eye contact, the sarcastic comment, the low expectation, or the perceived bias—that can derail any working relationship. There are so many ways we can step on someone else's toes. It takes a reflective teacher to be able to realize the effects of his or her actions and words.

Administrator Angela Schoonover: When you're teaching in the moment, you don't always realize things that you do. Like, a kid had come to me and said, "I felt like when you said this to me, I don't know, it made me feel really bad about myself." It was kind of eye opening. Kids need to be able to openly communicate with people that they're working so closely with. It's powerful.

HOW ARE MEDIATIONS AND TRADITIONAL DISCIPLINE BALANCED?

Mediation is not designed to replace traditional disciplinary consequences. When a student uses profanity with a teacher, that student will likely be given a punishment based on the school's code of conduct. Mediation is designed to expand and augment the consequences. Mediation is an avenue for students to learn how their behavior has an impact on the teacher and their classmates and provides students with a venue to take responsibility for their actions or at least to explain the context of their misconduct. Apologies are not required in mediation but often occur spontaneously and are always much appreciated.

At Centennial High School, teachers and administrators developed a list that identified and differentiated between behaviors that could be managed by a teacher within the classroom and those that warrant a referral to the administrator's office (see Table 3.1).

The list in Table 3.1 reminds nonteachers of all that can go wrong in a classroom. One might wonder, however, why some teachers write dozens of disciplinary referrals a year and others write almost none. How does this affect teacher–student relationships within a classroom? An administrator at Centennial High School eloquently described the effects of a high number of disciplinary referrals.

Administrator Angela Schoonover: The teachers who are quick to send a kid out are really outsourcing their discipline to someone else. When you outsource your discipline, students start to lose respect for you as a person. They see you as someone who doesn't care about them as people. I see that just through conversations that students have shared with me. When a teacher is willing to open up and work with a student but still set those high expectations, I think that is what you want to see; you want to see a teacher who has high expectations, but also cares for a student and is willing to work with them. When kids see that, they begin to respect the teacher. You can see it with certain teachers in the building that kids just love, and you can see the expectations are high and they're not going to get away with everything.

Table 3.1. Comparison of teacher-managed and office-managed student behavioral infractions

Teacher managed	Office managed
Excessive talking	Insubordination
Being off task	Fighting
Chewing gum/eating food/candy	Vandalism
Drinking (nonalcoholic)	Verbal/physical intimidation
Missing homework	Carrying weapons/making threats
Not being prepared for class	Gang representation
Name calling	Cutting class/repeated tardies
Public displays of affection	Theft
Passing notes	Drug/alcohol violations
Backtalk directed at adults	Directed profanity
Cheating/plagiarism	Harassment (including sexual)
Sleeping	Security threat/breach
Shut down/no compliance	Passing lewd notes
Minor disobedience	Repeated backtalk
Minor disruptive behavior	Repeated public displays of affection
Minor vandalism	Dress code violation
Electronic device	Creating a fake pass

SUMMARY AND NEXT TOPIC

This chapter provided an explanation of what mediation is and why it is important to mediate with teachers and students. Chapter 4 expands on this and provides comprehensive training on how to conduct teacher–student mediations using dialogues and examples. Throughout the book, I will be repeating the important mantra that schools are all about quality relationships. Every training I have ever attended and every observation that I have made point to the same fact: Students perform best when they think the teacher cares about them, and teachers' high expectations show respect for students.

4

How to Conduct Teacher–Student Mediations

Start where you are. Use what you have. Do what you can.

—Arthur Ashe

Sometime around mid-August or early September, teachers return to school for a new semester. Typically, the first 1–3 days are student free, and the faculty is bustling to get rooms set up, obtain lists of incoming students, and learn about relevant updates. There may be new staff and administrators present, so each year feels like a fresh start. People are generally smiling, upbeat, and refreshed from spending time with friends and family over summer break. This is a good time to introduce teacher–student mediation. This chapter describes that introduction and provides a step-by-step guide for how to conduct teacher–student mediations.

HOW TO INTRODUCE TEACHER–STUDENT MEDIATION

It was the first day of school in August of 2011 when Angela Schoonover, administrator at Centennial High School, explained Tier II interventions and supports to the faculty. Teacher–student mediation was introduced using a PowerPoint slide depicted in Figure 4.1, which serves as an example of one way to present mediation to teachers. At Centennial High School, mediation was a recommended intervention following three disciplinary referrals from the same teacher for the same student because disciplinary referrals could be deemed ineffective in improving the student's behavior. Despite the suggested

Teacher–Student Mediation	
Led by: School psychologist	
Description:	**Referral criteria:**
• Mediation helps eliminate problems occurring in a specific classroom with a staff member.	• Three disciplinary referrals from the same teacher, or upon request
	• Participation is voluntary.
• The school psychologist serves as a neutral (impartial) party.	**Determining response:**
• A mutually agreed upon plan is created by the teacher and student to help decrease unwanted behavior.	• No disciplinary referrals from the same teacher after the mediation

Figure 4.1.   Introduction to teacher–student mediation.

referral criteria, it is important to emphasize that mediation is voluntary and that a teacher, student, parent, or administrator can request mediation at any time. Counselors and social workers can also request mediations for students with ongoing conflicts with teachers or for those students who exclaim, "My teacher hates me!" Three disciplinary referrals were not a firm prerequisite to hold a mediation, but a general guideline for when intervention might be requested.

For purposes of data collection, the determining response was as follows: A mediation was deemed *effective* if the teacher did not issue any further disciplinary referrals to the student. A mediation was deemed *ineffective* if the teacher issued further disciplinary referrals to the student.

HOW TO REQUEST A TEACHER–STUDENT MEDIATION

Anyone may request a teacher–student mediation, including an administrator, teacher, student support staff, hall monitor, coach, student, or parent. In the initial stages of introducing mediation at Centennial High School, we requested that people who wanted to participate in a mediation fill out a Teacher–Student Mediation Request Form to provide background information on the problem. Figure 4.2 provides an example of how the form is completed, including notations by the mediator. (A blank template of this form is included in Appendix A.)

After the first year, the request form was used inconsistently, as people preferred to request mediations via email or in person. Furthermore, the background information was not always needed, as relevant issues and concerns would be revealed in the mediation meeting itself. Regardless of whether or not people used the form in requesting a mediation, we tracked the request data and noted the date of the mediation, who requested the mediation, the teacher and student names, student grade, student ethnicity, and whether or not the student received free or reduced price lunch. The collection and analysis of demographic data were aimed to provide feedback on who was using and/or benefitting from the mediation intervention.

Teacher–Student Mediation Request Form

Student name: _Zoe Miles_

Date of referral: _3/18/15_

Teacher name: _Ms. Oswald_

Referring party: _Ms. Lymon_

Reason for request _Zoe has received three discipline referrals and has multiple_
minor infractions for disobedience. Zoe gets angry and mumbles profanity
when she is asked to stop talking and open her book. She frequently puts her
head down. She recently left class without permission.

Who is asking for mediation? Please circle and/or provide name:

(Administrator) _____   Teacher _____   Counselor _____

Student _____   Parent _____   Other _____

Teacher is aware of request   (Yes)   No

Student is aware of request   (Yes)   No

Parent/guardian is aware of request   (Yes)   No

The person conducting the mediation will complete this portion and return it to the referring party:

Name of mediator: _Mr. Gerber_

Date of mediation: _3/20/15_

Additional information: _Mediation was helpful. Zoe and Ms. Oswald came away_
with a better understanding of each other, and they developed positive rapport.
They made a plan to improve classroom behavior.

Figure 4.2.   Completed Teacher–Student Mediation Request Form.

THE REQUEST IS IN—WHAT HAPPENS NEXT?

This section provides the reader with how-to training on performing a mediation. Rather than beginning every sentence with, "The mediator…," I speak directly to the reader with step-by-step instructions.

Step 1

Contact the teacher to ask if it is okay to set up the mediation and secure a time. Never assume a teacher's participation is voluntary unless it is explicitly stated. Figure 4.3 provides an example of a mediation invitation form returned by the teacher. I have found that emailing teachers the invitation form is more efficient than putting a paper version in a mailbox. The invitation can be embedded in the body of the email or sent as an email attachment. A reproducible template of the Teacher–Student Mediation Invitation Form is provided in Appendix A.

Sometimes an email invitation (and perhaps the desire to not participate in a mediation) prompts the teacher to personally resolve the conflict with the student. I might hear back: "No need to mediate; we worked it out." Or,

---

Teacher–Student Mediation Invitation Form

Date: _1/17/15_

Dear: _Ms. Ryder_ ,
           Teacher's name

I have been asked to do a voluntary teacher–student mediation with you and

Alexander Bordini .
           Student's name

Is this okay with you?   (Yes)   No   Not sure

If yes, please tell me when you are available for this meeting.

Dates: _Jan. 19 or Jan. 21_   Times: _10 a.m.–11 a.m. or 1 p.m.–2 p.m._

If the answer is *No* or *Not sure*, please let me know if you would like to speak further or if you have questions about mediation.

Comments/questions: _Thank you for the invitation for mediation. I am hopeful that this meeting will help me improve my relationship with Alexander in the class-room._

Thank you!

Ellen Branden, Mediator
     Mediator name

Figure 4.3. Sample Teacher–Student Mediation Invitation Form.

sometimes the teacher may call the parent about the student's behavior. Either way, the teacher addressed the concern, and the mediation does not move forward. The majority of teachers respond by listing available times and dates.

Step 2

Review the student's schedule and identify the best time for the student to participate. It is best to schedule as soon as possible after receiving the request.

Step 3

Go to the student's classroom and ask the teacher if you can briefly speak to the student in the hall. When the student comes out, say something such as the following:

Mediator: Hi, I am _____. I have been asked to do a teacher–student mediation with you and _____. Teacher–student mediations are a really great way to clear the air when there's a problem. It's really simple. I will just ask you and the teacher to speak only to me and answer the question, "What brought us here?" While one person is talking, the other person just sits back and listens. It is amazing how much you can learn just by hearing the other person's perspective. Then the other person has a turn. After both people have spoken, I ask you to speak to each other and develop a plan to move forward. How does that sound to you? Are you willing to be in a meeting like this? [ASKING is key because it is respectful and empowering to give the student the choice.] Ms. _____ said the best time for her to meet would be Thursday, during period 7. Would that work for you?

I have found that approximately 90% of the students whom I ask to participate in a mediation say, "Okay." They have usually been told about teacher–student mediation from the adult making the request, so my brief talk does not come as a complete surprise. Even without prior communication with the student, however, I find the vast majority to be amenable. When they agree to participate, I praise them for their openness and willingness to communicate:

Mediator: Okay, that's really great that you are willing to do this. Thank you! Do you have any questions? I'll send a reminder on the day of our meeting. See you then!

Step 4

Confirm the date and time with the teacher, taking care not to discuss the specifics of the conflict before mediation. Because one of the four principles of mediation is impartiality, the way I ensure my own impartiality is to avoid having an in-depth "intake" conversation with either party prior to the mediation. I do not want to act impartial. I want to be impartial. For example, if Mr. Lehman has given me a laundry list of Jose's transgressions prior to the meeting, he might expect some adult solidarity within the meeting. Children spot conspiring adults a mile away, and it would not be fair to have the mediation turn into a "two-against-one" meeting. I want to react with authenticity in the mediation. If something does not make sense or is complicated, I can ask for clarification. If something is funny, I can laugh. I want to hear both parties in real time so that my reactions and questions are genuine. Under these conditions, my reflective listening skills are earnest and not phony because I truly am hearing and reacting to everything for the first time. If approached by the teacher prior to the mediation, you can say something such as the following:

Mediator: I see that you want to give me background on Abigail. I appreciate that, except that when I wear my mediator hat, it helps my impartiality if I learn about everything in the course of the mediation meeting.

Even if the mediator has background knowledge and a prior relationship (including prior mediations) with the teacher and the student, it is important to approach each mediation meeting with a fresh set of ears.

Step 5

On the day of the mediation, verify that the student is at school and send the student a reminder note or personally visit the student to reconfirm the mediation time. Mediations are often scheduled during a teacher's prep period, lunch, or hallway supervision time. It is important to not waste a teacher's time waiting for a student who is not in school. Send a reminder email to the teacher the day of the mediation as well.

When it's time for the mediation meeting, one party may still have forgotten. In rare instances, students change their mind the day of the appointment. They might say, "Things are better. We don't need it anymore." The teacher may or may not agree. I may revisit the issue with the student and encourage the mediation. However, participation is always voluntary. If both parties believe things are worked out, I simply say, "That's great. I'm here if you need me in the future."

THE MEDIATION PROCESS

The meeting is scheduled and both parties arrive. The mediation process may begin.

I. Welcome with a Smile

Dale Carnegie's classic book *How to Win Friends & Influence People,* still a best-seller after more than 75 years in print and many updated editions, spends an entire chapter on the importance of a smile: "Actions speak louder than words, and a smile says, 'I like you. You make me happy. I am glad to see you'" (1981, p. 63). People entering a mediation do not know what to expect and likely are nervous. A smile puts them at ease and projects warmth and caring. The mediator sets the tone and must come across as friendly and open.

Mediator: Welcome to this mediation. Please sit here.

Triangular seating may be ideal so that the parties are not directly across from each other, but can easily face each other.

Mediator [smiling]: I am so glad you are both here! Mediation is a great way to resolve conflicts and clear the air. It's also a way to learn things about another person's perspective that you might not have realized before. I just want to start by thanking both of you for being here.

II. Review the Rules of Mediation

Explain the rules of mediation to the student and teacher so that they have an idea of how the meeting will proceed. You might say something such as the following:

Mediator: The rules for mediation are really simple. I will ask each of you to speak only to me and answer the same question: "What brought us here today?" While one person is speaking, the other person just sits back and listens. Then I will ask the other person the same question. Only one person speaks at a time, and, of course, there are no interruptions, put-downs, or nonverbal behaviors such as eye rolling. I will take notes, ask clarifying questions and summarize what I have heard. At the end I will ask you to speak directly to each other and develop a plan to move forward.

III. Review the Four Principles of Mediation

Clarify the four principles of mediation (impartiality, confidentiality, self-determination, and voluntariness) one by one so that everyone feels safe and open to discussing the issues at hand.

Mediator: I'd like to review the four principles of mediation.

- First, as your mediator, I am impartial. I don't take sides.

- Second, this meeting is confidential. What we discuss here is private.

- Third is the principle of self-determination. You get to decide what you do or do not want to talk about here, and you will develop your own plans to move forward.

- Fourth, this meeting is voluntary. You both agreed to be here, right?

Mediator: I just want to pause here a moment to thank you both again for being here. It takes courage to be in a meeting like this, and I really appreciate your willingness to give mediation a try.

An important way to set the participants at ease is to continually express thanks and praise throughout the mediation process. The expression of thanks and praise supports and affirms the participants' efforts to improve their relationship and helps maintain a positive tone in the mediation.

IV. Identify the Issues

The mediator starts by asking, "Who would like to go first?" Both participants may be nervous, and often the student does not opt to go first. Typically, the teacher will jump in; however, it is generally not important who starts the meeting. If the student and teacher turn to one another and try to speak to each other, redirect them by saying, "Remember to speak only to me. What brought us here today?" Each person may only speak to the mediator at this stage, as the mediator will solely focus on one speaker's full story, and then the second speaker's full story. The importance of this cannot be overstated:

- If the teacher and student start to speak directly to each other, they may soon exhibit the problematic communication patterns that existed before the mediation (e.g., "serious teacher" vs. "sassy child"), and the mediator is relegated to the role of bystander.

- Conflicts often arise from inadequate listening. When each party speaks directly to the mediator, the mediator reflectively listens and emphasizes certain key points, thereby enhancing the listening process for the participants. Simply stated, people listen better when they are not in the "hot seat."

- The mediator must show control over the mediation by setting the tone, climate, and tempo of the meeting. When the participants speak only to the mediator, the mediator has maximum flexibility to maintain the focus, productivity, and safety of the meeting. If interruptions occur, politely redirect by saying, "Remember, no interruptions. We really want to hear from you, and each person will have a turn to speak."

The following tips are useful when identifying each party's issues in a mediation.

Tip 1: Take Notes   Take notes on relevant details and verbatim quotes because you are reflecting on and not interpreting what is being said. An easy way to do this is to draw a vertical line down an 8.5" x 11" piece of paper, labeling one half of the sheet with the teacher's name, and the other half with the student's name. The notes are a tool for the mediator's use only and are confidential.

Tip 2: Ask Initial Background Questions Carefully   Ask initial questions carefully and avoid certain words and phrases that may sound judgmental. Use the word *what* rather than *why*. For instance, ask, "What happened?" instead of "Why did this happen?" *What* sounds more neutral and less accusatory than *why*.

Also, *why* invites an "I don't know" response. Also, avoid phrases such as "tell your side" or "give your version" because they suggest that there is an adversarial relationship between the teacher and student. On rare occasions, a student may request a mediation and the teacher does not know why. To help provide background information and context, it is helpful to ask about the setting, the time of day of the problem, and the length of the teacher and student's relationship. These are relevant details, and asking specific, concrete questions also helps to break the ice. Additional communication tips are shared in Chapter 5.

Mediator: Thank you for telling me what brought us here. Before we speak more about that, I'd like to ask a few more questions:

- What is the class subject?
- How many students are in the class?
- When does the class meet?
- How long have you known each other? (Weeks, months, years?)

Tip 3: Validate Each Person's Point of View   Use reflective, supportive, and nonjudgmental statements to validate each person's point of view.

Mediator:

- Oh, so you feel like the teacher is picking on you when you are not the only person talking.
- I think I understand what happened...
- I know this can be difficult, and I appreciate that you are talking about it.
- You're saying that you have asked the student many times to stop speaking in class, and you took him into the hallway for a talk, but it did not really help for very long.

Tip 4: Pause and Summarize What You Hear   Pause at various times during the meeting to summarize what you have heard. This helps modulate the rhythm of the mediation so that someone is not speaking too fast or for too long. You can gently raise your hand or finger and say, "Let's just pause for a second so that I make sure I understand what you just said."

Tip 5: Identify Specific Details on What Led up to the Problem   This is very helpful because usually there is one incident that derailed the teacher–student relationship. What happened with these two people? Identifying the details allows a mediator (and each participant) to understand the arc of the story and learn about relevant factors that are affecting the relationship.

Mediator:

- It sounds like things were going well for many months. What happened that changed things?

- So let me see if I understand this—you are saying that a lot of new people joined your group in the class...

- Oh, so you had been absent and were talking because you were trying to figure out what was going on.

- You are saying that this class is far from your locker, and you always need to get a snack because you're hungry at 11:30. That is why you were late. Your lunch isn't until 12:30 and you get cranky if you don't eat something?

If the student reports untoward behavior from the teacher, or vice versa, the mediator stays calm and impartial:

Mediator:

- So, you were talking to your friend, and you are saying that Mr. Lehman said, "Shut up." What happened next?

- You overheard Jennie whisper that you are "such a b*tch." Did I get that right?

   Tip 6: Provide the Teacher with an Opportunity to Identify Feelings   The mediator can ask about the class; the preparation for the class; personal expectations; and how it feels when students are not engaged, rude, or disruptive. It's also important to ask the teacher how the specific student's actions feel.

Mediator:

- Do you spend a lot of time thinking about the lessons for this class?

- What is it like to teach when students are talking in class?

- Are you hopeful that students will work hard and be engaged during class time?

- How did it feel when Scarlett did not open her book for a few days?

Some students can be more empathetic than others. Some care very much about the teacher's feelings, and others not as much. Regardless, mediation is a powerful tool that shows students how much the teacher actually sees each of them in class. Many students in mediation are astonished about the details teachers actually know about them.

Tip 7: Ask the Student to Identify Feelings Ask the student to identify feelings that result from the specific conflict. Again, write down verbatim quotes in your notes. For example

Student: Mrs. La Grange says I never do my work! That's totally not true!

Mediator: You are saying that Mrs. La Grange says you never do your work, and you are feeling like that is not true. Tell me more about that and how you feel about it.

Student: I did the frog assignment! I feel mad!

Mediator: Oh, you are feeling mad because you did the frog assignment. Were there some other assignments that you did not turn in? I just want to understand this a little better.

Student: Yeah, a few.

Mediator: Okay, so you are feeling mad that Mrs. LaGrange said you *never* do your work, when you did the frog project. You are also saying that there is some work that you have not turned in.

Student: Yeah, I know there's more stuff I need to do.

It is not the mediator's job to fact check during the mediation. The principle of self-determination dictates that the teacher and student may decide whether or not to focus on or question particular facts. It is their call, not the mediator's.

Tip 8: Highlight Positive Statements or "Mine for Gold" Highlight any positive statements from the teacher and student about each other. Probably the most powerful moment in a mediation is when the student or the teacher hears positive observations or feedback. These statements dispel the notion that there is mutual dislike or that one party hates the other. This is a critical component of the mediation because it helps generate mutual positive regard.

Student: I am not trying to say that Ms. Carlyn is a bad teacher. I do not have a problem with her in that way. I mean, she is a good teacher because she explains stuff well.

Mediator: You think Ms. Carlyn is a good teacher that explains stuff well. Cool!

Teacher: One day, Ray helped me carry some packages into the school. That was really helpful.

Mediator: Oh, Ray was helpful to you when he carried the packages!

If there has been no mention of anything positive, seek it out. I call this "mining for gold."

Mediator: Tell me about a time when Sunny did well in class.

Teacher: Actually, Sunny got off to a good start the first few weeks of class. She always brought her book and did her work.

Mediator: Oh, so you saw some good work habits from Sunny. She brought her book and did her work. Was there a certain assignment that she did well that you could comment on?

Mediator: What do you like about the way Ms. Soledad teaches?

Student: That's easy. She tells funny stories.

Mediator: Oh, so you like the funny stories that Ms. Soledad tells. What was your favorite one?

Mediator: So, it doesn't sound like you have a problem with Mr. Patel.

Student: Yeah. I like Mr. Patel. He cares.

Tip 9: Praise and Acknowledge Personal Responsibility Always acknowledge and praise participants when they take responsibility for their own actions.

Student: I admit it. It was rude of me to say, "Who cares about the stupid assignment" when I was in class.

Mediator: You are saying it was rude of you to make that statement. That is big of you to take responsibility for your behavior. I appreciate your honesty.

Teacher: Believe me. By eighth hour, I can be stressed. Sometimes I'm not at my best.

Mediator: Yes, by eighth hour, people can be tired, and may not always be at their best. Whatever you do, do not come around here during eighth hour if I've missed my lunch! I'm like an angry bear in a cave!

Tip 10: Help Break Any Tension It is okay to break tension by being silly or funny or momentarily digressing from the discussion of the conflict. Not all conflicts have easy resolutions, and the larger goal of the meeting is to restore respect and goodwill. Making self-deprecating remarks, pausing to ask about hobbies, or sharing a little story that universalizes classroom experiences helps to relax the participants. Consider the following example.

Mediator: I had this best friend in high school named Susie. Susie and I thought we were slick. We would sometimes whisper in class and pass notes. (Yes, in those days, we passed notes!) Of course we were smart enough to do all this when the teacher's back was turned. Then Susie became a high school teacher, and the very first thing she told me was, "Teachers see everything. We see everything!"

Tip 11: Avoid Restarting Negative Teacher–Student Conversations   Be cautious about asking, "What do you want to see happen?" too early in the mediation because it could turn into a repeat of previous teacher–student conversations. For example

Mediator: Mr. Ulrich, what do you want to see happen?

Teacher: I just want Jason to come to class prepared, to do his work, and to be quiet.

Or, consider a student's answer:

Mediator: Jason, what do you want to see happen?

Student: I want Mr. Ulrich to stop picking on me.

Although there is nothing inherently wrong with this dialogue, it can potentially restart the "here we go again" cycle and diminish the impact of the goodwill and positive statements that were generated during the mediation. A better time to ask such a question would be after goodwill has been clearly established. By then, the student's takeaways should ideally be

- The teacher cares about me
- The teacher notices what I do in the class
- What I do in the class really matters to the teacher (and to the other students)

The teacher's takeaways should ideally be

- The student has some things going on that I didn't realize. I'm going to try a different approach.
- The student cares more about our relationship than he or she lets on
- The student is capable of showing me respect
- The student and I came to an understanding and can move forward now that we have resolved our conflict

Tip 12: Ask for Any Remaining Statements   At the end of each person's full statement, check to make sure all has been said.

Mediator: Is there anything else you would like to say before we ask _____ to speak?

This protects against the mediator assuming that everything that needs to be said has been said.

V. Summarize What the Teacher and Student Have Said

Once both parties have spoken, provide an overall, humanizing, and impartial summary of what happened and how people felt about it. Be mindful of vocal inflections, and advocate for both parties. If possible, try to summarize in a way that shifts the point of view back and forth rather than discussing one party's viewpoint and then the other.

Emphasize the positive statements and the goodwill that each party had displayed toward one another. Use your notes and as many verbatim quotes as possible so that it does not feel like you are misinterpreting the statements made by either party. For example

Mediator: I am now going to summarize what I heard each of you say. We started with Mr. Ramirez, who said that what brought us here was that Mimi got three discipline referrals. He said that "she pretty much talks non-stop" during math class. Mr. Ramirez said that he felt "really frustrated" by that and has "tried to talk to Mimi about it in the hallway." He said that after that, "her behavior improved for a few days." When Mimi got talkative again, Mr. Ramirez said he called home and spoke to Mimi's father. Her behavior improved for a whole week after that, and Mr. Ramirez said that he saw some "promising work" from Mimi during that time.

Mimi said that she knows she talks a lot, and that it is really hard for her in that class because it is right before lunch. She said she is new to the school and trying to make friends. She said that if she talks to a certain group of kids, then she could go with them to lunch and sit with them. She said she talks to them so she won't feel lonely at school. Mimi said she was sorry about all the talking. She said, "I know it's rude."

We talked a little about the class in general, and Mr. Ramirez said that from the promising work that he saw from Mimi, he knows she can be a "top student" once she makes up her mind to focus in class. Mimi said she thought Mr. Ramirez was "a good math teacher" and that she likes math. In fact, she cares about her grade in that class. She said, though, that she gets upset sometimes when she gets disciplinary referrals and other people are talking. Mr. Ramirez said that he knows other people are talking; the reason Mimi keeps getting the disciplinary referrals is that she often talks after he says, "If one more person talks, they are going out."

We have identified in the mediation that Mr. Ramirez would like Mimi to do more of the promising work he has seen she is capable of and that she can even be a top student. We also heard that Mimi wants to do well in math, she likes math, and she thinks Mr. Ramirez is a "good math teacher." She has been upset about being singled out when other people are talking, and in the mediation, we learned that she was sent out because she talked immediately after Mr. Ramirez drew a line and warned the class that the next person that talked would be sent out. We also heard that Mimi is new to the school and is trying to form some friendships. Because this class falls right before lunch, it has been important for Mimi to be a part of a social group so that she can join them during lunch.

Be sure to include praise and thanks in the summary, such as the following:

Mediator: This has been helpful because we learned so much that we did not know before, and I want to again thank you both for participating today. You showed courage by being here and a real willingness to improve things.

VI. Ask Both Parties to Develop a Plan to Move Forward

Every time I do a mediation, I see the wisdom of self-determination, which allows the teacher and student to develop a plan that is suitable for their needs. They know the class—the students, the rules, the culture, the rhythms, the jokes. These are all things I would never know as an outsider. The mediator is not there to direct the student or teacher, nor is the mediator to act in the role of "consultant." He or she should simply ask, "At this point in the mediation, I am going to ask both of you to speak to each other and develop a plan to move forward." Under the best-case scenarios, the teacher and student launch into a fruitful discussion and make detailed arrangements. The mediator should continue to listen and jot down some notes but takes a back seat to the teacher–student conversation. Let us return to the example of Mr. Ramirez and Mimi.

Mr. Ramirez: I know that you are new to the school and want to have friends to sit with at lunch. I was a new kid myself once, so I know how it feels. I am getting ready to change some seats around in the class. How about if I group you with one of your new friends, and you work on math during class time? You will also be sitting right next to her when the bell rings, so you can make your lunch plans then.

Mimi: That would be good. I am also having trouble understanding the new unit. Could you help me with that?

Mr. Ramirez: Sure! I'd be happy to help! Come in during study hall or before or after school.

VII. Develop a Written Plan or Contract

First, summarize what you have heard the teacher and student agree to.

Mediator: Okay, you two have decided that Mr. Ramirez will change the seating so that Mimi is close to one of the students in her new friend group. She will talk about math with that student during small-group time but will be in a good position when the bell rings to make lunch plans. Mimi has agreed to speak about math during class time and has asked for math help. Mr. Ramirez is happy to help during study hall or before or after school.

Next, you might decide to develop a written plan or contract. This can be a helpful step, but it is not always necessary. Over time, I have modified my thinking about developing a written contract at the close of the mediation meeting, as I observed that teachers and students were often uninterested in developing a contract. They said they did not need it. They did not want to shift the positive mood and were satisfied with the verbal agreements they mutually developed in the meeting. Often the mediations seemed to focus on the teacher's and student's need to develop a better rapport and understanding of each other's perspectives, and a written document was not needed. Also, under the principles of self-determination, the decision whether or not to write a contract should be based on the wishes of the teacher and student.

As a result of teacher feedback (to be discussed in Chapter 7) and discussions with the Tier II team at Centennial High School, I have modified my practice to include a follow-up email. The benefit of an email is that it provides something tangible that each party can reference later to review what was agreed upon. The email, designed to be printed so that the teacher and student both get a copy, summarizes the joint agreements developed in the mediation. I also invite the parties to give feedback about the mediation and provide a menu of choices for follow-up. For example, you might ask whether the participants would like to do a check-in at a designated time, or if they would like to have an additional meeting on an as-needed basis.

VIII. Conclude the Meeting with Thanks and Praise

It is important to conclude the meeting on a positive note and praise each person's efforts.

Mediator: Thank you both so much for being here today. The communication was honest and respectful. It seems like you have a good plan to move forward. Great work! Mr. Ramirez, I will send you an email with a summary of the plans you made here today, and I ask that you please print a copy for Mimi. That way you each have a record. If there is anything else I can do for either of you, just let me know. I'm happy to help.

While the notes and the mediation are fresh in mind, send the teacher the email agreement. (Figure 4.4 provides an example of the email agreement for Mr. Ramirez and Mimi. A blank, reproducible Teacher–Student Mediation Follow-Up Email agreement also is included in Appendix A.) It is not important to provide a blow-by-blow summary of everything that was said, but if there was something positive that is worth repeating and that would be encouraging to the student or teacher, it can help to state that.

When mediations are concluded at Centennial High School, the teacher and student usually leave my office at the same time and sometimes continue to converse in a friendly manner. Teachers rarely seem to need to see me following the mediation to debrief because the mediation experience tends to

From: Ellen Braden

Sent: Tuesday, September 10, 2015 3:30 p.m.

To: Robert Ramirez

Subject: Follow-Up to Our Teacher–Student Mediation

Dear Mr. Ramirez,

Please print this email and provide a copy for Mimi.

Thank you again for participating in the mediation. Here are the plans you developed:

1. Mr. Ramirez will change the seating so that Mimi is close to one of the students in her new friend group.

2. Mimi agrees to talk about math during class time and will be near her friend so that she can make her lunch plans at the end of class.

3. Mimi asked for extra math help from Mr. Ramirez, and Mr. Ramirez said he is happy to help Mimi during study hall time or before and after school.

Please share feedback below and note if you would like additional follow-up:

_____ Meeting to debrief about the mediation or discuss next steps

_____ Follow-up check-in: 1 week   2 weeks   quarterly   (please circle)

_____ Another mediation

Additional comments: _____

Thanks again,

Ms. Braden

Figure 4.4.   Teacher–Student Mediation Follow-Up Email for Mr. Ramirez and Mimi.

cover the necessary bases. I let everyone know that my door is always open and that I am available.

Once the participants leave my office, I quickly add the teacher and student names and demographic information to our Tier II team data spreadsheet. I also keep my own handwritten roster. I keep one folder for all the mediations for the year. In that file, I store the original notes I took during the mediation, stapled to a copy of the email I send to the teacher. Mediators should develop an organization and data collection system that work for them.

AFTER THE MEDIATION MEETING

After the meeting has ended, the mediator must uphold the principle of confidentiality. It is not always easy to uphold this principle within a school setting because parents or administrators may ask about the outcome of the mediation. When asked, I share positive general statements about the student:

- "Sandy was amazing in mediation. He fully participated!"

- "Brittany had a very good mediation with Mrs. Tanaka, and they now have a plan to move forward."

- "The mediation was successful between Shu-lin and Mr. Colgate."

In the rare cases that the mediation did not go well, I also speak in generalities:

- "The mediation did not get off the ground. I am going to meet with the student individually instead."

- "Unfortunately, the mediation was not effective. I will be speaking with Ms. Bailey about some other ideas that might work better than mediation."

I do not speak to others about a teacher's behavior in mediation. Teachers must view the mediator as trustworthy, and it would be inappropriate for me to comment on their demeanor or effectiveness. During mediations, the vast majority of teachers are incredibly kind, sensitive, and caring. They show genuine interest in the student's well-being and a detailed knowledge of the student's activity in the class. The fact that teachers are willing to participate in mediation with students speaks to their openness, goodwill, and integrity. Occasionally, mediations expose less-than-perfect teacher behavior. Apologies are never required in mediation, yet I have been deeply moved by watching teachers sincerely offer apologies to students. The students seem surprised and touched and readily accept the apologies. Students, too, offer genuine apologies in mediations, and these are greatly appreciated by teachers. These are powerful moments in mediation and one of the many ways that such spontaneous, unscripted interactions between teachers and students can be truly healing and restore the respect.

TIPS FOR CONDUCTING TEACHER–STUDENT MEDIATIONS WITH YOUNG STUDENTS OR STUDENTS WITH SPECIAL NEEDS

Referrals to mediation should be made on a case-by-case basis, and for some children, a more traditional intervention, such as a counseling session or a parent–teacher conference, may be more appropriate. Some special considerations need to be weighed when conducting teacher–student mediations with students who have special needs. For example, because mediations are verbal meetings, it is important to first consider a student's level of communication skills. Students with ASD may have specific difficulty with changes in routine and considering another person's perspective, so having a familiar adult present and/or providing premeeting coaching on what to expect at the mediation may be helpful. A student with a cognitive impairment may have difficulty grasping abstract concepts such as "hopes" and "expectations," but that same student might readily grasp the more concrete concept that one's actions can hurt or anger another person. That student would also be able to describe a specific incident that hurt or angered him or her. The following tips may be useful for younger students or students with special needs.

Tip 1: Hold an Intake Meeting

If mediation is deemed appropriate, the mediator may wish to hold individual intake meetings with the student and teacher prior to the mediation in order to help crystalize the issues. At the student intake meeting, the student may be interviewed to identify the main issues to be discussed at the mediation. Consider the following sample interview format used with Ricky, a student with a mild cognitive disability.

Mediator [smiling]: Hi, Ricky. I'm Ms. Anthony. Thank you for meeting with me. I'm here to ask you a few questions:

- How old are you?
- What grade are you in?
- What do you like to do when you are not in school? [Smile, be responsive, and work on developing a rapport with the student.]

Mediator: Now let's talk about school.

- What do you like about school?
- What do you not like about school?
- If you could change one thing about school, what would it be?
- Anything else you'd like to add about school?

Mediator: Now let's talk about your class.

- What do you like about the class?
- Is there anything you do not like about the class?
- If you could change one thing about the class, what would it be?
- Anything else you'd like to say about this class?

Mediator: Now let's talk about your teacher.

- What do you like about the way Mr. Vraney teaches?
- Is there anything you do not like about the way Mr. Vraney teaches?
- If you could change one thing about the way Mr. Vraney teaches, what would it be?
- Is there anything else you'd like to say about Mr. Vraney?

Sometimes, with younger or special needs students, direct questions do not reveal enough. The direct question may be confusing or make the student uncomfortable—perhaps the student may be reluctant to give an answer for fear of repercussions. An unrelated, open-ended question can often bring forth relevant information. For example, instead of asking, "What do you want?" you can ask the "three-wishes" question.

Mediator: Thank you so much, Ricky. I have one more question: If you could have any three wishes right now, what would they be?

Mediator: Thank you so much for giving me this information, Ricky. It has been nice to get to know you and your thoughts and feelings about school, your class, and Mr. Vraney. We are going to have a meeting with Mr. Vraney and we will work on making things better for everyone. How does that sound?

At the intake meeting with the teacher, it is important to have a conversation such as the following:

Mediator: Mr. Vraney, I really appreciate you meeting with me. Thank you for being open to a mediation meeting with Ricky. I want the meeting to be a positive experience where social skills, communication skills, and problem-solving skills are modeled. The role of a mediator is to be impartial, so right now I'm wearing my mediator hat.

I have had a chance to meet with Ricky to get some ideas of his experiences, and I wanted to speak with you for about 10 minutes and ask you about your experiences. This will help me keep the mediation meeting with you and Ricky focused and structured.

Take notes in both intake meetings, and use the notes and verbatim quotes in the actual mediation where appropriate.

Tip 2: Provide "Feeling" Words

Sometimes, younger students or those with special needs are not familiar with a "feeling words" vocabulary to describe their emotions. See Table 4.1 for an alphabetical list of feeling words to share with students.

During the mediations or intake interviews, ask the students to select the feeling that matches their experience and/or consider using pictures with facial expressions.

Mediator: You said you took Ms. E's cookie and knew it was wrong. Show me how that made you feel [pause]. Okay, you chose *guilty.* You felt guilty because you took the cookie and because you know it is wrong to take something without permission. It sounds like you know when something is right or wrong.

Table 4.1. Alphabetical list of feeling words

angry	frightened	sad
annoyed	frustrated	scared
anxious	furious	shocked
ashamed	guilty	shy
bored	happy	sick
confused	hurt	sorry
cranky	jealous	spaced out
disappointed	lonely	surprised
disgusted	loving	timid
distracted	mean	tired
embarrassed	nervous	unfocused
envious	peaceful	vengeful
excited	playful	withdrawn
explosive	proud	worried

The mediator may also want to help clarify and simplify the teacher's responses so that students fully grasp what occurred.

Mediator: Mrs. Khan, you said you spent a lot of time preparing the reading lesson and that you picked a giraffe story because you knew Oscar liked giraffes. When Oscar walked away, you said you felt disappointed. Were you disappointed because you really hoped Oscar would enjoy the story and it looked like he didn't like it? [Pause and wait for answer.] When he got up and walked away, you said you also felt a little frustrated? Please tell me more about that feeling.

Tip 3: Ask an Adult to Represent the Student in the Mediation

In some cases, it may be appropriate for an adult other than the mediator (i.e., a safe, impartial adult in the school) to represent a student in a mediation with the teacher. Prior to the actual mediation, the representative interviews the student and asks the questions similar to a mediator: "Please tell me what brought us here today." The representative asks the child clarifying questions; uses reflective listening statements; and helps identify the issues, the student's feelings, and the strengths in the teacher–student relationship. Then, the adult representative participates in the mediation in the student's role while the student quietly observes. Thus, if the student is unable or unwilling to participate directly, the representative models the appropriate social, communication, and problem-solving skills with the teacher and mediator in the meeting.

SUMMARY AND NEXT TOPIC

In this chapter, I have shown the "how to" of teacher–student mediation, including how mediation techniques can be used with younger students or those needing special assistance. In Chapter 5, I discuss the skills necessary to be an impartial mediator, with special emphasis on the importance of identifying one's own biases and beliefs in order to be more open and nonjudgmental. I also include a humorous "reflective listening pop quiz." Many educators can identify times we opt for the teachable moment to guide students rather than using reflective listening skills to show understanding of the students' points of view.

5

What Is Required of a Skilled School Mediator?

That which is spoken from the heart is heard by the heart.

—Jewish saying

Mediation is practiced worldwide for a variety of disputes and situations. Mediators can range from students who conduct peer mediation to attorneys who conduct complex negotiations. People learn how to mediate from professional training organizations, universities, community agencies, law schools, informal tutorials, online courses, and books. There is no single professional degree, license, or certificate required to mediate. What does exist, however, is a set of ethical guidelines for mediators, put out by the American Arbitration Association, the American Bar Association, and the Association for Conflict Resolution (2005). In Chapter 4, I reviewed the principles of mediation, which include mediator impartiality, confidentiality, voluntariness, and self-determination. Another ethical standard is mediator competence. Participants enter a mediation with the expectation that the mediator will competently lead the meeting.

The mediation techniques presented here do not require complex negotiation skills, and this book may suffice as preparation to conduct school mediations. However, one's own readiness to mediate will be decided by each reader, and like any skill, ongoing training and practice are encouraged. This chapter reviews the qualities of skilled school mediators. It is important to note that if, at any time, a mediator determines that he or she is unable to conduct a mediation competently, he or she must disclose this to the participants and find an alternative course of action. It is perfectly fine to say something like the following:

Mediator: I'd like to stop this mediation and talk about rescheduling it. I'm thinking that someone with more experience would be better suited to serve in the role of mediator. It is a positive step that you are both willing to be here, and I want to make sure you get the best possible assistance.

WHAT IS REQUIRED OF A SKILLED SCHOOL MEDIATOR?

I frequently conduct workshops on school mediation and notice that counselors, social workers, and school psychologists, with just one training, are ready to begin using these mediation techniques. These professionals already conduct numerous interventions with students, teachers, and parents in their schools and are eager to try a new approach.

Schools also have employees or community volunteers with sensitivity, intuitiveness, and compassion. Others are drawn to them for their patient listening, wisdom, and heartfelt advice. These individuals could also be school mediators. In the following sections, I discuss the characteristics of a skilled school mediator.

Trustworthiness and Impartiality

A mediator should be trustworthy so that teacher and student participants are secure in knowing that information disclosed during a mediation will not be used against them (with the exception of mandated child abuse reporting). Word-of-mouth reviews are often the way new interventions are endorsed in schools, and skilled mediators will earn trust among the school community by displaying impartiality and equal support of student and teacher viewpoints.

A question about a mediator's impartiality was raised at a training I did on mediation. An audience member looked troubled and raised her hand to ask, "How can you tell what really happened and who is telling the truth?" In response to this legitimate question, I responded, "It doesn't matter." Mediators do not have to administer disciplinary consequences, collect witness statements, or decipher events for purposes of uncovering the truth. In fact, there can be multiple truths. Healing any relationship begins with the acknowledgment that everyone's perceptions of events and beliefs have validity and are true. Such an acknowledgment paves the way toward understanding.

Here is an example: Monique, a timid and hard-working fourth-grade student, was thrilled. Thursday had finally arrived, and on this day she would be her teacher, Ms. Duke's, special helper—a reward for the excellent work habits Monique had demonstrated during the week. The activity for the day was to prepare a new bulletin board. Soon after commencing their work on the board, Ms. Duke ran out of construction paper and asked Monique to borrow some from Ms. Smiley, the teacher in the adjoining classroom. Monique excitedly ran next door, and upon entering the class, blurted, "Ms. Duke needs paper!" Unbeknownst to Monique (and Ms. Duke), Ms. Smiley's class was taking a timed, standardized test. Ms. Smiley was startled by Monique, ran over to her, and said in a loud whisper, "Stop right now! This class is taking a test! You need to leave!" Monique dashed out of the class, returned to Ms. Duke, and burst into tears.

In this example, one can readily see that the truth or who was "in the right" or "in the wrong" is irrelevant. Each person's perception and emotional reaction are what matters. A few days later, the school holds a mediation with Monique and Ms. Smiley. Each benefits from listening to the other's full story, gains an understanding of the other's perceptions and feelings about the event, and identifies how to prevent such events from occurring in the future. Apologies abound (even though they are not required), and good will is restored. Monique's mother is relieved, because thanks to the mediation, Monique will no longer have stress and fear about seeing Ms. Smiley in the school building.

The example of Monique and Ms. Smiley is a simple way of illustrating that the mediator does not need to find the truth. A skilled school mediator will convey empathy and understanding for each participant's experience but remain impartial by not endorsing one participant's viewpoint as better or more correct. Appearing impartial does not require the mediator to wear a poker face in order to avoid showing emotions or favoritism. Instead, the mediator shows equal support, respect, and acceptance for both participants as they relay their experiences.

Sometimes mediations cover topics that challenge or resonate with the mediator's own values or beliefs. Then more effort is required to remain impartial, and that effort comes in the form of self-knowledge.

Self-Knowledge and Cultural Sensitivity

It is necessary for mediators to be aware of their own background, beliefs, and potentially unconscious biases. Where we were born, how we were raised, and our education have an impact on our outlooks, beliefs, and philosophies. What if a mediator came from a background where his or her parents were divorced and experienced frequent moves? What if he or she had difficulty making friends, was teased, or was unpopular in school? Some mediators will have been straight-A students in school, whereas others might have struggled academically, gotten in trouble, or experimented with drugs or alcohol. Personal viewpoints and life experiences may slant the way a mediator views various conflicts and situations occurring in schools.

Knowing oneself and "owning your stuff," as therapists like to say, is important in order to identify areas in which additional training and education are needed, particularly when it comes to awareness and appreciation of cultural differences. Mediators must admit to and be willing to identify stereotyped thinking in themselves (i.e., the unconscious assumptions we may make about others based on their race, culture, or socioeconomic status). Identifying and challenging stereotypes are the first steps toward accepting another person's perspective with openness, understanding, and empathy. All participants in mediations deserve dignity and respect and to be fully understood as the individuals they are.

When mediating in schools, it is also important to consider how cultural, ethnic, or other lifestyle differences between student and teacher can sometimes lead to conflicts or misunderstandings. Some educators have grown up in ethnically homogenous communities and have not had opportunities for sustained personal contact with diverse groups of people until they work in schools. University training programs do not always require future educators to take a sociology course in poverty or racial discrimination. Nor do they require that aspiring educators take coursework in, say, African-American, Asian American, or Latino studies. Yet many educators will work in schools with populations of students with different socioeconomic, racial, and cultural backgrounds than their own. Does this create excitement or anxiety? What expectations are triggered? Many teachers may have been brought up with a specific set of values and expectations for life, including how people should behave. They bring earnestness to their work and a strong desire to be excellent educators who touch lives, yet they can vary widely in their cultural knowledge and experiences.

Outstanding educators who seek a deeper understanding of those different than themselves actively seek to broaden their breadth of understanding of their students' various backgrounds. They read books by diverse authors, attend workshops, and visit their students' neighborhoods and events. These educators are aware that they did not have experience with diverse people growing up, but that they do now, and their students directly benefit from their efforts to become more culturally sensitive. From a research study on the impact of culturally responsive educational practices on the psychological well-being of students of color, Cholewa, Goodman, West-Olatunji, and Amatea (2014) concluded that "academic instruction that attends to students both as learners and as people with rich cultural and individual experiences engenders an educational experience that allows students to develop academically, socially, and psychologically" (p 17). A skilled mediator will help foster teachers' abilities to gain knowledge about the rich cultural and individual experiences of their students.

Emotional Intelligence

As teachers and students tell their stories, many emotions may surface, and a skilled mediator exhibits emotional intelligence in order to maintain a supportive tone in the meeting. Just as a good stand-up comic reads the room to pick up on the vibe for how people respond to their comedy set, the mediator continually gauges the emotions of participants and redirects the conversation so as to maintain a safe, productive climate. "Emotional intelligence is the ability to perceive emotions, to access and generate emotions so as to assist thought, to understand emotions and emotional knowledge, and to reflectively regulate emotions so as to promote emotional and intellectual growth" (Mayer & Salovey, 1997, p. 87). Consider the following example: In a mediation with Coach Tisch, 15-year-old Camila shares her experience on the girls' basketball team when she missed a bus to an away game. As she speaks, her breathing quickens, and then she lets out a long sigh.

Mediator: Camila, I see that your breathing kind of changed when you told this story. How do you feel about this experience?

Camila: Frustrated!

Mediator [leans in and shows concern]: Well, I completely understand. Missing a game can be incredibly frustrating!

Camila: Yeah. It just was a terrible day.

Mediator: Tell me more.

Camila: I was super scared to face Coach Tisch and stopped going to practice.

Mediator: So you are describing that after this terrible day, fear set in, and you avoided going to practice because you were scared to face Coach Tisch?

Camila: Yes.

Mediator: Wow, it is great that you are here today even though you were scared to face Coach Tisch! That takes courage! I can see how much you care, Camila, and that really matters. You have described your feelings of frustration and fear. In just a few moments, Coach Tisch will share her feelings, and you will see the day's events from her perspective. From this understanding, I know you will be able to find ways to move forward.

In this example, the mediator exhibits emotional intelligence by observing Camila's nonverbal cues, asking about her feelings, projecting care and concern, and providing encouragement that Camila's feelings will be addressed during the mediation.

A skilled mediator will feel comfortable being spontaneous and should be ready to react in the moment—one might use humor; act silly; or interject a very brief personal story, anecdote, or question.

Mediator to student [sensing an opportunity to digress from the conflict discussion and allow for the participants to relax and get to know more about one another]: By the way, I don't know much about you. What do you like to do in your free time away from school?

Mediator to a geography teacher and seventh-grade student [sensing unproductive tension starting to mount in the mediation]: This topic is starting to create some tension. Let's take a break from it for the time being. We can return to it in a moment. I'm just curious, what is your favorite thing you ever learned in geography?

These interjections are brief because the point is to lighten the mood so that the mediation may proceed more easily and to model that in problem-solving conversations, it is okay to leave the topic at hand, keep talking on a lighter subject, and return to the topic when appropriate. Another helpful digression to use during times of tension or heightened emotion is to pause and ask about the feeling being displayed. This will be discussed more in the next section, Communication Skills. Here is a brief example:

Mediator: Are you okay right now? You seem a little upset.

Sometimes participants couch their true feelings with pat phrases, such as, "It's fine," "Whatever," or "It doesn't matter." The mediator can ask for clarification:

Mediator [with a kind tone of voice]: I'm hearing you say that it doesn't matter, but that's not what I'm picking up. Was there something that was said just now that bothered you? I'd really like to understand how you are feeling right now.

As always, a mediator can also adjust the mood by interjecting thanks or praise:

Mediator: I know it's not always easy to be in these meetings, and I appreciate your courage and willingness to give mediation a try.

Emotional intelligence also includes a mediator's awareness of one's own emotional reactions. There will be times when a mediator's personal feelings are triggered. The rule of impartiality will always apply, however, and the mediator should never appear to take sides because one person's story is more compelling than the other person's story. A mediator's personal disclosure of emotional reactions has its place, however, when it is in service of the mediation and is meted out equally. For example, a mediator can be deeply moved when a teacher or student spontaneously and unexpectedly expresses kindness and generosity.

Mediator: Wow. The way you just offered to carry Ms. Decker's boxes to her car after school was really sweet, Ralphy. I am touched by that.

Mediator: Ms. Suto—I hear you saying that you are willing to work with Fernando before school, after school, and during lunch to help him with his project until he gets it done. I just have to pause here. That shows such kindness and dedication. I feel happy when I see that.

When someone says something sad or upsetting, a mediator's personal reaction can model what appropriate expressions of sympathy look like.

Mediator to teacher: Mr. O'Grady, you mentioned that your father is ill and that is affecting your mood. I'm so sorry for you and your family. We heard from Miguel that he thinks you hate him, so now we know there are difficult things happening in your life. Thank you for letting us know. I hope your father has a speedy recovery.

Teacher: Thank you for that. Yes, I definitely want Miguel to know I do not hate him! I was grumpy the day we had our problem because my father was having surgery.

Communication Skills

Encouraging people to tell their full story and actively listening to that story are acts of profound respect. Speakers will feel they have been treated with dignity because someone thought their words were important. A skilled mediator listens and facilitates communication so that participants will feel safe enough to share their deep, honest feelings and gain empathy for one another.

A skilled mediator shows engaged listening by facing each participant when he or she is speaking, maintaining eye contact, nodding, and responding. Body posture is upright, and arms and hands are relaxed and not crossed. A mediator listens carefully to a speaker's words while also gauging the emotions underlying the words. The accurate perception of emotion is key because sometimes words and nonverbal signals do not match. A mediator identifies emotion from observing participants'

- Body language: Are the participants sitting up or slouching? Are they calm or fidgety? Are they turned toward the speaker in a relaxed, open way that seems to say, "I want to be here," or are they rigid and turned away with hands crossed, seeming to say "I wish I were anywhere but here"?

- Voice: When participants are stressed, they may speak faster and at a higher pitch. Sometimes voices get louder and communicate anger or frustration. At other times, voices may be barely audible and communicate fear or nervousness. Mediations may begin with people speaking in cold or monotone voices, but as comfort levels increase, voices become warm, animated, and humor filled.

- Eye contact: Does eye contact occur consistently, sometimes, or never? Sustained eye contact may communicate confidence and comfort, whereas a lack of eye contact may demonstrate unease, fear, or insecurities. Often, teenagers and children do not comfortably make sustained eye contact with an adult or each other, yet as long as they are willing to answer questions and speak, the mediation process can be effective.

- Length of responses: Are participants giving one word answers, or are they willing to elaborate? A one-word answer might convey reluctance, anger, or resistance, and a longer response might convey an eagerness to be understood. The length of responses will show their level of engagement.

A skilled mediator acknowledges participants' nonverbal communication to help identify underlying feelings and gently inquires if words and nonverbal communication do not match. Here are some examples:

Mediator: Fernando, I hear you say that everything is fine. I also see that your body is kind of tense and your hands are balled up into fists. Could there maybe be some tension or anger there as well?

Fernando: Yeah...I don't know...maybe.

Mediator: Ms. McGillivray, when you were talking about all the ways your lesson was interrupted yesterday, you made a lot of heavy sighs. How did you feel about all the interruptions?

Ms. McGillivray: Frustrated! And worried! I knew we had a lot to cover in a short amount of time, and I knew we weren't going to make it.

Mediator: Cheryl, you looked down right now and started talking a lot slower. How did this experience make you feel?

Cheryl: Really worried.

Skilled mediators will also want to be well practiced in the use of reflective listening skills. The highly regarded humanistic psychologist Carl Rogers pioneered reflective listening, also known as active listening. Active listeners are attentive to words, feelings, and nonverbal cues, and they convey to speakers that they grasp their point of view. Despite people's natural tendency to want to judge, evaluate, approve, or disapprove when other people express their views, Rogers wrote

> We can achieve real communication and avoid this evaluative tendency when we listen with understanding. This means seeing the expressed idea and attitude from the other person's point of view, sensing how it feels to the person, achieving his or her frame of reference about the subject being discussed. (Rogers & Roethlisberger, 1991, p. 1)

In training school mediators, I use the term *reflective listening* rather than *active listening* so that mediators can visualize holding a mirror that reflects back to the speaker. Reflective listening is done in the following way: The listener gives full attention to the speaker's message and underlying feelings and then repeats that message using the speaker's own words. Reflective listening is powerful because when people know that someone has truly heard them, it puts them at ease and facilitates continuing conversation and exploration of the topic. In his book *A Way of Being* (1980), Rogers wrote

> When I have been listened to and when I have been heard, I am able to reperceive my world in a new way and to go on. It is astonishing how elements that seem insoluble become soluble when someone listens, how confusions that seem irremediable turn into relatively clear flowing streams when one is heard. I have deeply appreciated the times that I have experienced this sensitive, empathic, concentrated listening. (p. 12)

Here is a humorous and often-told version of a conversation with a couple, Brenda and Joe:

Example 1 without reflective listening:

Brenda: Oh my gosh, my job is so stressful!

Joe: So quit!

Example 2 with reflective listening:

Brenda: Oh my gosh, my job is so stressful!

Joe: You are finding your job stressful?

Brenda: Yes. I'll tell you what happened today…

Employing reflective listening skills sounds simple, but it requires practice because it does not come naturally. It is human nature to do exactly the opposite because each of us is eager to react with our own stories or viewpoints. Indeed, reflective listening practices rarely occur in schools, with the exception of counseling sessions. That is because in adult–child communication, adults often feel that it is their duty to educate and create teachable moments at every opportunity. Even professional counselors need to brush up on reflective listening at times. Figure 5.1 includes a somewhat tongue-in-cheek pop quiz exercise to show the differences between reflective listening responses and the responses we may feel like saying.

In addition to developing strong reflective listening skills, it is important for a mediator to hone his or her expressive communication skills. A skilled mediator conveys acceptance and respect by speaking in clear, nonjudgmental language. Using open-ended questions invites participants to elaborate and describe their perspectives and feelings in their own words. Often, these questions start with *what* or *how* and enable a participant to elaborate on a topic. For example, the mediator might ask

"What were your thoughts as the test was going on?"

Rather than

"Didn't you realize that talking during a test would disturb others?"

Or, the mediator might say

"How did you feel about that?"

Rather than

"Did that upset you?"

As a further example, instead of asking, "Do you often come to class late?" it is better to say, "Tell me more about your schedule."

As stated in Chapter 4, though it may be tempting to ask, "Why did you do that?" a skilled mediator will try to avoid asking "why" because it can come across as accusatory and judgmental. It is better to say, "Tell me more about your thoughts on this," or "I want to understand your reasons for this." When

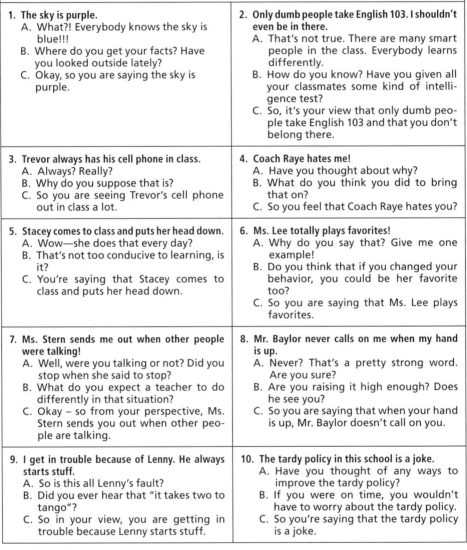

Directions: Form teams of four people and take turns as the person who reads the statement, and as the people who provide the A, B, and C responses. Experience the difference in how it feels to be told the C response as opposed to responses A and B. Notice how many times the statements are couched in absolute terms such as *always* and *never*. We may leap at the chance to refute such statements with our innate logic. However, that is not the correct way to reflectively listen. Reflective listening is nonjudgmental and is designed to keep people talking so that their thoughts and feelings are fully expressed.

1. **The sky is purple.**
   A. What?! Everybody knows the sky is blue!!!
   B. Where do you get your facts? Have you looked outside lately?
   C. Okay, so you are saying the sky is purple.

2. **Only dumb people take English 103. I shouldn't even be in there.**
   A. That's not true. There are many smart people in the class. Everybody learns differently.
   B. How do you know? Have you given all your classmates some kind of intelligence test?
   C. So, it's your view that only dumb people take English 103 and that you don't belong there.

3. **Trevor always has his cell phone in class.**
   A. Always? Really?
   B. Why do you suppose that is?
   C. So you are seeing Trevor's cell phone out in class a lot.

4. **Coach Raye hates me!**
   A. Have you thought about why?
   B. What do you think you did to bring that on?
   C. So you feel that Coach Raye hates you?

5. **Stacey comes to class and puts her head down.**
   A. Wow—she does that every day?
   B. That's not too conducive to learning, is it?
   C. You're saying that Stacey comes to class and puts her head down.

6. **Ms. Lee totally plays favorites!**
   A. Why do you say that? Give me one example!
   B. Do you think that if you changed your behavior, you could be her favorite too?
   C. So you are saying that Ms. Lee plays favorites.

7. **Ms. Stern sends me out when other people were talking!**
   A. Well, were you talking or not? Did you stop when she said to stop?
   B. What do you expect a teacher to do differently in that situation?
   C. Okay – so from your perspective, Ms. Stern sends you out when other people are talking.

8. **Mr. Baylor never calls on me when my hand is up.**
   A. Never? That's a pretty strong word. Are you sure?
   B. Are you raising it high enough? Does he see you?
   C. So you are saying that when your hand is up, Mr. Baylor doesn't call on you.

9. **I get in trouble because of Lenny. He always starts stuff.**
   A. So is this all Lenny's fault?
   B. Did you ever hear that "it takes two to tango"?
   C. So in your view, you are getting in trouble because Lenny starts stuff.

10. **The tardy policy in this school is a joke.**
    A. Have you thought of any ways to improve the tardy policy?
    B. If you were on time, you wouldn't have to worry about the tardy policy.
    C. So you're saying that the tardy policy is a joke.

Figure 5.1.   Reflective listening pop quiz and practice activity.

searching for underlying reasons for a behavior or action, say "How come?" or "How so?" The following sample questions demonstrate phrasing that is commonly effective in teacher–student mediations:

- "What has been your experience, so far, in the history class?"

- "What do you like about this class?"

- "What would seem fair to you?"

- "What would you like for us to understand about this?"

- "What good work have you observed from this student?"

- "How has the semester been going?"

- "What are your biggest concerns?"

- "What would you like to see happen?"

- "What would be helpful for you right now?"

- "How did you feel about that?"

- "Looking back, is there anything you would change about it?"

- "What would you like to see moving forward?"

- "How do you think the situation could be improved?"

Listening reflectively and respectfully and encouraging participants to tell their story allow both teachers and students to feel as though they are being treated with dignity. This is cathartic and powerful, and as people become comfortable opening up, there is the likelihood that an "aha" moment will occur. Therapists talk about "aha moments" when a person gains a new insight that is a missing puzzle piece to a story or situation. When students and teachers identify these missing pieces, the palpable sense of relief I see in the room can be exciting to witness.

Teacher: Wow! I didn't realize that the way I passed out the test booklet to you upset you! I had no idea that you thought I tossed it at you. That explains why you have acted differently! I'm so glad I know now!

It is joyful to witness when one mediation vastly improves the relationship between a teacher and student. Rogers (1980) wrote, "I can testify that when you are in psychological distress and someone really hears you without passing judgment on you, without trying to take responsibility for you, without trying to mold you, it feels damn good!" (p. 12).

Administrator Tony Maltbia [referring to mediations he has personally conducted at an alternative high school]: I never had a case that I used [teacher–student] mediation that it didn't solve the issues. It may have taken two meetings, but even between the two, there has been growth.

Warmth and Nurturance

The last quality for a skilled school mediator to possess is not a skill at all, but a willingness to nurture mediation participants by offering a snack. I keep a jar of granola bars, and along with a smile and a "Welcome," I say, "Who would like a snack? Help yourself." Offering a snack shows warmth and concern about someone's well-being. Providing food also helps prevent the irritability that affects many people with an empty stomach. Some teachers participate in a mediation during their lunch break, and they are hungry. Most students are always willing to accept a snack. Offering food is a caring gesture, a way to break the ice, and a way to convey thanks to the teacher and the student for their participation in the mediation.

SUMMARY AND NEXT TOPIC

In this chapter, I discussed the skills necessary to conduct mediations, with special emphasis on the importance of identifying one's own biases and beliefs in order to be more open and nonjudgmental. I presented a communications skills refresher, including a reflective listening pop quiz, and I have described how a well-run mediation can be transformative for both students and teachers. In the next chapter, I specifically describe how mediations help students and teachers problem-solve. The chapter begins by discussing many root causes of stressors that have an impact on teachers and students and that might potentially lead to their conflicts in the classroom. Sometimes, the reason for a student's acting-out behavior or the need for a mediation is a manifestation of a deeper problem, so I provide guidance on how one might respond. I also share real-life examples of mediations and problem-solving strategies to address specific mediation challenges.

6

Sources of Teacher–Student Conflict, Problem-Solving Strategies, and Sample Mediations

---

One child, one teacher, one book, one pen can change the world.

— Malala Yousafzai, 2014 Nobel Peace Prize Winner

How do mediations solve problems between teachers and students? This chapter explores possible root causes for problems teachers and students experience and discusses the importance of recognizing underlying feelings and needs that present in different classroom conflicts. The chapter also provides examples of real-life mediations, practice mediations, and problem-solving strategies for conflicts between students and teachers.

WHAT PROBLEMS DO TEACHERS EXPERIENCE?

Picture spending hours preparing for a lesson, only to have a student do everything possible to show a lack of interest, such as not bringing materials, talking to others, or looking at a cell phone. Imagine that when you try to redirect that student, you are met with contempt: eye rolling, words under the breath, or whispers to others. What if you faced this disinterest and hostility on a daily basis? Teachers are emotionally affected by their relationships with their students. Koomen, Verschueren, and Pianta (2007) reported on high levels of teaching stress and low levels of competence and job satisfaction due to poor teacher and student relationships.

Teachers are at risk for experiencing "burnout," which has three principal aspects: emotional exhaustion, depersonalization, and reduced personal accomplishment (Maslach & Jackson, 1981). Emotional exhaustion entails fatigue and feeling unable to muster the necessary energy to provide for students. Depersonalization involves feeling negative, cynical, or indifferent toward students, parents, or fellow staff members. Reduced personal accomplishment occurs when teachers feel as though they no longer effectively contribute to student growth (Maslach, Jackson, & Leiter, 1996). Burnout can slowly sap the vitality and optimism of any teacher, and when many teachers experience burnout, it casts a negative pall over an entire school.

Teachers are expected to professionally and sensitively respond to the diverse needs of students in their classrooms every day. Classrooms may range in size from 5 students in a self-contained special education room to 65 students in a PE class. Students often differ in terms of their socioeconomic status, knowledge of English, learning style, and interest in the specific subject. Some students will have identified disabilities. Unfortunately, there can be discrepancies in how teachers relate and respond to these students. Murray and Pianta (2007) cited the work of Montague and Rinaldi (2001) and reported that

> Historically, teachers have held more negative attitudes and directed more negative behaviors towards students with disabilities and low achieving students than towards high achieving students. Included in these findings are lower levels of emotional support, praise, and other positive behaviors and greater levels of criticism, ignoring, and negative behavior directed towards lower functioning students. (p. 109)

No teacher would readily admit, "I treat high achieving students better than students with disabilities," but what if this occurs unconsciously? If I were teaching a class, would I not respond more positively to students who follow all of my directions, work hard, study hard, and laugh at my jokes? A teacher naturally experiences disappointment when students do not engage in classroom activities.

Consider the following example: A seventh-grade teacher named Mr. Cohen baked a chocolate cake from scratch, using all fresh ingredients and the finest Swiss chocolate he could find. Mr. Cohen baked it at night and excitedly brought it to his class the next day. Mr. Cohen chose chocolate because he could not imagine anyone not loving chocolate. When the time came, he excitedly surprised his students. In his class of 30 students, 24 smiled, cheered, and said, "Yeah! Thank you!" They ate the cake and complimented Mr. Cohen on how delicious it was. Three students did not eat the cake at all. They did not smile or laugh. They refused to taste it. Three other students said, "Chocolate cake sucks!" Not only did they not taste it, they pushed it away. One of the three students took a slice of cake and dumped pencil sharpener shavings all over it. These three students were displaying anger because Mr. Cohen did not bring something else. Question: Will Mr. Cohen feel greater warmth and connection with the students who appreciated the cake?

If you substitute a lesson for the cake example, you might imagine that teachers experience irritation, annoyance, or anger on a regular basis. It may depend on the year, the time their class meets, the size of the class, the age of the students, and their years of teaching experience, but no teacher is immune from working with challenging teacher–student dynamics. In every school, there will be children who do not respond to the curriculum that is taught. And yet, teachers must work to win the hearts and the minds of all students in order to be successful. They must activate students' desire to learn by generating the right amount of rewards, incentives, and consequences. Teachers must show flexibility with different learners, and yet somehow not come across as playing favorites. They must provide organization and structure so that students understand expectations and receive timely feedback on their performance, and they are also responsible for students' social-emotional growth and well-being—good teachers develop personal relationships with students and show interest in students' lives outside the classroom. I sometimes think of teachers as performers because regardless of their mood, "the show must go on," and much like stand-up entertainers, they must "work the room" to keep everyone engaged and on board. Their profession requires tremendous dedication and a lot of energy.

At Centennial High School, most teachers instruct in five classes of approximately 25–30 students each and thereby connect with 125–150 students a day. Each class occurs during a 50-minute period, and there is a 4-minute "passing" period between classes. Teachers and students meet at the school, but the neighborhoods they inhabit, the religious institutions they attend, and their recreation and leisure activities may differ along racial or socioeconomic lines. It is no mystery how miscommunication and misunderstandings can occur in a school like Centennial High School, even with earnest effort and good intentions.

How do teachers keep from misinterpreting and misunderstanding students who are different from themselves? At Centennial High School, dialogues and workshops on the topic of culturally responsive education (CRE) to promote equitable success among diverse students are ongoing. Research by Cholewa et al. (2014) indicated that CRE practices decrease psychological distress and increase psychological well-being among students of color. Both CRE and teacher–student mediation contribute to the goals of equitable student success by promoting respectful teacher–student engagement, greater understanding about another person's feelings and reactions, positive acknowledgement, and high expectations.

WHAT PROBLEMS DO STUDENTS EXPERIENCE?

Now, let us consider students. What problems do students have, and what are some root causes for them? First, students are in a constant state of growth, with puberty bringing dramatic cognitive and physiological changes. During puberty, which may start before the teen years, students grow rapidly and experience shifts in emotion and behavior. A typically sweet, curious, and thoughtful child may begin displaying hostility, rudeness, or self-centeredness in adolescence.

Teen: I hate you!

Dishonest behavior may also set in, particularly in the adolescent years, as teens have the propensity to lie (Shenfield, 2014). They might cover up, omit the truth, stretch the truth, exaggerate, and mislead.

Teacher: Brody lied to my face when I asked him about the missing paintbrush.

Children are wonderful and challenging, yet the teen years pose additional pressures. An excellent book titled *The Teenage Brain* (2015) by Frances E. Jensen, M.D., describes the teenage years from the perspective of the author: a mother and neurologist. My personal observations from working with teens for 30 years are detailed in the following sections.

Significant cognitive growth broadens teens' abilities to ponder more complex, hypothetical, and abstract issues. There is growth in their deductive reasoning and problem-solving skills. They also display a surge in creativity. Walking down a school hallway is a visual feast given the wonderfully varied outfits teens put together, often on a shoestring budget.

Critical thinking skills are developed, which teens use to measure, evaluate, judge, and possibly criticize anybody or anything, on a daily (if not hourly) basis, at home and at school. Nobody likes a critic, and teens' voices and attitudes may create conflict. However, critical thinking is a vital life skill that educators promote and encourage. Teens will one day be in the position to make important decisions about life partners, jobs, major purchases, and health care, in addition to judgment calls about right and wrong. Although many teens have a strong sense of justice and fairness and may not hesitate to accuse an authority figure that is in violation, they do not always have a keen eye on their own transgressions. They also do not readily think of others' perspectives or the impact that their actions have on others and this lack of awareness frequently appears in mediations.

Larry: What is the big deal if I take out my phone? I finished my work, I am quiet, and I'm not disturbing anyone!

Mr. Sanchez: When Larry's phone is out, it distracts other students, it distracts me, and it causes me to stop the lesson to tell him to put it away.

Josie: Why does Ms. Victor care if I don't do my work? It's my grade! If I fail, I fail!

Ms. Victor: It is my job to teach geometry to Josie, every day. I take that responsibility very seriously, and all my students matter to me.

Teens grapple with their sense of identity, and peer acceptance is of paramount importance: Who am I? Where do I fit in? How do I act around different peers? Do I act differently in school, in the neighborhood, and in my home? If I act cool in the neighborhood, how do I act in the classroom? If my identity is of a sullen, angry teen that hates school, am I allowed to smile, laugh, and enjoy classroom activities? If I try to be perfect, what if I make mistakes? Must I keep up a front? Must I choose a script and stick with it? This confusion appears in teacher–student mediations when a student has taken on one identity and does not know how to gracefully switch roles. A teen may tell her friends, "I HATE Mr. Jacobson!" every day after class when students gather around to laugh at the latest stories of all the ways Mr. Jacobson is annoying. But what if that same teen actually starts to like Mr. Jacobson? Will her friends call her two-faced or fake? Must she stick with her stance for the entire semester? Or what about not wanting to appear too studious? Consider another example:

Ms. Barker: Tyran does not come to class with his materials.

Tyran: When I go to biology, I am coming from lunch and don't have time to go to my locker.

Adults may respond to Tyran's problem with the following thoughts: "How hard is it for you to say to your friends, 'Excuse me. I need to get my books?'" The truth is that it might be very difficult for Tyran to shift roles from playful lunch companion to a serious student who is mindful of retrieving books before class.

Teens experience heightened self-doubt, and the digital age contributes to the uneasiness teens feel about their actions and their appearance. For example, before social media appeared, two friends could have a misunderstanding and ultimately talk it out. Now, the misunderstanding might be posted online where onlookers comment and fuel the fire of the conflict. As another example, teens may experience a punch-to-the-gut feeling upon finding an unflattering or distorted photo image of them posted online as a joke. It is not so funny when one is the butt of a joke, or worse, when it is not a joke at all, but harassment or bullying. Imagine if the discovery of such online activity occurred in the 4-minute passing period between PE and English. The teen likely will become preoccupied, stressed, anxious, and have no way to address the issue that "everybody" is talking about. There would not be a lot of learning in English class that day. There would also be a chance that the student would verbally lash out at the hapless teacher. These occurrences often are revealed in mediations.

Ms. Wolman: I asked David the capital of Minnesota and he responded by blurting out some choice words. Frankly, I was shocked. I am just here to find out if I did something to set David off?

David: A lot happened before I came to Ms. Wolman's class. It had nothing to do with her, and I'm sorry I said that stuff. She didn't deserve it.

As previously stated in this book, teacher–student mediation does not require apologies, but they are acknowledged and appreciated when offered. These types of dialogue help the student and teacher understand what happened and move forward.

Teens display a wide spectrum of moods. These emotional reactions may be traceable to an event such as a family problem, a disturbance in a peer relationship, a friend or family illness or loss, a conflict or misunderstanding, or a previous or ongoing trauma. Emotional reactions may also be due to diet, mental health problems such as anxiety and/or depression, hormonal changes, sleep cycle problems, and/or ingestion of substances. The intensity of a teen's mood may vary according to the individual, but all teens experience strong feelings: "I'm angry and I don't know why." "Why am I crying at this commercial?" When teens display intense moods in a classroom, the teacher will be concerned, call home, and/or refer students to school support staff for additional help. Many teacher–student mediations occur because a teen's mood brought on a negative action and consequences. In such a case, mediation provides a very helpful opportunity to repair trust.

Teens are impulsive. Neurologists such as Dr. Jensen (2015) have taught us that a teen's prefontal cortex is not fully formed. The prefrontal cortex is the part of the brain that facilitates impulse control. Teens act in the moment, do not always think things through, and sometimes do not predict the consequences of their actions. Students with attention-deficit/hyperactivity disorder are particularly susceptible to impulsive behavior. They can create messes for themselves that hurl them into a storm of guilt, shame, confusion, regret, or anxiety, and they do not know how to mop up afterwards. In such moments, Ms. Harper's outstanding Civil War lesson could prove to be a great source of annoyance.

Teens send mixed messages, particularly to adults: I need you—I do not need you. Pay attention to me—Leave me alone. Help me—I can do this myself. I want to be alone—I am lonely. Don't look at me—Look at me. Everybody is staring at me—Nobody cares that I am here. One aspect of my job has been to meet with students others were concerned about. Referrals come from administrators, staff members, parents, and other students.

Administrator: I need you to talk with Hilary. She walked out of her class today.

Teacher: Could you meet with Dane? He just isn't himself lately.

Hall monitor: I think I saw cuts on Sharla's arm today.

Parent: I got in a really bad fight with Luke last night.

Student: I'm worried about my friend.

In most of these situations, I call the student to my office, introduce myself, and simply say, "Hi, I'm Ms. Gross, the school psychologist. You are not in any trouble. You are here because someone cared about you and asked me to just check in. How are you doing?" No student has ever bolted from my office in anger because someone cared about him or her. In fact, it is often just the opposite. Most students breathe deeply, almost in relief, and proceed to tell me, in great detail, about their feelings and experiences. The truth is that even if the teens sent messages that said, "Stay away," they were pleased someone noticed and took action. They are not invisible after all. One of the most powerful features of mediations is when students realize how much the teacher knows about their activities in the class.

Mr. Stiller: I noticed you worked well in the group with Maya and Eddie. You were really active in getting art materials for the volcano, and played a big role in making sure it ignited.

Jasper: Yeah.

Ms. Hollis: You did well in the lesson on multiplication. I saw that you had a harder time when we moved to division.

Randall: Yeah, division is harder for me. I think I need more help with that.

Keep in mind, however, that sometimes students really do not want the extra attention and need the teacher's understanding.

Ari: Sometimes I'm just having a bad day. I don't want to be called on.

Mr. Dealy: I get it. Thanks for letting me know.

During the teen years, mental health problems and the impact of disabilities often are more keenly felt. Because adolescence is a time of identity formation and increased self-doubt, both school settings and online social media sites offer many ways for teens to compare themselves to peers and find ways they fall short. Murray and Pianta (2007) cited U.S. Department of Education findings from 2003 to suggest that the students with "high incident disabilities"—specific learning disabilities, emotional and behavioral disorders, and mild intellectual disabilities—comprise 9% of the school-age population and approximately 70% of all students who receive special education. These students "share a heightened risk of experiencing a number of social, emotional, and behavioral difficulties" (p. 106). Students with ASD may also face heightened isolation and alienation when they do not fit in or gain acceptance from peers. Nurturing teacher relationships, however, can have a great impact on students with disabilities. Murray and Pianta (2007) cited the work of Murray and Greenberg (2001) that showed that students with high incidence disabilities "who had more positive relationships with teachers had lower levels of delinquency" (p. 107). A teacher's acceptance, understanding, and bond with a student can be a lifeline. I have seen hundreds of students flourish under the caring attention of teachers and aides, even when their peer relationships were unsatisfactory. I have also seen mediations that were effective with students with emotional difficulties, specific learning disabilities, autism spectrum disorder, and intellectual disabilities. Communication and problem-solving skills are universal needs, and finding common ground and understanding is helpful for everyone.

Teens are risk-takers. Jensen (2015) shared that

The chief predictor of adolescent behavior, studies show, is not the perception of the risk, but the anticipation of the reward *despite* [italics in original] the risk…gratification is at the heart of an adolescent's impulsivity, and adolescents who engage in risky behavior and who have never, or rarely, experienced negative consequences are more likely to keep repeating that reckless behavior in search of further gratification. (pp. 107–108)

Mediation helps identify the reward the student seeks in a simple way: by asking what it is the student wants. Disciplinary consequences should also play a role, however, because negative consequences will often serve to deter risk-taking behavior.

WHAT ARE THE POSSIBLE ROOT CAUSES OF PROBLEMS PRESENTED IN TEACHER–STUDENT MEDIATION?

Having considered possible challenges teachers and students experience, it is important to recognize that the specific problems presented at a mediation are often associated with deeper needs and feelings. Table 6.1 explores possible needs and feelings associated with common issues brought to a mediation for students. When reviewing this list of presenting problems for students, recall that under MTSS, we are generally describing the approximate 20% of students (Tier II or Tier III) who do not consistently respond to schoolwide (Tier I) interventions and supports. Table 6.2 explores presenting problems and possible underlying needs, feelings and issues from a teacher's perspective.

The root causes for problems are numerous and varied, and one teacher–student mediation session will not always resolve the issues at hand. New insights and "aha" moments do not always lead to behavior change, but they are a place to start. Someone must first grasp what another person wants, needs, or feels to begin to solve a problem. To explain this further, consider the following example with two adults: Mona and Lee are having a conflict. Mona knows her partner, Lee, is a neat freak, but she is naturally sloppy. In their marriage counseling, Mona has come to understand how important it is for Lee to live in a neat house. In fact, on a scale of 1–10, with 10 being very important, Mona gains the insight that for Lee, a clean house is rated a 10. Will this insight lead to change? Will it solve the problem once and for all? For Lee, the solution is for Mona to also be a neat freak. For Mona, the solution is for Lee to not nag when the house is less than perfect. Here is a case in which effort matters. Mona can show Lee that she cares about his anxieties over a neat house by making an effort toward maintaining a cleaner living environment. They may even reach a suitable compromise and arrange for certain rooms in the house to be given higher priority for neatness. Learning that his wife is frustrated and stressed over his constant critiques of the house, Lee will also show effort by not nagging as much. Both will appreciate the effort of the other, yet know that it will be easy to slip back into old habits, necessitating another talk and renewed efforts.

Table 6.1. Presenting problems for students

Presenting problem	Deeper student need, feeling, or issue
The student is constantly disruptive in class.	I want adult attention!
	I want peer acceptance, and I am going to do whatever I can to get it.
	I am not trying to be bad, but I have a short attention span, and I am easily distracted.
	I am not doing schoolwork. I'm busy talking and texting my friends! It is important. Besides, the stuff we are doing in class is boring.
	I didn't start it, but other kids were talking to me, so I had to answer.
The student exhibits a disrespectful attitude toward the teacher.	I wish the teacher liked me. I don't feel like she even cares.
	I already know how to do these math problems. I shouldn't have to show my work. Can't I be more challenged? I am bored.
	I do not feel respected by this teacher, so I am not going to show respect.
	The teacher insulted me, and I refuse to work for him. I got in trouble and other people were doing the same thing.
	I'm different from the other kids in the class. When is the teacher going to realize that? I want the teacher to talk to me more and understand me.
The student's grades have dropped.	I'm going through some family problems. I'm not always going to be able to focus in class. I would like to know the teacher cares about me, though.
	I can't do my schoolwork because scary things are happening in my home and I'm frightened.
	The work is too hard. I'm confused and embarrassed because other students seem to get it. If I ask for help, other students will think I'm dumb.
	I only work hard if the teacher gives out stuff like candy and stickers. (Student lacks intrinsic motivation and wants extrinsic rewards.)
	Why should I work so hard? Nobody at home would even notice. In fact, I don't care about this or much of anything.
	I only come to school because I have to. It never feels good to me.
The student comes to class and puts head down.	I don't want the teacher to call on me! If I look down, I will be invisible. I didn't study and I don't know the answers.
	I'm so tired. I work at Go Burger and I had to close last night, and then I had to wake up early to help with my little brothers.
	I'm struggling with depression. It took everything I had to even be in school today. I feel like I'm in a hole and don't know how to climb out.
	I have anxiety and am terrified that I will have a panic attack in class.
	I got high before coming to school.
	I am hungry. I'm not getting enough to eat at home.
	I'm not following what is going on in class.
The student says the teacher is racist, or the teacher plays favorites.	I really want to be a part of the class, but other kids seem to fit in better.
	The only time the teacher says my name is when I'm in trouble.
	I wish the teacher had higher expectations of me and challenged me more.
	I wish the teacher knew more about my background. We just don't connect.
	I wish the teacher seemed happier to see me, smiled at me, and laughed at my jokes like she seems to do with other kids.

Table 6.2. Presenting problems for teachers

Presenting problem	Deeper teacher need, feeling, or issue
The teacher explains behavioral rules and expectations, but students do not follow them.	I feel frustrated. I explain the rules clearly. Why doesn't everybody just follow them?
	I feel angry. Every day I go through the same thing with Whelan. Every day! We are just not getting along. I want him to stop being so rude to me.
	I feel defeated. I have spoken to Carla in private over and over. I have also spoken to Carla's father. She only improves for a day or two, and then it is back to the same disruptions.
The teacher has underperforming students.	I'm not going to say I have given up, but Alvin just does not care. There is not a whole lot I can do about a student who does not attend class regularly or come for extra help.
	I feel powerless. I know Chelsea comes from a challenging background, but there is nothing I can do to change that. I try to reach out to her in class, but it is not making a difference.
	I feel confused. I try to motivate Jenni by praising her work and offering her extra help, but she doesn't respond.
	I feel angry and fed up. I am not focusing any more attention on Lance. I have a classroom of students who care about their work, and they need my time.
The teacher is not connecting with students.	I'm feeling completely stumped. I try to talk to Kacey and ask her if she needs help, and she glares at me. She often comes to class late and doesn't bring her materials.
	My classroom is too hot. When will we get air conditioning? And did I mention that it is freezing in the winter? I'm just not at my best in that environment.
	I am less than at my best with a class size of 30. I am not a miracle worker. I can't get to everybody every day!
	I'm not connecting to all of my students because I'm going through some personal issues right now. It's been a rough year.
	I'm sorry for not connecting to all my students, but how can I be positive, when last week a student stole my phone?
	I'm not connecting to my students the way I want to. I just got assigned to teach this new class, and I am learning the material for the first time! I was up late every night this week, and I am exhausted.
The teacher is accused of being racist or playing favorites.	I feel confused. I cannot be flexible with my different learners and see to their individual needs without appearing to play favorites.
	I know that I am unfamiliar with Lew's background, but he has to meet me halfway and participate a little more in class.
	I feel rattled when Jana gives me back talk. I kind of avoid her after that.
	I'm very frustrated. Elijah comes to class and puts his head down. If I wake him, he just gives me attitude for the rest of the class. If I don't wake him, he doesn't learn and sets a bad example for other students. I end up sending him out of class, and that just makes his attitude worse.
	Marty called me a racist for sending him out of class, but he wouldn't be quiet when I gave three warnings! I know others were talking as well, but I specifically asked *him* to stop. I expect more from Marty. We usually get along well.

The example of Lee and Mona's marriage counseling can be used to represent the ebb and flow of how problems are processed in a classroom as well. One mediation will not stop Jeremy from taking out his phone and constantly whispering to his friends in class. The mediation can, however, humanize the teacher–student relationship and enhance or repair the respect and rapport so that Jeremy will be more likely to show effort toward improvement. Invariably, there will be one step forward, two steps back, but as long as both parties do not lose the will to demonstrate effort, the path will go in the right direction.

QUICK FIXES AND PLEASANT SURPRISES

Despite the reality that mediation does not provide an instant solution, there are times when a teacher and/or student genuinely misread a situation. In those cases, mediation can provide an instant fix. Such mediations are extremely gratifying and easy. Take for example, a situation I experienced at Centennial High School. It was late April, and the semester was winding down. Andrew, a quiet and mature sophomore, was sent to the office with a disciplinary referral for inappropriate cell phone use. Andrew's fury was palpable. He told his administrator that he was done with Ms. Reynolds and would never go back to her class. The administrator suggested mediation. With a bit of coaxing, Andrew agreed to the mediation and actually liked the idea of telling Ms. Reynolds what he really thought of her. Ms. Reynolds agreed to the mediation as well.

As the mediator, I was nervous going in. I had only briefly met Andrew to verify his consent to participate in the mediation. He seemed to be looking forward to the mediation a little too much. I did not want Ms. Reynolds, a younger member of the faculty, to feel insulted by Andrew during the meeting. The mediation began with Andrew asserting, "I'm done and I don't care if I fail the class." He described getting a disciplinary referral at the beginning of class for having his phone out. "I do not like her playing favorites," he said, referring to Ms. Reynolds.

Andrew went on to explain that he knows phones are not allowed in class, but his phone takes extra long to turn off. He was not trying to violate the rule. What really triggered Andrew's impression of favoritism was that the same day, another student named Lewis lashed out at Ms. Reynolds. And she only gave Lewis a warning followed by a talk in the hallway.

Andrew: How come I got a disciplinary referral for my phone, and Lewis, who told off Ms. Reynolds and is always bad in class, only got a talk? And here I am—a good student who always does my work—and I get the referral?

Andrew said he was prepared to spend the rest of the semester sitting in the back of the room doing nothing. It became clear that Andrew believed he had earned "good student" collateral by exhibiting sound work habits throughout the semester and that he should not be treated like other students who do not seem to care.

Since it was April and everything until this point had been fine with Andrew and Ms. Reynolds, I wanted to "mine for gold" and have Andrew identify some positive reactions to the teacher and the class prior to the event. I used reflective listening skills to validate Andrew:

Mediator: You see yourself as a good student who follows the rules. You were slow to put the cell phone away, but that was because of how long it takes for your particular phone to turn off. You thought it was unfair that Ms. Reynolds gave you a disciplinary referral when you see other students with their phones out. On the day you got really upset, you saw Lewis really lash out at Ms. Reynolds, but she just took him out in the hall, and he didn't get a disciplinary referral. Because of that, you think that Ms. Reynolds is unfair and playing favorites.

Andrew: Uh huh.

Mediator: I just want to understand a little more. Did you have Ms. Reynolds for the first semester as well as this one?

Andrew: Yeah.

Mediator: Okay—so how did that go? What was your grade?

Andrew: I got a B.

Mediator: That is a good grade! So your first semester with Ms. Reynolds went okay? [Reinforcing the solid foundation of their relationship and their history.]

Andrew: Yeah, it was fine.

Mediator: Would you say that before this problem, you were learning geometry pretty well from Ms. Reynolds?

Andrew: Yeah—she is a good math teacher.

Mediator: Oh, so you like the way she teaches math? [Restating praise to emphasize the positive.]

Andrew: Yeah—she explains things well.

Mediator: Okay, Andrew. It sounds like things were going along pretty well with you and Ms. Reynolds. You were earning a B in the class, and mastering geometry. Last Wednesday, you got a disciplinary referral for having your cell phone out, and you have explained why it was out and how you felt about getting the disciplinary referral. I am just curious about something. Were you feeling like you should not have gotten a referral because you usually are such a good student and that maybe you should have gotten more leeway? [I am wondering if Andrew perceived the disciplinary referral as an insult.]

Andrew: Yeah—I thought Ms. Reynolds would know I am not trying to break the rules.

Mediator: So it sounds like you really wanted Ms. Reynolds to know that you are a student who cares about the class and your work, as you have shown during the entire semester, and that it would not be your intention to violate the phone rule. It just takes your phone extra long to power off. Is there anything else you would like to say before we ask Ms. Reynolds to speak?

Andrew: No.

All of my fears about Andrew being rude to Ms. Reynolds were put to rest. In fact, he was calm, polite, and soft-spoken. I was relieved and very impressed with Andrew. Before continuing on with the mediation, I was sure to provide thanks and praise.

Mediator: Before I ask Ms. Reynolds what brought us here, I just want to thank you both for your willingness to participate in the mediation. These meetings are not always easy, but I think they really help clear the air, and I am so glad you both are here. Thank you.

Next, I turned to Ms. Reynolds.

Mediator: Okay, Ms. Reynolds—what brought us here?

Ms. Reynolds: I did write a disciplinary referral for Andrew at the beginning of class. I issued a warning, but I still saw the phone out. I try to be consistent with my policy. That policy is spelled out clearly, and all the students know the rule.

Mediator: Okay—so you are saying that you have a firm policy that all the students know about. After issuing a warning, Andrew still had his cell phone out, and you wrote a disciplinary referral.

Ms. Reynolds: Yes. The other incident Andrew is referring to was that another student had an outburst, and I removed him to the hallway. I can totally see how Andrew thought of that as favoritism. Here is the best way I can explain it: Sometimes I find it necessary to build a more positive relationship with a student in order to improve that student's behavior. That might involve having a private talk in the hallway. I can see how another student might think that is unfair, but our school administrators are encouraging us to really try to understand where students are coming from and work on building positive relationships.

Mediator: Oh, so you sometimes take students out in the hall, rather than sending them to the office, because you are trying to build a more positive relationship. You can see how another student would see that as favoritism, though, because students do not always know the back stories.

Ms. Reynolds: Yeah—and I have never taken Andrew in the hall because it was not necessary.

Mediator: Oh—you never needed to take Andrew in the hall. How would you describe Andrew as a student? [I sought positive statements and "mined for gold."]

Ms. Reynolds: Andrew is a bright student. He does his work in class and does all his homework. He scores well on tests. He is not chatty. I can see he has a strong work ethic. He is concerned with doing well, and he asks for help if he needs it.

Andrew noticeably relaxed more in his seat. It was clear that this positive acknowledgment of his character and performance by Ms. Reynolds had restored his dignity.

Mediator: Oh, wow. You have so many nice things to say about Andrew! I heard you say that he is a bright student. He does his work in class. He does all his homework. He scores well on tests. He is not chatty. He has a strong work ethic, and he is concerned with doing well and he asks for help. That is fantastic! [I read these remarks from my verbatim notes.] Is there anything else you would like to add?

Ms. Reynolds: No.

Mediator [referring to my notes]: Okay—I am going to summarize and then ask both of you to speak to each other to develop a plan to move forward. Andrew is a strong student. He works hard, cares about his grade, does all his work, asks questions, and completes his homework. He also has a cell phone that takes extra long to put away. Ms. Reynolds explains things well, and things have been fine in the class between the two of you all year, until the cell phone incident. Ms. Reynolds tries to be consistent with the cell phone policy and issues a warning before giving a student a disciplinary referral. Andrew identified favoritism because the same day he received the disciplinary referral for the cell phone, another student had an outburst, and the teacher just took him out in the hall for a talk. Andrew couldn't figure out how something that was a more serious infraction got a talk, and he—a hardworking student—got a disciplinary referral. Ms. Reynolds explained that sometimes it is necessary for a teacher to try to understand where students are coming from and build a positive relationship, but that other students would not necessarily know that. Does that cover it? [Pause.] Now, I am going to ask each of you to speak directly to each other and develop a plan to move forward.

The minute they look at each other, they smile. Ms. Reynolds says she is sorry that Andrew got upset, and that she understands how he could feel that way. Andrew, who feels terrific after hearing Ms. Reynolds' words, smiles warmly and says gracious things back to her. It is instantly clear that respect has been restored, and these two can go back to their teacher–student relationship.

Mediator: Would the two of you like to develop a plan to move forward?

Ms. Reynolds: I understand that your cell phone takes longer to put away. Just say, "Give me a minute" and then I will know what is happening.

That was the extent of their plan. This entire mediation took 10 minutes.

Other nice surprises occur in mediations. There are often vulnerable, poignant, and human moments that are shared and honored by the teacher and the student. I have seen teachers share their own mistakes and vulnerabilities:

Mr. Burl: You are right. I did get mad at you when Noah was doing the same thing. I'm really glad you brought it up here. I didn't think about it at the time, but you are right…it was unfair. Now that I think back, I think it was because Noah was also respectful and funny, and that made me treat him a little different. That is wrong, and I apologize for it.

Ms. Farrow: I was going through something personal because my own daughter had recently gotten really sick. I know that I was not at my best.

Students also will often use the mediation as a way to admit their mistakes and apologize:

Liz: I talk, I am rude, I don't quiet down, and I have my phone out too much. It has nothing to do with the way you teach. I just have to be better.

Evan: I am really sorry. I should not have walked out of class without asking.

I have also been touched when a student in mediation offers gentle advice to a teacher:

Courtney: It kind of seems like you are reading to us, and the class might act better if we did more hands-on stuff.

Because of the high emotions that can be brought into a mediation, sometimes there are tears, sometimes hugs:

Sabrina: Well, there are things you don't know about me, Ms. Nishi. My mom and I have to move at the end of the month, and it has been really hard for us. [Tears well up in her eyes.]

Ms. Nishi: Oh, Sabrina. I am really sorry you are under that kind of pressure. Thank you for telling me. [Ms. Nishi pauses, looks at Sabrina with warmth in her eyes, and asks to give her a hug. Sabrina readily agrees. It is a poignant, healing, and beautiful moment.]

A few words about touch: The ways humans touch each other is affected by their background, culture, and personal experiences. In some cultures, greeting strangers with a kiss on each cheek is the norm. In some religions, any touch among unmarried males and females is forbidden. Some people are quick to touch and hug, others find it invasive and uncomfortable. Now consider touch among teachers and students. For obvious and good reasons, students are not allowed to push, hit, or verbally threaten teachers. Any of those infractions can lead to expulsion. I have seen students expelled, however, when teachers blocked a doorway and the students shoved the teacher's arm away in order to walk away before doing or saying something they'd regret. I have also seen students threaten teachers because the teachers innocently tapped or placed a hand on their shoulder. Some students become highly agitated when a teacher "gets in their face" or steps in too close and "violates their personal space." A teacher may naturally lean in to help a student seated at a desk. When is it too close? Some touch is nurturing. Some touch is unwanted or uncomfortable. How can teachers gauge a student's reaction to touch when it is so dependent on personal background and preferences? My rule of thumb is not to touch anyone without explicit consent: "Can I shake your hand?" "Can I give you a hug?" "Do you mind if I stand/sit here or would you like to move to those desks over there?"

Mediations can offer a suitable venue for issues of touch and personal space to be discussed.

Gavin: I hate it when someone comes up from behind and touches me. I shouldn't have yelled at Mr. Bach, though.

Mr. Bach: Gavin, I realize now that I shouldn't have tapped you that way. I'm really glad I know that now.

Kaelyn: Instead of saying, "Kaelyn, lift your head!" I wish Ms. Sakai would just come over to my desk.

Mediator: So you would like Ms. Sakai to come over to you if your head is down?

Kaelyn: Yeah. Maybe she could lightly tap me on the shoulder, or ask me if everything is okay.

Elliot: It's nothing personal against Mr. Cleveland, but I don't like coming in for tutoring help because teachers lean over me and get up too close.

Mr. Cleveland: Would it help if we set up two desks side by side, and then I wouldn't have to lean over you?

Because touch and personal space issues vary from person to person, the mediation helps to identify what will work best for the two parties.

PROBLEM-SOLVING STRATEGIES AND MEDIATION CHALLENGES

It is nearing the end of the mediation meeting, and both parties have had a chance to express their points of view. The mediator has reflectively listened to the stated problems, validated both participants, summarized, and offered thanks and praise. It is now time for the participants to speak directly to one another and to develop their plan to move forward. The vast majority of the time, the mediator can play a passive role, and the teacher and student will develop their own plans. The principle of self-determination allows the teacher and student to devise creative solutions for themselves.

Teacher to student: I notice you get kind of restless at times. Would it help if you were responsible for feeding the salamander every day?

There are times, however, when the teacher and student do not know how to have that conversation and look to the mediator for guidance and ideas. The following strategies often are helpful to employ in mediations:

- Identify the best ways for the teacher and student to communicate or signal each other.

   Terence: Sometimes I am just having a bad day, and I have trouble doing good work.

   Mr. North: I understand that you sometimes have bad days. Is there a way you could let me know when those days are happening? I could let you work outside, or go to the library, or get a drink of water or something. I know the class gets intense sometimes—it does for me, too!

   Mediator: Some people have a special gesture, use a Post-it note, write something on the board, or just walk over and tap a shoulder or tap the desk. Terence, maybe you and Mr. North could talk about the best ways to communicate on those difficult days.

- Identify the area of the classroom where the student works best.

   Mediator: Sometimes in mediations, teachers and students find it helpful to talk about where in a class the student works best.

   Mr. Patrick: I noticed that you worked best when I had you in a group with Jasmine and Mila. Do you agree? Or can you tell me someone else I could group you with?

   Taylor: I like sitting by myself. Can I just have a seat off to the side?

   Ms. Fuller: Since we changed seats last week, you seem to be more distracted.

   Dylan: Yeah, I probably should be moved near the front.

- Identify concrete next steps.

   Mediator: Karen, you mentioned during the mediation that you had fallen behind on your work.

   Karen: I know I have two tests to make up. Could I set up times when I can take those tests?

   Ms. Chu: Sure, Karen. You also missed the lesson on DNA, but if you come after school today, I can show you what you missed and help you get caught up.

Challenges in Mediation

In my experience with more than 200 teacher–student mediations, I have experienced just a few challenging situations. The first challenges were when the students didn't play nice—in other words, they were polite, and even cooperative within the mediation meeting; however, they did not catch on to the idea that this meeting was to problem-solve and generate good will. Instead, they remained fixed in their original position.

Madison: I don't like the teacher and I never will!

 Ms. Dawson was new to high school teaching (after working in adult settings) and taught an industrial design class. Madison was a freshman and had definite ideas about what she liked to draw. The problem was that she only drew what she wanted and not what Ms. Dawson assigned. Prior to going to the mediation, Ms. Dawson had called home many times, and Madison had received disciplinary consequences from school and home. This had upset Madison. Ms. Dawson was strict, and as a teacher new to working with adolescents, she thought it was her duty to monitor Madison's behavior and comment on every mistake. From Madison's perspective, Ms. Dawson needed to "get out of her face," "stop picking on her," and "leave her alone!" During the mediation, I tried every single way I could to help identify the problems, understand the root causes, and mine for gold, but Madison would not budge from believing that she would never like Ms. Dawson. It seemed that the bridges had been burned and there was no way to repair them. Was Ms. Dawson too rigid, and Madison too stubborn? Perhaps, yet despite my many attempts to direct the conversations in a positive, constructive direction, it became clear that the mediation needed to stop, and it did. Ms. Dawson accosted me after the mediation: "I thought you said this would be safe!" All I could do was apologize and assure her that additional interventions would be implemented. I reported to the referring administrator that the mediation did not go well. I also met with Madison individually. Fortunately, Madison was doing fine in all of her other classes and generally got along well with her teachers. She had made the decision to do her own art in the class despite the consequences, even if she earned a failing grade. We discussed how her actions might affect the teacher and other learners. In addition, the administrator scheduled a parent–teacher–student conference in which classroom rules and consequences were reviewed.

 I share this example to show that there is an element of risk to all mediations. The vast majority of the time, things go smoothly because it is a voluntary meeting and presumably participants would not attend if they were not open to work toward improvement. This meeting was "safe" insofar as Madison did not use profanity to insult Ms. Dawson, but the mediation alone could not repair a 14-year-old's negative feelings and perception of injury at the hands of the teacher.

 Here's another example of a student not playing nice:

Ryder: I don't like the teacher. I can't tell you why. I just don't.

Ryder was a junior who disliked his science teacher, Ms. Russo. I could iden-tify no reason for his attitude toward her. Ms. Russo dutifully attended the mediation with openness and a real desire to improve the relationship. Ryder would not make eye contact with her and was unwavering from his statement that nothing would change the way he felt. Again, I tried to identify the arc of the relationship and events of the class and what could have gone wrong. I even asked Ryder if Ms. Russo reminded him of someone else. Ryder was not failing the class, and there were no behavioral issues to address. The problem was one of attitude, and he was immovable. I asked to speak with him at a private follow-up meeting, and I was still unable to identify any reason for his strong feelings or any means to improve his attitude toward Ms. Russo. The key takeaway here is that mediation is not successful when one party with-holds their honest thoughts and feelings. I later debriefed with Ms. Russo. She said she found solace in the fact that Ryder was performing well academically and that he now knew she cared enough to devote time to a mediation. As an experienced teacher, Ms. Russo knew that not every teacher–student relation-ship is ideal.

When mediations are ineffective because a student will not budge on his or her opinion, additional options can include a parent–teacher meeting, administrative involvement, or a change to another teacher. Or, as many teach-ers and students alike tell themselves: "Just get through the rest of the semes-ter" because at times, everyone must cope with challenging relationships.

Another challenge in mediations is when a quiet, vulnerable student is paired with a brash teacher. Every school has at least one teacher with a strong personality: a character that instructs with high animation, humor, and sar-casm. These teachers can be immensely popular. However, not every student will feel a sense of belonging in such classrooms and may feel scared or intimi-dated. In such mediations, it is necessary for the teachers to tone down and the students to step up, thereby meeting half way. In other words, the teachers will hopefully shed their tough veneers to reveal a softer side, and the students will hopefully tap into their inner strength to find their voices. However, it does not always work according to plan. In a case in which the student becomes emo-tional (starts to cry or stops talking), the mediator may pause, acknowledge the emotion, and offer words of solace.

Mediator [hands student a tissue box]: This meeting is touching on some deep stuff that's painful. Let's just take a minute…are you okay to continue?

Stopping the mediation is always an option.

Mediator: I'm thinking that we should stop the mediation and Kendall and I should just talk one on one. Is that okay with everyone?

Mediator: Justin, instead of continuing with this mediation, would you like to have a one-on-one meeting with your counselor, Ms. Balaban? I can see if she is available.

Another challenge in teacher–student mediation occurs when a student does not speak. This is rare, but it can happen that a student agrees to come to the mediation but once in the meeting says almost nothing. The mediator may gently coax the student to speak, using encouragement and praise. If the student still says little to nothing, the mediator can ask if the student would like another adult in the room. If another adult is brought in, that adult may be in the role of an observer so that the format of the mediation remains the same. Another option is for the mediator to stop the mediation and briefly speak to the student outside of the room. The mediator and student can then rejoin the mediation, and the mediator will share the student's concerns and proceed with the meeting.

A final example of a challenge in mediation, though not a huge difficulty, arises when one of the parties asks to bring another adult to the mediation. For example, a student may have a class taught by a team or co-teacher, and both adults wish to attend. I ask that only one adult attend, or, that if both adults attend, one stay in the role of observer. Similarly, a parent may be aware of the conflict with a teacher and ask to attend the mediation. I ask that the parent only attend to observe. It is critical to protect the integrity of the mediation structure by not having it become a two-against-one format. At the very end of the mediation, when the teacher and student are developing their plans, the adult observer may ask to speak. By then the mediation has run its course, a positive tone is assured, and it is okay for the observer to speak. It is not advisable to invite the adult observer to speak before the mediation is completed because the mediator may lose the ability to maintain the right pacing and climate.

PRACTICE MEDIATIONS

This section provides practice mediation scenarios that can be used in workshops to train mediators and to familiarize attendees with how the mediation process works. I recommend that adults switch among the teacher, student, and mediator roles. I find that adults are genuinely surprised by the emotions they feel in each role they play.

Practice Mediation #1

Student: Jeremy, a 15-year-old sophomore, has stopped working in his English class, and his grade has dropped from a C to an F. He is upset because last week the teacher wrote him a disciplinary referral and sent him to the office. Jeremy knew that another student was much more disruptive and was offended that he was the one that got sent out. He has completely shut down.

Teacher: Mr. Cole, an experienced teacher, thinks that Jeremy is a good student and that he is definitely not the worst offender when it comes to talking too much in class. The day of the disciplinary referral, Mr. Cole issued a warning to the class: "The next person who talks gets sent out!" The next one to speak after the warning was Jeremy, and Mr. Cole sent him out.

Practice Mediation #2

Student: In her third period reading class, Shay, a sixth grader, is withdrawn and morose. She puts her head down and has not been turning in work. When the teacher approaches her, she "has an attitude." Shay thinks the teacher hates her. However, she is withdrawn in class because she is going through some personal challenges at home.

Teacher: Last year, Ms. Owen had an ugly confrontation with Shay when she was serving on hall duty. This year she is Shay's teacher and thinks that Shay recalls that event and that is why she has an attitude. (Note: Shay has no recall of that event in the hallway.)

Practice Mediation #3

Student: Kayla, a high-achieving African-American junior in an AP English class, is extremely upset, and so is her mother. During a lecture, Ms. Watson, an experienced teacher, quoted a historical document that had the "N" word. However, she used the actual word when teaching the class about it.

Teacher: Ms. Watson issued disclaimers prior to reading the document and conveyed that in no way did she approve of the historical document she was teaching. She wanted to use the real word to be accurate to the history of the time.

Practice Mediation #4

Student: Brody is a 13-year-old eighth grader who is small for his age. He sits in the back of his science class and wears his hat, even though he is reminded daily to take it off. He rarely opens his book or does any work. He has a D- in the class. (It is revealed during mediation that the class discussions move too quickly and he is not following the lessons. He is confused and discouraged.)

Teacher: Mr. Meese, a very caring teacher nearing retirement, is extremely frustrated with Brody. Why does he insist on wearing his hat and not taking out his book? He has tried talking to Brody privately, with no success. He has had it and is now turning to mediation to come up with a solution.

Practice Mediation #5

Student: Amir, a new student, comes from a Middle Eastern background and abides by his family's cultural practices. He has vowed that he will never return to Ms. Sidler's economics class. He reported that the last time he went to the class, Ms. Sidler "slammed the door in his face" and he reports that in his culture, this is an unforgivable show of disrespect.

Teacher: Ms. Sidler strictly follows the tardy policy. She taught the students her expectations: When the bell rings, students must be in their seats, and may not enter the class while the bell is ringing. She feels she has not singled out Amir in her implementation of this policy—when the bell rings, she closes the door, even if students are approaching. They must get a tardy pass from the hall monitor before returning to class.

Practice Mediation #6

Student: Nicole, an overweight sixth grader, reports that she hates her math teacher, Ms. Saroyan, because Ms. Saroyan "plays favorites." She says that Ms. Saroyan only cares about the cute kids in the room, like Bonnie. She is always helping Bonnie, but Nicole says that the teacher ignores her when her hand is up.

Teacher: Ms. Saroyan is a first-year teacher. Unbeknownst to Nicole, Bonnie is a student with special needs who does need extra help. Ms. Saroyan is trying to figure out how to balance her time with Bonnie and all of the other students.

Practice Mediation #7

Student: Abigail is an immensely popular freshman and is very socially active. She has the reputation of being in the "eye of every storm" with regard to drama. In her Spanish class, the teacher has frequently reprimanded her for being on her cell phone and talking. Unbeknownst to the teacher, Mr. Rich, Abigail has never experienced success in an academic setting. Her reading skills have been weaker than her classmates' for her entire school career. Spanish is very challenging because she has trouble reading English words, let alone unfamiliar words in a different language.

Teacher: In private, Mr. Rich puts it bluntly: "Abigail does not shut up!" She talks constantly! If she is not talking, she is texting on her cell phone. She does not bring her materials to class and refuses to answer any questions when called on. Her grade is rapidly dropping. Mr. Rich has called home about this, and the improvement in Abigail's work habits only lasted a day. He is at his wit's end.

Practice Mediation #8

Student: Jimmy is 8 years old, and for the last 6 weeks, he has spoken to his mother about how much he dislikes his teacher, Ms. Bond. Now he's confused, because his mother came back from a meeting with Ms. Bond and said nice things about her. Jimmy knows that this meeting is to try to give

Ms. Bond another chance, and to help him do better in the class. He used to like Ms. Bond, so he is curious about what will happen next.

Teacher: Ms. Bond is a novice fourth-grade teacher who recently had a mediation with Jimmy's mother. That mediation cleared up a parent–teacher conflict that had been rubbing off on Jimmy, and alerted Ms. Bond to some background issues that had upset Jimmy. Now, Ms. Bond wants a mediation with Jimmy because she knows that he has been unhappy with her, and she wants to rebuild their relationship. (She learned from his mother that he likes racecars.) Ms. Bond also wants Jimmy to understand why other students besides him get to take turns caring for the turtles, and get called on during the math lessons.

Practice Mediation #9

Student: Che is a seventh grader who dresses in fashionable, colorful attire, and whom many describe as flamboyant. Che is open about the fact that he is gay. This semester, Che has asked to be called "Cher" and to be referred to as "she." Most of Cher's teachers comply with this request, but not Mr. Qualley, the science teacher. Cher has stopped attending Mr. Qualley's class.

Teacher: Mr. Qualley says he is fond of Che and is sorry that his attendance has gone down. He states the belief that he should call students by the names on his roll sheet and discussed this with the principal and Che's parents. He thinks that to call Che "she" in class would draw unwanted attention to Che and distract other learners. He also admits that he is personally uncomfortable with the idea of using the name "Cher." Mr. Qualley has told the principal and Che's parents that he doesn't think that a seventh-grade class is the place for "social experiments." There is no school policy on the matter, and the adults have suggested mediation so that Che and Mr. Qualley can better understand each other and develop a plan.

Practice Mediation #10

Student: Marc, a senior, is a tall, husky football player. He is nearing the end of his high school career and is nervous about the future. Midway into the semester, his favorite history teacher steps aside to make way for a student teacher, Mr. Frank. Marc is upset because he really hoped to end his senior year with his favorite teacher. During Mr. Frank's first week, Marc is talking with friends instead of paying attention. Mr. Frank approaches Marc from the back, taps him three times on the shoulder, and says, "You need to get to work." Marc leaps up, and towering over Mr. Frank, yells, "You need to get your $%^&* hands off of me!"

Teacher: Mr. Frank is shocked by Marc's behavior. He was eager to begin his student teaching assignment, build positive relationships with students, and share his enthusiasm for history. The last thing he expected was to be confronted and intimidated by a student. Mr. Frank, however, is open and reflective. He has spoken to his supervising teacher, college instructor, and the principal. He has come to understand that coming up from behind students and/or tapping them should probably be avoided. He knows that Marc is in his final semester before graduating and is open to mediation to get things back on track.

In every mediation training workshop I have done, adults have a visceral reaction to their role-play experience. Some enter the role play with healthy skepticism, imagining a certain student they know who would never respond to mediation. It is gratifying to watch the astonishment as adults realize how powerful the experience can feel. Some stop the role play midstream to say, "Wow, I'm feeling really touched right now," or, "There is something really healing about this." Nothing drives home the potential of mediation to people more strongly than when they experience it for themselves. Those practicing a mediation also learn that it is not their job to fix the complex problems for the participants and see how following the mediation format allows the participants to reach their own solutions after gaining a greater understanding of one another.

SUMMARY AND NEXT TOPIC

This chapter presented possible root causes of problems brought by teachers and students to mediation and how helpful it is when those emotions and issues are brought to the surface. Once that understanding has occurred, mediation creates the opportunity for teachers and students to demonstrate greater effort toward resolving a problem. Though one mediation does not instantly solve all conflicts, there can sometimes be quick solutions, pleasant surprises, and profound healing moments during a teacher–student mediation. This chapter also introduced common mediation challenges and shared various problem-solving strategies that may be offered at a mediation. The sample mediation scenarios at the end of this chapter help further familiarize the mediation process and provide opportunities for role playing and practice.

In the next chapter, I discuss how to assess the effectiveness of a teacher–student mediation program and collect feedback on how both students and teachers feel about mediation. Many wonder if teachers are resistant to mediation with students. The next chapter presents frank feedback from surveys given to both Centennial High School students and teachers and discusses how to improve a mediation program based on survey results.

7

Feedback on Teacher–Student Mediation

A person who never made a mistake never tried anything new.

—Albert Einstein

How do we determine whether an intervention is effective? In education, it is trendy to proclaim something as a *best practice*, but as my graduate program taught me, this can be a subjective determination. Often, words such as *research-based*, *data-based*, and *evidence-based* give a quantitative stamp of approval to our practices. We often don't think to argue with this kind of data, yet numbers are not always foolproof.

Perhaps it is due to my early training as a school psychologist, but I have always been skeptical of numbers being applied to the soft science of human behavior and emotion. My first misgivings came when I was learning how to administer intelligence quotient (IQ) tests. I chose a lawyer friend to practice on. He scored within the *gifted* range on a Stanford-Binet (IQ: 138). He scored within the *average* range on a nonverbal test of intelligence (Leiter IQ: 99). How can the same person be gifted or average, depending on the test? There are many reasons. It depends on the test construction, its reliability, and its validity. It also depends on the test taker's mood, motivation, and fatigue level. Moreover, the setting where the test is administered affects performance—was it well lit and quiet enough? Were people walking in and out of the room? The examiner's attitude and demeanor may also play a role and have an impact on test performance. The classic work on "stereotype threat" by Steele and Aronson (1995) described the difference in performance of black college students on standardized testing in different contextual settings. In settings where the test takers were vulnerable to negative stereotypes, their performance was lower. Additional scholarly work on stereotype threat replicated the findings with other groups, including females, Hispanics, and white males (see www.ReducingStereotypeThreat.Org).

It is important to sometimes think beyond the data and not let numbers dwarf the larger picture. Consider the data obtained from schools: grades, attendance records, graduation rates, disciplinary referrals, and suspension numbers. Also consider a school's teaching strategies, disciplinary practices, social-emotional interventions, and available resources. We cannot easily construct a clean cause-and-effect line directly from, say, a powerful individual counseling session with Joel to Joel's improved academic functioning because to do so would ignore the numerous other influences on Joel's behavior. Joel's family, teachers, friends, coaches, and pastor, not to mention Joel's individual, personal motivation, may all positively affect his performance.

Despite the difficulty of measuring and quantifying the positive effects of social-emotional supports and interventions, social scientists do so every day. For a "gold-standard" example, see the research obtained in Durlak and colleagues' (2011) meta-analysis of 213 school-based, universal SEL programs involving 270,034 kindergarten through high school students. Their work confirmed the positive impact social-emotional programming has in schools. As stated in Chapter 2, collecting and analyzing data and making improvements based on the data is an ongoing practice when implementing RTI within MTSS. It was therefore our responsibility when implementing Tier II supports to collect as much information as possible on the effectiveness of teacher–student mediation.

The data we collected for Centennial High School's Tier II meetings showed that for 3 years straight, approximately 80% of students who participated in teacher–student mediation did not receive any additional disciplinary referrals from their teacher following the mediation. (These results are presented in Chapter 8.) Thus, the numbers strongly suggested that mediation was an effective intervention, which jived well with my personal observations. However, because the Tier II mission at Centennial High School involved evaluating and improving interventions in an ongoing way, additional data were needed. What did Centennial teachers and students think of teacher–student mediation? It was time to ask them.

The Tier II team discussed the use of a survey to obtain additional feedback from teachers. Surveys yield raw numbers and percentages but also allow respondents to express their impressions, viewpoints, and personal takeaways. Counting disciplinary referrals following a teacher–student mediation is one way to measure outcomes. Survey feedback is another dynamic and informative way to gauge response and identify areas for improvement. In December 2013 (year 2 since the inception of Tier II interventions), I sent an invitation to 35 teachers who had participated in mediations to complete a survey, and my Tier II team members helped me construct the survey questions. Below is an example of the survey prompt I sent to colleagues who had participated in mediations.

Dear Teachers,

If you are receiving this email, it is because you have participated in a teacher–student mediation. We would like to get frank feedback on your experience and observations so that we can make improvements as needed. Below is a link to a very brief survey that will allow you to participate anonymously.

Thank you so much for your help!

In this Chapter, I present the results of the 2013 anonymous survey conducted at Centennial High School. Note that anonymous surveys hold the risk of respondents expressing feedback that they would not say in a different format. On this survey, teachers wrote many positive statements, and they also provided constructive criticism. Only one or two people who participated in the survey were completely negative. (SurveyMonkey.com allows one to analyze both individual and group responses to surveys.) All teacher responses to teacher–student mediation are very informative and are presented here to provide an example for how schools adopting mediation might also obtain survey feedback to improve effectiveness.

TEACHER REACTIONS TO TEACHER–STUDENT MEDIATIONS

This section outlines the survey results from the 25 teachers who responded to our 2013 survey. The first survey question asked how many mediation meetings the teachers had attended. Figure 7.1 shows that nearly 63% of teachers participating in mediations had participated in two or more meetings. This suggests that teachers found the mediations effective and/or useful and were willing to participate in meetings with additional students after their first one.

As seen in Figure 7.2, 40% of the teachers viewed themselves as driving the decision to mediate. Other data that I collected and present in Chapter 8 (Figures 8.2, 8.7, 8.12, and 8.17) indicate that administrators were the source of referrals to mediation. The difference in this data suggests that unbeknownst

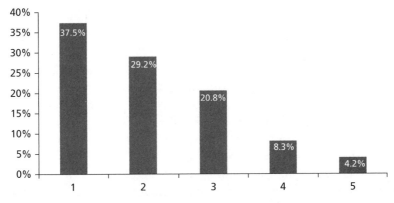

Figure 7.1. Survey results: How many mediations have you participated in? (24/25 responded.)

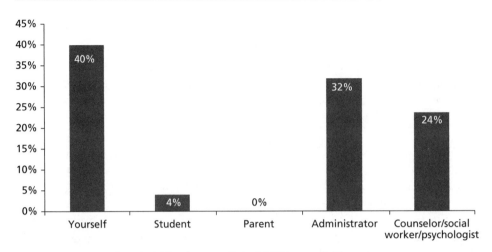

Figure 7.2. Survey results: Who initiated your mediation? (25/25 responded.)

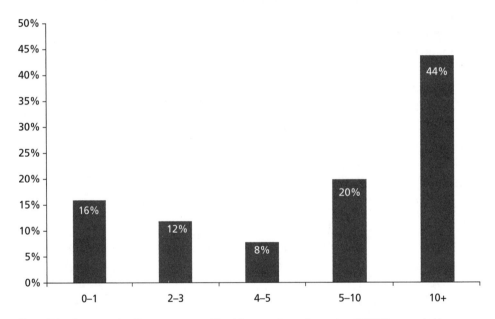

Figure 7.3. Survey results: How many years of teaching experience do you have? (25/25 responded.)

to me, either the teachers requested the mediation, or the administrator and teacher jointly agreed to propose mediation. In either case, the administrator conveys the requests to me. This question will be modified in future surveys to better understand who initiates mediations.

As shown in Figure 7.3, 64% of teachers participating in mediation had more than 5 years of teaching experience, and 36% had 5 years or less of teaching experience. The data indicated that both experienced and novice teachers used mediation. Many veteran teachers do an outstanding job of building positive relationships, maintaining classroom discipline, and obtaining exemplary results from diverse students, but some do not display such skills. There

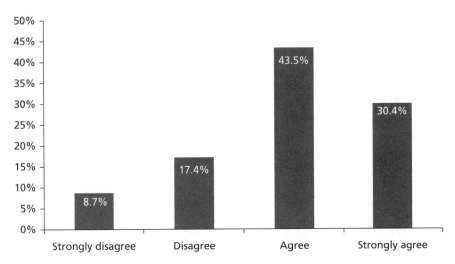

Figure 7.4. Survey results: When asked to participate in a mediation, I was enthusiastic and eager. (23/25 responded.)

are also wonderful teachers who claim to be "not-so-wonderful" with certain classes: "You would not think I was a great teacher if you came into my seventh period class!" Similarly, some novice teachers can be open-minded, energetic, and brimming with fresh ways to engage students and build respectful relationships with them, whereas other novice teachers may be nervous and lack the life experience or confidence to know how best to build positive relationships and resolve conflicts with diverse students. Sometimes veteran teachers advise novice teachers to "lay down the law" and send out troublemakers to set an example that bad behavior will not be tolerated. I have seen this approach backfire in some cases because the students who did not respond have ongoing conflicts with the teacher, and no rapport is established.

As shown in Figure 7.4, the results indicated a 74% agreement versus a 26% disagreement with the statement, "When asked to participate in a mediation, I was enthusiastic and eager." The wording of this question was slightly tongue-in-cheek because I imagined that many teachers might be reluctant to participate in a mediation with a student. I was pleasantly surprised that I was mistaken in that assumption, as nearly three times as many teachers felt positively about participating in mediation. However, comments in response to this question showed some mixed reactions:

Teacher: I was at the point where I didn't know what else to do. I felt like this was my only option to have a successful rest of the year with the student.

Teacher: I was not asked. I was told to participate. And one day after the incident!

I am not always aware of how the discussions between the teachers and the administrators occur. Perhaps the student had met the criterion of three or more disciplinary referrals from the teacher and the administrator did not communicate with the teacher prior to requesting mediation. This is why it is imperative for the mediator to emphasize to the teacher that mediation is always voluntary. Another teacher also commented:

Teacher: When the mediation replaces a consequence, it sends the student a message that disciplinary action by the teacher was being brought into question, even if it is in accordance with school policy.

Again, I cannot speak for how the administrator requested this teacher's participation in mediation, which may have had an impact on his or her impression, but this feedback underscores another area to improve: Administrators may need additional training on how to propose mediation to teachers so as to promote collaborative problem solving. Following is an example of an effective way that an administrator might address a teacher:

Administrator: Hello, Ms. Ohanian. I received the disciplinary referral you wrote on Howard. Throwing books, saying, "This class sucks!" and leaving the class without permission are unacceptable behaviors. I have assigned him a 1-day in-school suspension. I have also asked our social worker to enroll him in an anger-management skill-building group (Tier II intervention). I'm getting ready to call his parent, but I wondered if you might be willing to participate in a teacher–student mediation with Howard. Sometimes kids are triggered by things we don't know about, and a mediation helps to figure that out. It would also be a way for him to learn about your perspective. This is a completely voluntary meeting, it's highly structured, and an impartial mediator facilitates it. We have seen great outcomes with these meetings. What are your thoughts?

In addition to providing training to administrators, informational brochures, website postings, and faculty meeting presentations are also ways to impart correct information about teacher–student mediations. Often word-of-mouth endorsements are the most powerful way for new school initiatives to take hold, but misperceptions can also be spread that way. Despite one teacher's comments about mediation replacing a consequence, it is unlikely that students think that mediation is meant to undermine a teacher's discipline. In fact, many students know when they have crossed the line and often say so in the mediation meeting. Mediation is not meant to replace a disciplinary consequence, rather it is to provide additional support by serving as a safe, structured way for the teacher and student to problem solve. These meetings are not trials or legal court proceedings where the mediator renders a verdict at the end. The mediation is simply held to learn the perspective of each party and to identify positive steps for the future. I asked one of our administrators how he decides when to issue a disciplinary consequence and when to use a Tier II intervention.

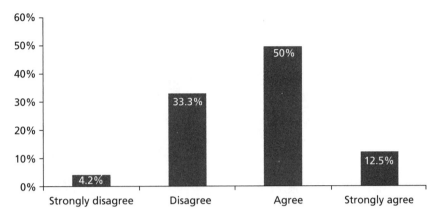

Figure 7.5 Survey results: During the mediation, I learned things about the student's perspective that I had not previously known. (24/25 responded.)

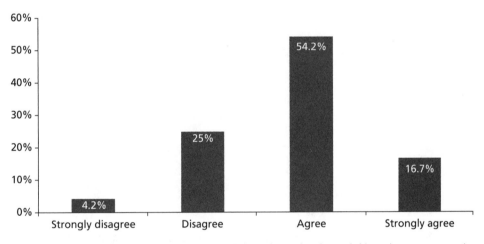

Figure 7.6. Survey results: During the mediation, I believe the student learned things about my perspective that he or she had not previously known. (24/25 responded.)

Administrator Ryan Cowell: I almost never replace a disciplinary consequence with a Tier II intervention. There's a place for a consequence....As soon as I see something particularly concerning, or multiple incidents with students in a class or the building, the first thing I start thinking about is the [Tier II] intervention.

As shown in Figure 7.5, a clear majority—62.5%—agreed that they learned something new about the student's perspective, and 37.5% disagreed. One teacher commented, "Students' ability to be frank and discuss their situation was always enlightening."

According to Figure 7.6, more than twice the respondents—70.9%—agreed that the student learned something new about the teacher's perspective,

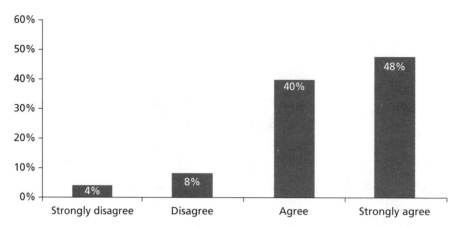

Figure 7.7.   Survey results: The mediator treated me with respect during the mediation. (25/25 responded.)

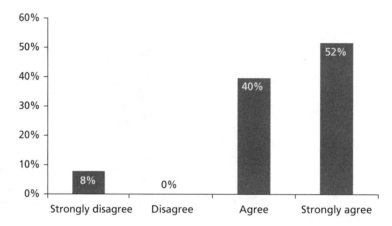

Figure 7.8.   Survey results: The mediator treated the student with respect during the mediation. (25/25 responded.)

whereas 29.2% disagreed. Though many teachers believe that they have made their expectations clear to all students, the majority of teachers felt that the student gained additional insights about their point of view during the mediation.

Figure 7.7 indicates that the majority of teachers—88%—reported that they were treated with respect during the mediation. As shown in Figure 7.8, most teachers—92%—indicated that students were treated with respect during the mediation.

As shown in Figure 7.9, 56% of teachers agreed that the mediation improved their relationship with the student, whereas 44% disagreed. The following are some comments teachers made:

- "Still rocky, but it led the way to have more open discussions. Also gave me a chance to change things in my teaching that were really bothering the student."

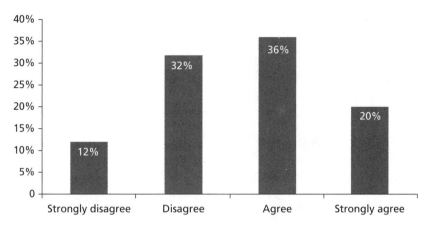

Figure 7.9. Survey results: The mediation improved my relationship with the student. (25/25 responded.)

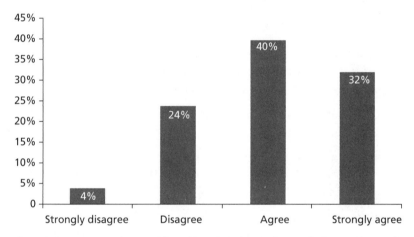

Figure 7.10. Survey results: I would recommend teacher–student mediation to other teachers. (25/25 responded.)

- "One relationship drastically improved. One relationship has not changed."

- "Most of the students have gone back to their old ways after a few weeks, so it helped for the short term but not the long term."

I took these comments to heart and changed the follow-up practices after mediations, which I discuss later in this chapter.

Figure 7.10 shows that 72% of teachers agreed with the statement that they would recommend teacher–student mediations to other teachers. According to Figure 7.11, the majority of teachers—87%—saw mediation as a positive step toward improving behavior and learning. Not only did this result encourage continuing with mediation, but it also provided a ringing endorsement that mediation was worthwhile. Teacher comments on the strengths of mediation included the following:

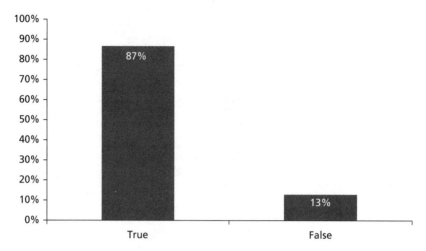

Figure 7.11. Survey results: The addition of teacher–student mediation to Centennial High School's Tier II interventions is a positive step toward improving student behavior and learning. (23/25 responded.)

- "It gave me suggestions to change things in my teaching to help the student I was having problems with. Led me to see that things I personally was doing were contraindicating to the student."

- "The opportunity to communicate with clear heads and be objective is very valuable."

- "It provides a space where students and teachers who have had conflict potentially can talk rationally outside of the context in which they are experiencing difficulties."

- "Always very helpful."

- "I think that mediations are helpful. Perhaps it is helpful for the student to feel that his/her voice is heard."

- "Get to know student(s)."

- "Mediator was positive and [the mediator] led the mediation with knowledge and concern for both parties."

- "It is a good way to clear the air."

- "It is an opportunity for student and teacher to have a talk with someone else in the room facilitating."

Teachers' comments on the weaknesses of mediation included the following:

- "Getting together in a timely fashion is a challenge."

- "Doesn't resolve root conflicts, just makes others aware. So conflict may still be there, but dormant."

- "The impact has not been long term."

- "The student did not really provide any input. It did not seem like it was her idea or that she was interested in the mediation."

- "There is not follow-up to see how things are going."

- "I sometimes think that the student thinks that requesting mediation will somehow make the rules change for that student. Two of the three students that requested mediation are students who really do not know how to behave in class. I felt that the mediator supported me in those times, explaining why there needs to be some order in a classroom so that learning can take place. I do not feel that the students really saw that perspective. In one of these cases, the student readily admitted that he did not see that perspective, and saw absolutely nothing wrong with his behavior."

- "The student was a little reluctant to go at first, so it seemed hard to get anything out of him at first. Because we were bringing up past issues, he got a little defensive. I think it was handled really well by the mediator, though."

These survey results were presented to the Centennial High School faculty and discussed at Tier II meetings. The Tier II team suggested that students also be surveyed for their reactions to mediation.

STUDENT REACTIONS TO TEACHER–STUDENT MEDIATION

Student data were collected in the spring of 2014. Fourteen students were asked to complete a written survey. All 14 students answered, "Yes" to the following questions:

- "Did you say what you needed to say?"

- "Did you feel you were understood?"

- "Did you feel you were treated with respect?"

- "Did you learn more about the teacher's feelings and thoughts?"

To the question, "Did the teacher learn more about your feelings and thoughts?" 12 students (or more than 80%) said, "Yes." Two students (less than 20%) said, "A little." Students gave a range of answers to the question, "How did you feel coming into the mediation?"

- "Irritated"

- "Upset"

- "A little frustrated"

- "Nervous"

- "I didn't feel like it would work"

- "Get it over with"

- "Didn't need it"

- "Thought I would regret saying something"

- "Good"

- "Calm"

- "I get the opportunity to be listened to"

As the students completed the surveys weeks after the mediation, they were able to provide feedback on the effect of the mediation. In response to the question, "Will this mediation help you and the teacher?" students responded

- "We don't have a problem as much"

- "Helped communication"

- "Haven't gotten sent out or in trouble"

- "We both understand each other now"

- "Get along great"

- "Get along better"

- "Got a calculator and plan worked"

- "I felt like I could get my point across and I'm being listened to"

- "Things will be a lot easier in class now"

The student feedback provided a clear endorsement that despite student's initial skepticism or reluctance to attend, mediation proved to be an effective way for them to be heard and understood.

RESPONDING TO FEEDBACK

As much as I wanted to believe that nearly all mediation experiences were positive, it was important for me to obtain actual feedback from participants. Despite my verbal proclamations that I welcome feedback, I learned that people do not necessarily share their true reactions unless anonymous survey questions specifically prompt them to do so.

I therefore decided to continue to use surveys to obtain additional feedback from mediation participants. As I was concluding the mediation, I would hand the teacher and student an exit survey that could be completed at their convenience because I am always seeking ways to improve the mediation process. (See Appendix A for printable feedback survey sheets for both teachers and students.) I rarely got those surveys returned to me. I also found that asking the teacher or student for feedback directly following a mediation might seem abrupt and not allow them time to process the mediation experience.

I concluded that the best option was to invite feedback at the end of my summary email. As discussed in Chapter 4, following each mediation, I send an email to the teacher to summarize the plan the teacher and student developed. Figure 7.12 is an example of what such an email might say for Ms. O'Neil, a social studies teacher, and Brad, a 10th grader. At the end of this email are questions about follow-up and an invitation for feedback on the mediation process. (A reproducible Teacher–Student Mediation Follow-Up Email is available in Appendix A.)

From: Ondine Gross

Sent: Wednesday, November 20, 3:00 p.m.

To: Alyssa O'Neil

Subject: Follow-Up to Our Teacher–Student Mediation

Dear Ms. O'Neil,

Please print this email and provide a copy for Brad.

Thank you again for participating in the mediation. Here are the plans you developed:

1. Brad agrees to put away his phone and give Ms. O'Neil his full attention when she is giving instruction.

2. If Brad is having a bad day that affects his mood, he will let Ms. O'Neil know about it.

3. Ms. O'Neil will change Brad's seat to be closer to the front to help him focus.

4. If Brad needs to be redirected, Ms. O'Neil will come to his desk and gently tap it rather than calling out Brad's name.

5. Brad has a make-up test, and he will take the exam on Thursday after school.

Please share feedback below and note if you would like additional follow-up:

_____ Meeting to debrief about the mediation or discuss next steps

_____ Follow-up check-in: 1 week   2 weeks   quarterly   (please circle)

_____ Another mediation

Additional comments: _____

_____

_____

_____

_____

Thanks again,

Ondine Gross

Figure 7.12. Sample Teacher–Student Mediation Follow-Up Email inviting feedback on teacher–student mediation.

Though it is sometimes difficult to obtain responses, and surveys are not always returned, it is important to invite participants to provide feedback whenever possible so that appropriate adjustments can be made to the mediation process. Collecting and analyzing data is an ongoing agenda item in Tier II meetings to help identify areas for improvement and future needs. Some of the identified needs at Centennial High School that are specific to mediation included

- Continuing to train others to expand the use of teacher–student mediations

- Continuing to track data and obtain meaningful feedback after the mediation in regard to student progress

- Continuing to publicize the teacher–student mediation program to all stakeholders

Seeking administrative feedback can also be helpful. I interviewed our principal in November 2014 about any resistance to mediation he may have encountered.

Principal Greg Johnson: I've never, ever, heard a teacher complain about it. A teacher has never griped to me about it.

Within a few years, new initiatives or interventions gradually become embedded into the culture of the school. I asked Principal Johnson if he felt that mediation had a positive impact on school climate. He replied:

Principal Greg Johnson: The fact that we do it [teacher–student mediation] is a good thing. It speaks to the overall culture and climate of the school. It's made more effective because of all the other things [MTSS] we have in place. It's good to know that it exists, and it's also good to know that it exists as part of a structure.

Another administrator commented as follows:

Administrator Tony Maltbia: I found that there is no better way to mend relationships between students and teachers than to go through mediation when it's done the correct way.

SUMMARY AND NEXT TOPIC

In this chapter, I have shown that teachers are amenable to mediation as a way to reduce conflict and get to know their students better. I shared teacher and student survey responses and discussed how to make improvements to the mediation program based on the feedback. This chapter also touches on how mediation can improve school climate and operate as part of a larger system of supports.

In Chapter 8, I specifically delve into the teacher–student mediation program at Centennial High School. I present data showing growth in the use of the intervention, as well as the age, race, and gender of student participants. African-American students participated at the highest rate of any demographic group at Centennial High School, whereas the majority of teacher participants are white. The rate of positive outcomes is encouraging and suggests that mediation is a viable means to improve dialogue and understanding across racial lines.

8

Promising Data

Mediation Is Effective

You measure the size of the accomplishment by the obstacles
you had to overcome to reach your goals.
—Booker T. Washington

In this chapter, I present data on the usage and growth of teacher–student
mediation at Centennial High School. The data offer valuable insight into who
participates in and benefits from teacher–student mediation, detail how mediation works and has grown, and provide a strong evidence base for its effectiveness. Data on teacher–student mediation collected during the first 3 years
of program implementation (2011–2014) were to assess

- Numbers of students referred for mediation and the response (i.e., effectiveness as measured by no disciplinary referral from the same teacher
  following the mediation)

- Referral source (administrators, teachers, students, or other staff)

- Grades of the students referred (freshmen, sophomores, juniors, or seniors)

- Gender of the students (male or female)

- Ethnicities of the students (White, African-American, Asian, Hispanic, or
  multiple)

- Ethnicities of the teachers (White, African-American, Asian, Hispanic, or
  multiple)

Recall from Chapter 2 that teacher–student mediation at Centennial High School occurs as part of MTSS; however, mediations can be offered even when tiered systems of support are not organized in a school.

YEAR ONE: 2011–2012

In a school of 1,454 students, 38 mediations were held in the first year, and 32 (84%) mediations were effective because the teacher wrote no additional disciplinary referrals for the student. From my perspective, the flow of referrals was manageable. As shown in Figure 8.1, there were on average 3–5 mediations per month, and because each mediation only took one 50-minute class period, it was easy to work mediation meetings into my busy schedule. Mediations were most heavily used in October and November, and the spring months of February, March, and April.

As shown in Figure 8.2, of the 38 referrals, 68% (26) came from administrators, 16% (6) came from teachers, 8% (3) came from students, and 8% (3) came from student services staff.

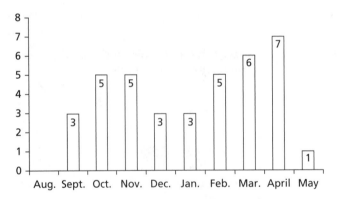

Figure 8.1.   Year one (2011–2012): 38 mediations (84% effective).

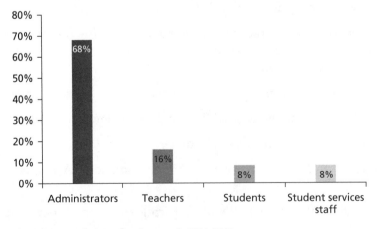

Figure 8.2.   Mediation referral sources in 2011–2012.

Figure 8.3 shows that 66% (25) of the participants were freshmen, 18% (7) were juniors, 13% (5) were seniors, and 3% (1) were sophomores. The administrators at Centennial High School are assigned different grade levels. That year, the administrator for sophomores was new to the school and did not initially use the teacher–student mediation option, so the number of sophomores referred for mediation was noticeably low.

As shown in Figure 8.4, the first year brought 66% (25) male students to mediation and 34% (13) females.

The overall racial demographic profile of Centennial High School in the 2011–2012 school year (posted by the Illinois State Board of Education at www.IllinoisReportCard.com) was 48% White, 34% Black, 8% Asian, 6% Hispanic, and 3% two or more races. Figure 8.5 indicates the ethnicities of mediation participants during the first year: The majority of students referred to mediation were African-American, and this trend continued in subsequent years. For the first year, there were 71% (27) African-American students, 26% (10) White students, and 3% (1) Asian student who participated in mediation. The ethnicities of teachers participating in mediation in 2011–2012 were as follows: 95% (36) White, 3% (1) African-American, and 3% (1) Asian.

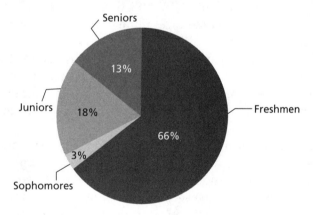

Figure 8.3. Mediation participants according to grade level in 2011–2012.

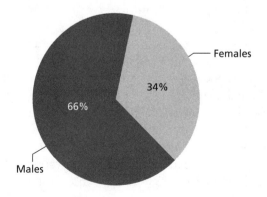

Figure 8.4. Gender of mediation participants in 2011–2012.

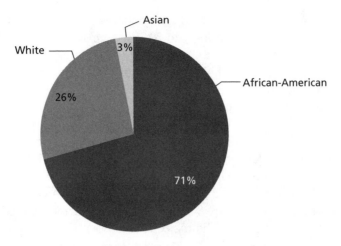

Figure 8.5. Ethnicities of mediation participants in 2011–2012.

YEAR TWO: 2012–2013

In the second year of mediations, 2012–2013, the overall school enrollment was 1,459 students, and an almost identical number of students were referred for mediation as in the first year. Of the 34 mediations held, 76% (26) were effective. Figure 8.6 shows that the intervention was heavily used in the fall months of September, October, and November, which is different than the first year. This difference suggests that Centennial High School staff became more familiar with the intervention of mediation and began using it at the start of the school year.

Similar to the first year, Figure 8.7 shows that the single largest source of referrals came from the administrators: 65% (22) from administrators, 20% (7) from teachers, 9% (3) from student services staff, and 6% (2) from students.

As shown in Figure 8.8, the second year of mediation brought more balance among freshman and sophomore students, with 38% (13) sophomores, 35% (12) freshmen, 21% (7) juniors, and 6% (2) seniors participating. The trend of younger students using teacher–student mediation was similar to the first year.

Figure 8.9 shows that the second year of mediations saw a nearly even split among the 53% (18) male and 47% (16) female students.

In the 2012–2013 school year, the school student demographics posted by the Illinois State Board of Education (www.IllinoisReportCard.com) included 49% White, 33% Black, 9% Asian, 6% Hispanic, and 4% two or more races. As shown in Figure 8.10, the ethnicities of participants in year two once again showed a disproportionately large number of African-American students referred for mediation relative to the school demographics: 76% (26) of the students were African-American, 18% (6) were White, and 6% (2) were Hispanic. The ethnicities of teachers participating in mediation in 2012–2013 were as follows: 97% (33) White and 3% (1) African-American.

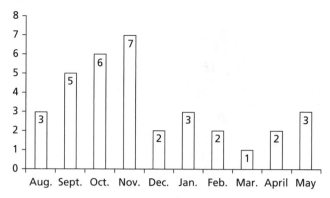

Figure 8.6.   Year two (2012–2013): 34 mediations (76% effective).

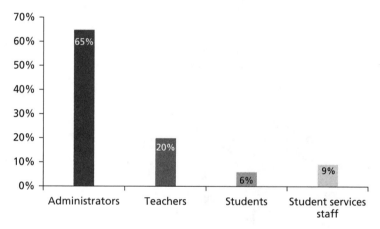

Figure 8.7.   Mediation referral sources in 2012–2013.

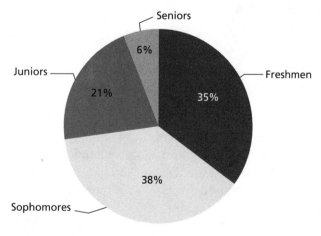

Figure 8.8.   Mediation participants according to grade level in 2012–2013.

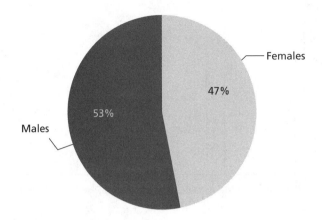

Figure 8.9. Gender of mediation participants in 2012–2013.

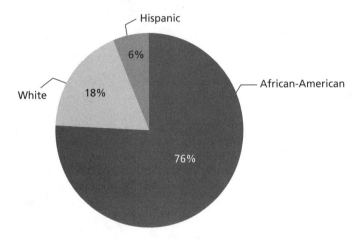

Figure 8.10. Ethnicities of mediation participants in 2012–2013.

YEAR THREE: 2013–2014

In the third year of mediations, the total school enrollment was 1,425. There was a significant increase in the amount of students referred for mediation. As shown in Figure 8.11, the total number of mediations was 57, and 50 mediations (nearly 88%) were effective. Almost 60% (34) of the mediations occurred in the fall semester, with the peak in the months of October, November, and December. The remaining 40% (23) of mediations occurred during the spring semester and especially in the peak months of February and March.

As shown in Figure 8.12, the trend of administrators making the majority of mediation referrals continued in the 2013–2014 academic year: 68% (39) from administrators, 19% (11) from teachers, 7% (4) from students, and 5% (3) from student services staff.

As indicated in Figure 8.13, no seniors were referred for mediation in the third year, 14% (8) of participants were juniors, and the majority of mediations

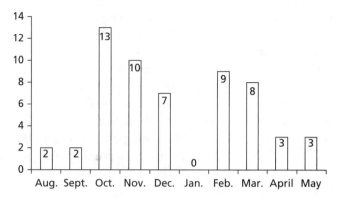

Figure 8.11.   Year three (2013–2014): 57 mediations (88% effective).

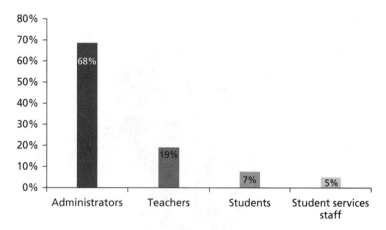

Figure 8.12.   Mediation referral sources in 2013–2014.

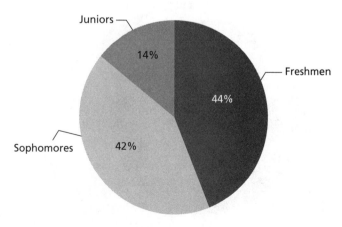

Figure 8.13.   Mediation participants according to grade level in 2013–2014.

involved freshman and sophomore students. There was nearly an even split between the freshman participants at 44% (25) and the sophomores who made up 42% (24) of mediation participants.

Figure 8.14 shows that males outnumbered females who participated in mediation during the third year, with 65% (37) males and 35% (20) females.

As shown in Figure 8.15, we saw similar trends in the third year with regard to the ethnic profile of the students referred for mediation: 68% (39) African-American, 26% (15) White, 4% (2) Hispanic, and 2% (1) students with multiple ethnicities. The ethnicities of teachers participating in mediation in 2013–2014 were as follows: 91% (52) White, 5% (3) Hispanic, 2% (1) African-American, and 2% (1) Asian.

In the third year, we also began to collect demographic data on each student participant's socioeconomic status based on whether the student met the requirements for enrollment in the free or reduced lunch program. Of the 57 students referred for mediation, 79% (45) were receiving free or reduced lunch.

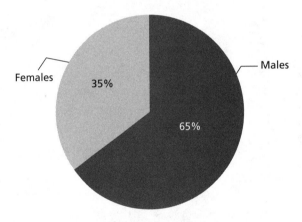

Figure 8.14. Gender of mediation participants in 2013–2014.

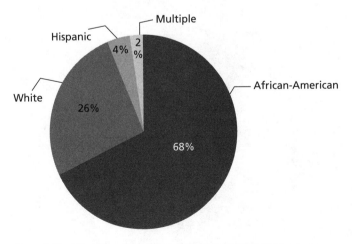

Figure 8.15. Ethnicities of mediation participants in 2013–2014.

SUMMARY OF DATA

When the results over the 3 years of mediation are considered, the growth in the use of mediation becomes apparent, as shown in Figure 8.16. The use of teacher–student mediation by administrators is shown in Figure 8.17. Administrators made the vast majority of mediation referrals throughout the first 3 years of mediation. Typically, the referral for mediation is made because a student is sent to the administrator with a disciplinary referral for an infraction such as disobedience (i.e., not following teacher directions or leaving the classroom without permission), disrespect, disruptive behavior, obscenity, or verbal abuse toward staff. After calling home and delivering the consequence from the code of conduct, the administrator suggests a Tier II intervention. Teacher–student mediation is suggested (often after the administrator consults with the teacher) as a voluntary

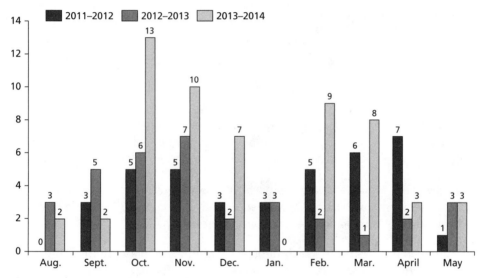

Figure 8.16. Yearly comparison of number of mediations

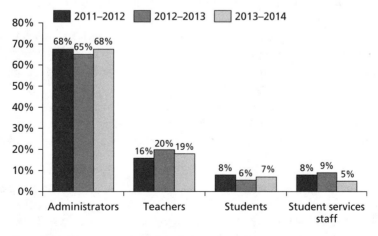

Figure 8.17. Yearly comparison of mediation referral sources.

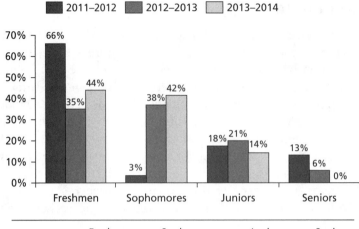

	Freshmen	Sophomores	Juniors	Seniors
2011–2012	25 (66%)	1 (3%)	7 (18%)	5 (13%)
2012–2013	12 (35%)	13 (38%)	7 (21%)	2 (6%)
2013–2014	25 (44%)	24 (42%)	8 (14%)	0 (0%)

Figure 8.18. Yearly comparison of mediation participants according to grade level.

option to help the teacher and student obtain an understanding of what went wrong and how to decrease or eliminate the unwanted behaviors. Parents typically are grateful when an administrator does more than deliver a consequence.

Administrator Tony Maltbia: It's always helpful to have a way to try to come to a problem with a solution. Most parents have tried everything they can try. Providing solutions and options gives parents hope.

As seen in Figure 8.18, freshmen and sophomores made up the larger portion of participants each year. Possible reasons for the declining participation of older students are that over the 4 years of high school, there is growing maturity, greater development of social and problem-solving skills, and more supportive relationships developed in the school.

There are significantly more males being referred for mediation than females, as shown in Figure 8.19.

Figure 8.20 shows that African-American students most frequently participated in mediations over the 3-year period.

Analysis of these 3 years of data reveals that administrators used the program extensively (as shown in Figure 8.17), and the majority of referrals was for African-American male students (Figures 8.19 and 8.20). I asked Administrator Tony Maltbia about this:

Administrator Tony Maltbia: As an African-American administrator who witnesses the disproportionate number of black male referrals, it [teacher–student mediation] has been my most useful go-to tool besides what I myself do. This has been a very useful intervention because it has evened the playing field by not giving the teacher the bigger platform or all the control in the meeting.

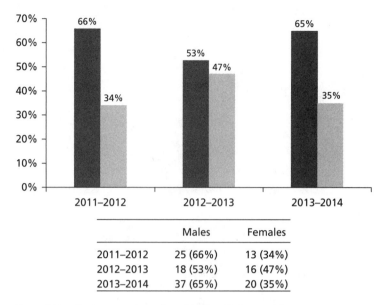

	Males	Females
2011–2012	25 (66%)	13 (34%)
2012–2013	18 (53%)	16 (47%)
2013–2014	37 (65%)	20 (35%)

Figure 8.19. Yearly comparison of gender of mediation participants.

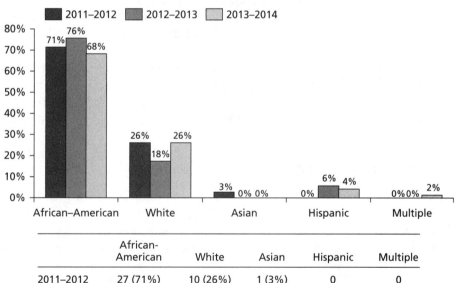

	African-American	White	Asian	Hispanic	Multiple
2011–2012	27 (71%)	10 (26%)	1 (3%)	0	0
2012–2013	26 (76%)	6 (18%)	0	2 (6%)	0
2013–2014	39 (68%)	15 (26%)	0	2 (4%)	1 (2%)

Figure 8.20. Yearly comparison of ethnicities of mediation participants.

The students feel like they have a voice if they want to get some things out they feel frustrated about. It teaches a lifelong skill of how to solve problems.

Figure 8.21 summarizes the growth and success rate of all mediations over the 3-year span. The use of mediation continues to grow as an intervention at Centennial High School and has since spread throughout the Champaign district, which suggests that teacher–student mediations can be replicated in

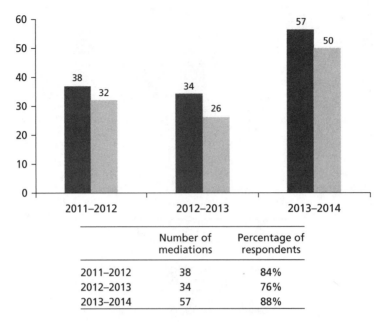

	Number of mediations	Percentage of respondents
2011–2012	38	84%
2012–2013	34	76%
2013–2014	57	88%

Figure 8.21. Yearly comparison of number of mediations that were effective.

other schools using existing staff. In addition to training staff at all secondary levels, in 2014–2015, I provided a mediation training to preschool (ages 3–5) and young adult (ages 19–21) special education staff, including specialists working with the students with learning disabilities, ASD, emotional disabilities, and mild to moderate cognitive disabilities. The feedback for this training was unanimously positive and indicated a high interest in using mediation for these populations.

NEW AREAS OF RESEARCH

In their 2013 study on teacher–student relationships, Wang, Brinkworth, and Eccles cited compelling research showing that positive relationships with teachers (characterized by warmth and trust) promote students' psychological resiliency and emotional well-being. They noted that more and more focus is being placed on relationship-building skills for teachers at the elementary level, but "teacher–student relationships at the secondary school level have been relatively neglected" (p. 702). They cited the work of Gehlbach, Brinkworth, and Harris (2011) and promoted the practice of social perspective taking in both teachers and students to improve the teacher and student bond. They wrote, "Evidence indicates that changes in students' social perspective taking accuracy are associated with improved teacher-student relationships from both the teacher and student point of view" (Wang, Brinkworth, & Eccles, p. 702). They continued, "Thus, one approach to fostering more positive teacher-student relationships could be to intervene with students and teachers to improve their ability to discern the thoughts and feelings of each other" (p. 702). The teacher–student mediation technique proposed in this book aims to provide this opportunity.

SUMMARY AND NEXT TOPIC

As the data demonstrate and the research suggests, the mediation process is extremely helpful to resolve teacher–student conflict and provide a venue for positive relationship building. In Chapter 9 I discuss how student mediation facilitated by a trained adult mediator can be used to resolve conflicts between students. This mediation technique can also be helpful in addressing bullying and preventing fights. I share a step-by-step student mediation technique, problem-solving strategies, and examples of student contracts. I also provide data from Centennial that indicate that 88% of the students who participated in student mediations had no further conflicts with each other that required disciplinary consequences.

9

How to Conduct Student Mediations

Few things can help an individual more than to place
responsibility on him, and to let him know that you trust him.
—Booker T. Washington

Student arguments occur everywhere—in structured settings such as classrooms and in unstructured settings such as hallways, playgrounds, cafeterias,
bathrooms, locker rooms, and buses. Lesbian, gay, bisexual and transgender
students are at a heightened risk for harassment and bullying (Kull, Kosciw, &
Greytak, 2015). Conflicts among students can range from minor misunderstandings between friends to threats, fights, or bullying. Bullying, defined
here, is intentionally aggressive behavior that involves an imbalance of power
and that is sustained over time (Hazelden Foundation, 2015).

Student conflict must be effectively addressed in schools because it often
results in a disruption of the learning environment, injury to individuals, and
damage to property. Further consequences for student conflict may include
parent meetings; punitive discipline; and even arrests, restraining orders, or
jail time. A change of classrooms or even schools is occasionally required to
stop serious conflict. Student conflicts may also produce psychological repercussions including chronic stress, academic underachievement, school avoidance, anxiety, depression, and withdrawal. Child suicide can be the most
distressing and alarming consequence of student conflict and bullying (Goldblum, Espelage, Chu, & Bongar, 2014).

A primary method to stop conflict in schools relies on adult supervision and, when affordable, security cameras to monitor student activity. Most students know better than to erupt in front of an adult. Although adult supervision is a primary deterrent to student conflict, nothing completely stops students from getting into verbal and physical altercations with one another. Students may choose to fight at school because adults do stop them before they cause severe bodily harm to one another. But adults cannot be everywhere at once. We also need students to help.

As discussed in Chapter 2, the Centennial High School Tier I team sought to teach and reward students who assisted in the reduction of student fighting: "If you know of a conflict between you and another student or between other students, talk to an adult." It makes sense to intervene quickly when a conflict is still brewing but has not yet erupted, and having many eyes and ears on the problem is helpful. All students are entitled to feel safe at school. Because most students do not want to be seen as a "snitch," they are afforded anonymity when reporting on a fellow student. When administrators present themselves as humanistic, helpful, and trustworthy, and when reporting such behavior is positively acknowledged, students are more likely to help keep schools safe.

School deans and administrators frequently mediate student conflict. In fact, nearly every adult in a school has at one time or another intervened with two (or more) angry students. Many student mediations follow a "get people in a room to talk" model. Sometimes, a moderated 3-minute conversation between two students ends a conflict. Who would argue with such efficiency in a busy school? But if the goal is to teach and model anger management, conflict resolution skills, and social skills, should more thought go into how student mediations are handled?

We sought to answer these questions at Centennial High School. In an effort to systematize student mediations and include counselors, social workers, and the school psychologists as mediators, we piloted adding student mediations to our Tier II interventions in the 2012–2013 school year. Unlike peer mediation (in which trained students are the mediators), this student mediation technique relies on a trained adult mediator. The request for a student mediation usually comes from an administrator, and whether or not to hold a mediation is determined on a case-by-case basis. Student participation is voluntary, and this principle of mediation is always followed. The request may be made because a student reported to an adult that a fight was about to erupt, or students might have told an adult that someone was bothering them or had threatened them in person, through friends, or through social media. Thus, the most pressing reasons for student mediations were to prevent fights. Figure 9.1 is an example of a completed request form for student mediation and the notes by the mediator following the meeting. (A blank Student Mediation Request Form is provided in Appendix A.)

We began collecting data on student mediation in the 2013–2014 school year. Collecting and analyzing data on effectiveness allowed the team to discuss, modify, and improve on the intervention at the twice-monthly Tier II

Student Mediation Request Form

Student "A" name: _Julian Hopkins_

       Grade _9_   Date of referral: _9/17/15_

Student "B" name: _Vince Nash_

       Grade _9_   Referring party: _Ms. Fromin, Admn._

Reason for referral: _Students had loud, verbal altercation in hallway yesterday that disrupted classrooms. Both were sent home. I suggested mediation, and students and parents are on board. Boys are friends who had some kind of falling out._

Relevant background information:

  _X_ Student "A" is aware of request   _X_ A's parent/guardian is aware of request

  _X_ Student "B" is aware of request   _X_ B's parent/guardian is aware of request

The person conducting the mediation will complete this portion:

Name of mediator: _Diane Greer_

Date of mediation: _9/18/15_

Students developed and signed a no-harm contract: _X_yes   _no_

(Please attach contract.)

Additional follow-up: _Students, parents, and administrator given copy of contract._

Parent contact: _Administrator will follow up with parents._

Additional contact with student A: _As needed._

Additional contact with student B: _As needed._

Contact with the following staff: _Administrator will inform teachers._

Mediator notes: _Boys were cooperative. Cleared up a misread incident at baseball game._

Figure 9.1. Sample Student Mediation Request Form.

meetings. Also, we got a broader picture of how resources (e.g., people's time) were being used. For purposes of data collection, effectiveness was measured when there were no further conflicts (as measured by disciplinary referrals or suspensions) between the two students. As shown in Figure 9.2, data from 2013–2014 revealed that of the 54 student mediations conducted with 117

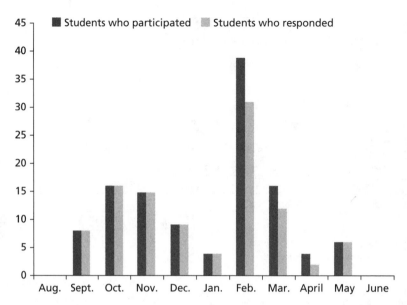

Figure 9.2. Student mediation outcomes at Centennial High School, 2013–2014.

students, 103 students (88%) had a successful outcome. The team considered this to be an immensely successful Tier II intervention.

WHEN IS STUDENT MEDIATION APPROPRIATE?

Not every student conflict is suitable for mediation. Often the best directive to two students is to stay away from each other and have no contact in person or online. But what if the adult directives do not work because the students see each other in classes, on the bus, or in the community? Or, more likely, what if the students are still emotionally entangled? In such cases, mediation may be appropriate. Care must be taken, however, not to fan the fires of student drama or to inadvertently reward students who are constantly involved in conflicts, fights, and confrontations. Some students may enjoy mediations a little too much because of the adult and peer attention they bring or because they are able to avoid typical classroom routines in order to participate.

Indeed, safety considerations and common sense must always prevail. In clear cases of a powerfully aligned bully and a weaker victim, adult intervention and consequences for the student doing the bullying may be the wiser course of action rather than mediation. Mediation should never be a venue for a bully to exert power over another student. Although the mediation itself could be safe and structured, harassment could continue outside of the meeting. I offer some caution here, however, in labeling a student as a bully. It is important to consider each child carefully (both bully and victim) and to never stereotype a child based on preconceived assumptions, as those assumptions may reflect biased judgments on a student's racial or socioeconomic background or may fail to account for underlying problems the child is facing.

Children behave aggressively for a variety of reasons, including child abuse and/or neglect, hunger, substance abuse, physical or mental health problems, or perhaps a need for acceptance or belonging. When considering underlying reasons for student conflict, it is important to identify the circumstances, time of day when we see certain behaviors, and the locations (e.g., at home, on the playground, in the hallways, in classrooms). What are the internal (e.g., hunger, fatigue, medication wearing off) and external (e.g., behavior of others, inadequate structure or supervision) influences that could trigger the agitated behavior? In rare instances, triggers are not readily identifiable, as there are some children who do exhibit disordered thinking and/or derive power and benefits from hurting others. Thus, careful screening of students for their suitability to participate in mediation is advised. That screening, typically done by an administrator, includes calling the parents of the students to discuss the mediation process and to ask whether they think it is a good idea. The administrator also discusses mediation with the students individually to assess their willingness to participate. Student participation is always voluntary. Many students are eager to be given a safe way to stop or redirect unwanted peer behavior.

HOW DOES STUDENT MEDIATION DIFFER FROM TEACHER–STUDENT MEDIATION?

The format of student mediation generally follows the same guidelines as teacher–student mediations, but there are differences in implementation because the participants are children.

First, embedded in the mediation are teachable moments as the mediator models problem-solving and prosocial communication skills. Persistent problematic behavior occurs because children lack the understanding of better ways to handle themselves. In some cases, children may be re-enacting a maladaptive behavior they have observed at home. The mediator seizes the opportunity to improve the students' skill set. For example, every student knows the feeling words of *mad, sad, scared,* and *happy.* How many students use and understand words such as *embarrassed, guilty, disappointed, humiliated, frustrated, overwhelmed,* or *confused*? The mediator may use such words to expand students' descriptive vocabulary and understanding of their own feelings.

Second, unlike teacher–student mediations, the goals are different when mediating with students. Student mediations are not necessarily designed to restore or repair the relationship. Rather, most are to stop the maladaptive behavior between two students. I say *between two students* because in a majority of cases, the maladaptive behavior goes both ways. Maladaptive behavior can include verbal rudeness and harassment, threats, name calling, and mocking. It can include nonverbal actions such as pushing, shoving, tapping, throwing things at a person, or bumping into another person in the hallway. Maladaptive behavior may also include group whispering, pointing, and giggling, and all-out exclusion. Teens, particularly during the middle school years, have a deep need for acceptance and belonging, and if the norm is to judge and bad-mouth others, teens may engage in such behaviors to fit in.

Third, unlike teacher–student mediations in which participants exercise self-determination and develop their own plans, student mediation partici-pants often look to the adult mediator to provide guidance and assistance. The mediator usually helps write an agreement or contract for the students to sign.

As students reach puberty, they are affected by changes in their bodies, social and familial challenges, and identity formation. The level of student conflict often increases during this time. The majority of student mediations in schools will therefore occur with secondary level students. The format and examples presented in this chapter will be suitable for a secondary setting. However, variations on the student mediation format, including for use with elementary students, students with special needs, and students who are highly agitated, are presented at the end of the chapter.

WHAT KINDS OF STUDENT CONFLICTS ARE BROUGHT TO MEDIATION?

Conflicts among middle and high school students may occur for seemingly trivial reasons, such "he said–she said" misperceptions or jealousy, yet these arguments and misunderstandings can feel very consuming for teenagers and have a great impact on them. Often, the students in conflict know each other from their communities or from online contact. Some conflicts are between former friends. Some are between friends of friends. Some are between stu-dents who run in different groups or gangs, or even their loyal affiliates. And, some are between total strangers who looked at each other the wrong way.

The buzz created by student conflict is tantalizing to many students, and teenagers who keep the drama alive often earn attention from their peers.

Ramona: What did he do today?

Harvey: She said what?

Some student conflicts derive from a game that went too far. This game involves hurling insults and has been called many different things: flaming, slamming, and talking smack, for example. Even if the students are friends, on any given day, insults can go too far and someone can get hurt or angry.

William: Don't talk about my cousin!

Sometimes student mediation may be used to mend the rupture caused by an abrupt ending to a close friendship. Perhaps the friendship did not weather the transition from middle to high school (e.g., dropping the steadfast and loyal elementary school friend to get into the crowd of cooler teen friends). There may be nostalgia for the former friendship or even regret over the way things ended. The mediation allows students to explain their actions and pos-sibly apologize, absolve their guilt, or make amends.

Finally, many conflicts are fueled by put-downs or arguments on social media. Students are often savvy enough to not identify the person they are insulting by name, but hiding the identity of the victim leads to more confusion:

Delia: The thot [translation: "ho" or whore] in my third period class needs to keep her mouth shut.

Holly: That B [bitch] better not be talking about me.

Stuart: Dude better watch his back today.

One can imagine the drama that ensues when students think they are being talked about. Sometimes, the victims become the aggressors and post statements about the students who originally posted, leading to ongoing online arguments. Needless to say, students preoccupied by what is happening on social media do not concentrate on academics. Their emotions range from angry and hurt to scared and confused. Algebra is the last thing they want to be bothered with.

FORMAT OF STUDENT MEDIATIONS

This section presents the format for leading student mediations to help resolve a variety of teenage conflicts.

I. Welcome with a Smile

Mediator: I am so glad you are both here! Mediation is a great way to resolve conflicts and clear the air. It is also a way to learn things about another person's perspective that you might not have realized before. I just want to start by thanking you both for being here.

II. Review the Rules of Mediation

Mediator: In this mediation, I will ask each of you to speak only to me and say what brought us here. When one person speaks, the other person can sit back and listen. Then the other person gets a turn to speak. This is helpful because you will probably learn things you didn't know before. After each person speaks, I will summarize what I heard and ask each of you what you would like to see happen. Then, I will ask you to both speak to each other, or to me, and form an agreement. The rules for mediation are simple:

- Only one person speaks at a time.

- No interruptions, put-downs, or nonverbal behavior such as eye rolling.

- This mediation is between the two of you and is confidential.

- Please do not talk about people who are not in the room.

- I am impartial. I do not take sides.

- We are all here voluntarily, right? [Wait for nods.]

- The agreement you make is yours, and I am not here to influence your decisions; however, we are here to keep everyone safe and allow you to focus back on your schoolwork. Are there any questions?

III. Identify the Issues

Mediator: Who would like to go first and tell me what brought us here today? Remember to speak only to me.

Most students are willing to follow the mediation format and are pleased to tell their stories to the mediator. Sometimes the students' stories involve many details and events, and the mediator will want to take notes on the most relevant facts and emotional reactions. Similar to teacher–student mediations, the mediator uses reflective, nonjudgmental listening statements to validate each student's point of view. The mediator manages the pacing of the meeting by pausing frequently to summarize, identifies specific details, and names the feelings and reactions of the students:

Mediator: Okay, you are saying that Tabitha stares at you during third period math class, and you are trying to figure out why. How does it make you feel when she stares at you?

Mediator: When everyone was throwing around your hat after school yesterday, you said it made you really mad. That is your favorite hat! When Ezra didn't give it back to you, it disappointed you because you thought he was your friend, and he didn't have your back. Am I getting that right?

Below are helpful tips for the mediator to keep in mind while issues are being identified.

Tip 1: Identify the History of the Two Students A knowledge of the students' history with each other provides a context for the conflict and helps identify the level of emotional investment each may have. Teen relationships usually fall within one of the following categories:

- Never met before: The students are completely new to each other and do not have classes with each other.

- Classmates but nothing more: The students see each other daily in class, but have no relationship outside of that.

- Acquaintances: The students know each other's names because of a vague social association. They are either currently classmates, know of each other from previous classes, or know of each other because they are acquaintances of acquaintances.

- Former friends: The students had a close relationship at one time. To determine how close, the mediator might question each participant about the nature of their relationship:

Mediator: So, did you go to each other's houses? Did you have sleepovers?

If these students spent time at each other's houses, they also presumably know family members, so it may be assumed that if they are no longer close, there was a rupture of some kind.

- Current friends: The students are close friends, but something happened that caused a rift. They are hurt or possibly feel betrayed.

Jackie: I thought I could trust Libby, but I was wrong.

The rift among current friends may be hours, days, or weeks old. These students are receptive to mediation because they want to repair the damage, but they lack the tools to do so. Sometimes these former friends "broke up" for an understandable reason. Perhaps the parents did not feel the children were good influences on one another, or one parent did not like the influence of the other student and encouraged ending the friendship. Regardless of the reason, the goal of the mediation is not to influence the outcome, but rather to facilitate a peaceful acceptance of whatever the outcome will be.

A true benefit of student mediation is that the structure creates an opportunity for students to honestly express kindness and humility. Away from the clamor of their peer group, students are often willing to take responsibility for their own behavior and even offer apologies that are unsolicited by the mediator.

Marcie: I know I've been treating you badly. I guess I was hurt when you didn't want to go to my game on Saturday. I see you hanging around with Veronica now, and I'm not going to lie...I feel kind of left out...but I don't like Veronica, so I don't even want to be with both of you.

Lulu: I get it. I know it was bogus of me to not go to your game. I'm sorry. And I know you don't like Veronica. She is my friend, too, though.

Sometimes students admit to their negative online postings:

Ruthie: I started the rumor about you being nasty with all those boys. I know it's not true. I'm sorry.

Angela: I just want to know why you did it.

Tip 2: Express Thanks and Praise Throughout a Student Mediation The mediator should always praise students' willingness to participate in mediation and acknowledge when they take responsibility for their actions.

Ken: I have an anger management problem. I should not have gone off on Toby like that.

Mediator: Wow, Ken. That's big of you to admit what you did...and to apologize. I never force people to apologize in these mediations, so that's really cool. I want to take a minute to thank you both for being here. It shows a lot of maturity and a willingness to learn how to solve problems peacefully.

Tip 3: Do Not Add Additional Students to a Mediation   It's usually best not to add additional students to a mediation unless you can maintain control of the meeting. I have sometimes found that once a mediation is underway, some students become conciliatory to one another and identify a third or fourth student that should be in the meeting:

Ronisha: I don't have a problem with her. Nina is the one that should be here.

Tony: I don't know why you called Cade here. It should be Brian and Horace.

A decision to bring in additional students to participate in the mediation must be made on a case-by-case basis. With more students in the room, there is more opportunity for interruptions, loud voices, and chaos, and the mediator has less control over the pacing and climate of the meeting. Earlier in my career, I had a meeting with two students. They wanted to add more students, so it became a meeting with four. Those four wanted to add additional students, and soon, the room held 10 people. I have tried not to repeat that mistake. The purpose of the mediation is to restore calm to two angry, hurt, or misunderstood students. A room full of angry, hurt, or misunderstood students can become unruly very quickly. If students suggest adding others, I offer separate mediations for additional pairs. Unless I am totally confident in my ability to create a safe and constructive problem-solving environment, or there are additional adults in the room, I keep the mediation to two students.

Tip 4: Allow Students to Talk to Each Other if They Can Still Follow the Rules   Although many students like the structure of one person speaking to the mediator at a time, occasionally they ask to speak directly to each other.

Frankie: Is it okay if we just talk to each other?

This is fine, particularly for former friends, but only after the structure and ground rules of the mediation have been firmly established. They must still follow the rules of no interruptions and no put-downs. The students may be relieved to be freed from the structure of the mediation format. They may speak fast, use teen jargon, and reference many situations that the mediator knows nothing about. I do not try to take notes, but listen carefully to ensure that the students are not, for example, going to plot revenge against a different student. I also make sure they are not insulting a student that is not in the room. Even when I take a less active role, I recognize the students for engaging in effective communication. I also encourage them to model positive problem-solving skills for other students once they leave the meeting.

Tip 5: Do Not Try to Find "the Truth"   It is not the mediator's job to identify "the truth" or "what really happened," as each student's perception may differ. (Plus, administrators obtain those facts as required.) As the students tell their stories, the mediator does help to identify the details of what led up to the events, the students' reactions, and the aftermath of the conflict. Many conflicts occur because a situation was initially misunderstood and snowballed into a larger issue.

IV. Summarize What Both Students Have Said

Once both students have spoken, the mediator has the opportunity to relay the arc of the story of what happened between the two students. The summary is impartial and is aimed to create a way for each student to understand the other student's perspective and emotional reactions. The mediator's vocal inflections describe the actions, confusions, and mistakes impartially, but also in a humanizing way to generate sympathy or empathy for the other.

Mediator: Okay, I am going to summarize what has been said here. Claire—you got upset, and maybe a little jealous, when a friend told you that Michelle hugged Nate in the hall outside the boys' gym. You asked Nate about it, and he said it didn't happen, but another friend, Javier, told you it did happen. This confused you and made you even angrier. So Claire, you put it out there on social media that some "B" was about to get hurt. Michelle, you are an acquaintance of Claire. You saw that and didn't think it applied to you, but three other people told you it was about you, and that Claire was going to fight you. Michelle—this truly confused you. You didn't have any problems with Claire. You felt you were being accused of something and you didn't even know what you did! This frustrated you and made you mad, so you started posting that if some "B" was going to fight you, then bring it on. Michelle, you only learned just now at this mediation that Claire was upset with you for hugging Nate. You explained to Claire that you used to know Nate in elementary school, and the hug was to congratulate him for his soccer win. Claire, that was information that you didn't know before today. Michelle, you also said you don't even like Nate in that way and you are sorry that the hug gave the wrong impression. Michelle, you said you understood why Claire got angry because you said that you don't like it when females hug your boyfriend. Claire, you said you overreacted, and that you are sorry that you made online threats against Michelle. Did I get that right?

V: Identify Next Steps: What Do Students Want?

Depending on the nature of the conflict and the earnestness shown by the students in the mediation, the mediator will either:

- Ask the students to look at and speak to each other to say what they would like to see happen and to develop a plan to move forward

or

- Ask the students to continue to speak to the mediator to say what they would like to see happen

Mediator: At this point in the mediation, I'm going to ask each of you to look at and speak to each other. You learned a lot of new information in this mediation that you can talk about. And, you can say what you would like to see happen now.

Often, a student will say something such as the following:

Michelle: Yeah, we're cool now. I get what happened.

Claire: Yeah…just want to say sorry, again, about what I said about you online.

When students want to say that they are regretful, the mediator acknowledges the genuineness of that action.

Mediator: These mediations do not require anyone to apologize, so the fact that you said *sorry* shows that you really mean it. It is sincere, and that's big of you to take responsibility for what you did that hurt Michelle. It seems like the misunderstanding has really been cleared up. Great job!

The mediator invites the students to look at and speak to each other to reinforce what was accomplished in the mediation. I think of it as equivalent to sealing a deal with a handshake. If students have spoken directly to each other, they are less likely to flip positions once they are done with the mediation and back with their friends. However, I also notice that students who are in conflict often do not look at one another—unless the opposite occurs, and students glare at each other to intimidate or show power. So, when students are encouraged to look at one another within the safety and structure of a mediation, there is often some hesitation. The students might act shy, look down, or giggle. Perhaps they don't make eye contact in general in their lives, due to shyness, cultural reasons, or even lack of practice associated with using text messages to communicate rather than face-to-face conversations (Shellenbarger, 2013). Students may also lack the vocabulary and social skills for reconciliation. Sometimes the dialogue between the students is very brief and to the point ("Yeah, okay, we're cool now, right?"; "Sorry"; "My bad"), and the students quickly look back to the mediator. Others may refuse to speak directly with another student but may agree to sign a contract. If the level of hostility (as determined by body language and tone of voice) remains intense throughout the mediation, it may be inadvisable to suggest having the students address one another. For instance, if the purpose of the mediation is to stop a fight, a conversation such as the following might take place:

Mediator: Now that we have heard from both of you, I want each of you to tell me what you would like to see happen.

Owen: I just want him to leave me alone. I don't want him to talk to me or about me.

Mediator: Okay, I'm hearing that you don't want Jay to talk to you or about you to other people. Jay, what would you like to see happen?

Jay: I'm fine with that. He leaves me alone, I leave him alone.

Mediator: It sounds like you both want the same thing. I trust that you both know how important it is to honor the agreement you are making today. I will draw up a contract that reflects what you both want and ask that you sign it.

A direct conversation between the two students strengthens the commitment; however, when that is not forthcoming or advisable, the mediator writes up a contract.

VI. Develop a Written Contract or Agreement

The mediator writes a simple contract during the mediation meeting for both students to sign. The students sign the agreement, the adult mediator signs as a witness, and copies are distributed to students and the involved adults. Contracts are personalized in order to be meaningful to the students. Occasionally students will balk at the idea of contract, saying, "It doesn't mean anything. It's just a piece of paper." The mediator's response could be as follows:

Mediator: You are right. It is just a piece of paper. But this paper represents you giving your word. It is a promise that you will be of good character and be true to your word. Also, when you think about it, a lot of contracts are just pieces of paper. You sign a contract when you rent an apartment, take on a job, or get married. That's just paper too, but it means something—even in a court of law.

This chapter provides three examples of contracts. (Printable blank student contracts are available in Appendix A.) The contract in Figure 9.3 is a simple contract if the two students are former friends or current acquaintances. It is clear from the mediation that they do not want to fight one another, and this contract is a way for them to formalize that promise to each other. It also helps them to identify the adults they will turn to should the need arise.

The sample contract in Figure 9.4 might be used if the two students were equally harassing one another and mutually agreed to leave each other alone.

Finally, the contract presented in Figure 9.5 would be used if one student is identified as the perpetrator of threatening and harassing behavior toward another student.

VII. Conclude the Meeting with Thanks and Praise

To conclude the mediation, the mediator thanks the students for their maturity and willingness to problem-solve in a constructive way. If I heard something in the mediation that I can turn into a brief teachable moment, I do so, but I refrain from lecturing the students and instead link my statements to the students' behavior in the mediation.

Mediator: I am pleased by how you both conducted yourselves in this mediation. I think communicating when there is a misunderstanding really pays

---

Student Mediation Contract #1

I, _Owen_____ ,

and I, _Jay_____ ,

participated in a mediation today that resolved our conflict. I promise not to fight. If I become

angry at anything the other does, I will handle it peacefully and/or tell an appropriate adult, such

as _Ms. Rogers_____

or _Mr. Patrick_____ .

Student signature: _Jay_____

Student signature: _Owen_____

Adult mediator (witness): _Mr. Gleason_____ Date: _12/1/15_____

Figure 9.3.   Sample Student Mediation Contract #1 between former friends or acquaintances.

off. When we don't communicate and hold things in, I always think of a teapot. Imagine a teapot on a stove…the heat is on, but pretend that something is blocking the steam from coming out. What happens? It explodes. People can explode in anger when they keep their feelings inside, and sometimes they even take it out on the wrong person. I think we saw how that happened here.

Mediator: Thanks again for coming today. I think you both learned a lot by hearing the other person. [Mediator holds up a tissue box on its side between the two students, so one student is facing the opening with tissues and the other sees the back of the box.] See this tissue box? One person can look at it and say it has a hole that tissues come out of. The other person can look at the same box and say the box is perfectly smooth—there's no hole and there's no tissue. And you know what? They are both right! They are looking at the same box, but from different perspectives. That happens all the time with people. We can swear something is true, and someone else can swear something is true, and we can both be right. Sometimes, there

---

Student Mediation Contract #2

I, _Owen_ _____ ,

and I, _Jay_ _____ ,

participated in a mediation today that resolved our conflict. I promise that I will not speak to or

about the other, in person or online. I will not ask anyone else to insult or fight the other, in

person or online. I will not touch (shove) or do any nonverbal behaviors (stares, pointing, laughing

at, looks) to the other that are disrespectful or negative. If there are any future conflicts, I will

handle it peacefully and/or tell an appropriate adult such as _Mr. Patrick_ _____

or _Ms. Rogers_ _____ .

Student signature: _Jay_ _____

Student signature: _Owen_ _____

Adult mediator (witness): _Mr. Gleason_ _____ Date: _12/1/15_ _____

Figure 9.4.   Sample Student Mediation Contract #2 for cases of mutual student harassment.

are many truths depending on our point of view. That is why it is so helpful to communicate—to truly listen to understand someone's perspective and feelings, and to share our own. That's what you did today.

Mediator: I am really impressed by the way you both behaved in this mediation today. Sometimes students think the best way to resolve a problem is to fight. But there is a reason that in our school, the older the students get, the less they fight. As students mature, they learn a better way to resolve their conflicts and don't want to do anything that can get them suspended, expelled, or arrested. They care about their education and have learned that schools have to be a safe place for students to learn. Today I saw how capable you both are to resolve your differences. You communicated really well and I think you are learning, just like the older students, that fighting is not the answer. Thank you again.

Student mediations rarely occur in a vacuum, as peers are often aware when two of their classmates are meeting. Whether for a reconciliation between

---

Student Mediation Contract #3

I, _Jay_____ ,

promise that I will not fight _Owen_____

at school or in the community. If I am physically attacked first, I will defend myself, but I will

not make threats in person, by text message, or on social media. I will also not ask anyone else

to insult or fight _Owen_____ in person or online. I will

not touch (shove) _Owen_____ or do any nonverbal

behaviors (stares, pointing, laughing at, looks) that are disrespectful or negative. I make this

promise because I care about my education and future and do not want to get suspended or

expelled. If there are any future conflicts, I will handle it peacefully and/or tell an appropriate

adult such as _Mr. Patrick_____

or _Ms. Rogers_____ .

Student signature: _Jay_____

Student signature: _Owen_____

Adult mediator (witness): _Mr. Gleason_____ Date: _12/1/15_____

Figure 9.5. Sample Student Mediation Contract #3 for cases in which one student is the perpe-trator of harassment, aggression, or bullying.

two former friends or to thwart a potential fight, the mediation provides a face-saving way for both students to stop the conflict on acceptable terms and to be a role model for their peers. At the close of the meeting (or once the contract is signed), the mediator must encourage the students to tell their peers that the conflict is over.

Mediator: I know there has been a lot of buzz about this conflict. When you leave this mediation and people come up to you to ask about it, simply say, "It's over…we worked it out….it's squashed."

At the close of student mediations, the mediator informs the referring administrator of the outcome, and parents are also contacted. When appropriate, the referring administrator is invited to the meeting to personally congratulate the students for resolving their conflict in a mature, responsible manner.

WHEN STUDENT MEDIATION IS INEFFECTIVE

Not all students respond to student mediation. They may become emotional and want to leave the meeting. They may say, "This is stupid," or "This isn't going to work." The principle of voluntariness applies, and they may make the choice to discontinue the mediation. In such cases, the mediator may say something like the following:

Mediator: We had hoped that setting up a safe way for you two to communicate would stop the anger and hurt between the two of you. I hope you change your minds. Mediation is always available, and we are here to help. In the meantime, I want to remind you that disruptions to learning and fighting in school are unacceptable. Students who fight get very serious consequences. Can we just take a few deep breaths and think about continuing this meeting? I know you both care about your education. I hope you both say that we can continue.

When students refuse to participate further in mediation, the mediator promptly alerts the building administrator that the mediation has stalled (and the potential for violence may still exist). Students in conflict are not dismissed from adult supervision without administrator notification and approval because steps must be taken to ensure student safety. Often, the administrator will join the meeting to encourage the continuation of the mediation. With more background information, and a stronger relationship with the students, the administrator can be effective in reinforcing how beneficial it is to resolve conflicts peacefully. The administrator will also remind students of the disruptive consequences of continued conflicts and that parents will be notified. Often the students choose to continue the mediation and are praised for that decision. If the administrator opts to remain in the room for the continuation of the mediation, this can be very helpful, even if the structure of the mediation loosens up. It is okay if the mediator takes a more passive role in the meeting and contributes where appropriate. The goal is to make effective inroads with the students.

Another safety measure when one or both students stops the mediation, stating that nobody can stop them from fighting, is for parents to be notified and for a school psychologist, counselor, or social worker to conduct a threat assessment. A threat assessment is an extended interview to determine the student's level of risk of harm (to self or others) and to identify any deeper causes for the students' problems. Fortunately, the majority of students are willing to participate in student mediation because the process brings them relief from the fears, stress, and tension of ongoing conflict.

I am a proponent of using trained adults to lead student mediation because the consequences of student conflict, harassment, and bullying are extremely serious. It is therefore critical for adults to carefully monitor the moods and actions of students, and adult-led student mediation creates such an opportunity. Some school districts opt to use peer mediators or peer juries within a restorative justice program. Because teens yearn for peer acceptance and understanding, these interventions can be effective, as in Oakland School District's example (Oakland Unified School District, 2015). In any peer-led program, however, much training must occur, and a trained adult needs to directly supervise such meetings to ensure safe proceedings.

As we move forward with our student mediations at Centennial High School as a Tier II intervention, our biggest challenge is to make sure that each student mediation meeting is recorded in the data system. This does not always happen where administrators are concerned, because for obvious safety reasons, school administrators must be nimble and react quickly to intervene with students.

Principal Greg Johnson: This kid comes to me, and is crying...is upset...there could be a fight after school...but it's really involving these two other people that's not the crier. You've got to go interview quick and pull them together and just try to deal with it in the moment, and who knows if you have the right people for the intervention to go. You just do it. It's part of the job. So it's tough to pull that data down. We would have to think more about how to do it. That's a good Tier II honest conversation. It really is.

Student safety comes first. It could be helpful for administrators to have several staff who can perform student mediation as an evidence-based Tier II intervention. The student mediation format usually takes less time than a regular (50-minute) class period and it does not require the hiring of additional staff. The Centennial High School data referenced previously showing an 88% success rate was a very promising endorsement for the continued use of student mediation as a Tier II intervention.

Student mediation can also be equally effective with younger students or students with special needs. These mediation techniques are discussed in the following section.

MEDIATING WITH ELEMENTARY STUDENTS AND STUDENTS WITH SPECIAL NEEDS

When conducting student mediations with elementary students or students with special needs, the mediator may wish to hold separate and individual intake meetings with both students prior to the mediation in order to crystalize the issues. Benefits to having an intake meeting prior to the actual mediation include the following:

- The students meet and develop a rapport with the mediator.

- Students are told about the format of the mediation and are prepared for what may occur.

- Students' questions are answered, and their needs are identified and validated.

- Students are given feelings words and concepts that might more precisely describe their experience.

- Meeting with the mediator can be calming and help to de-escalate tension.

At each intake meeting, the mediator remains impartial, takes notes, and uses reflective listening skills. Following is an example of an intake meeting introduction with Phoebe, age 7.

Mediator: Hi, Phoebe! I'm Mrs. Whitaker and I am here to help you. How are you feeling today?

Phoebe: Okay.

Mediator: Are you and Jack having a problem?

Phoebe: Yes. He bothers me.

Mediator: Oh…he bothers you? Please tell me more about it.

As stated in Chapter 4, some students are not familiar with feeling words (an alphabetized list of feeling words is provided in Table 4.1). For younger children, the mediator may use a poster or handout that illustrates facial expressions and feelings and ask the students to select the feeling that matches their experience. Or, the mediator may provide the possible feeling words as in the following example of 6-year-olds Jade and Terence. Jade is upset because of playground problems with Terence.

Jade: Terence threw the ball at me, and I didn't like it!

Mediator: Oh, you didn't like it when Terence threw the ball at you. Tell me more.

Jade: I thought he was going to throw it to Lucy.

Mediator: So you were you surprised that he threw it at you instead of Lucy?

Jade: Yeah, and I couldn't catch it in time.

Mediator: I think I understand. You did not catch the ball because Terence surprised you by throwing it at you instead. Were you embarrassed when you didn't catch it?

Jade: Yeah. I could have caught it if I knew it was coming, and I don't like messing up in front of my friends.

Mediator: Well, I'm glad we are having this talk, so I can understand your feelings better. It sounds like you felt embarrassed when you missed the ball and that you did not like being surprised. Is that right? [Wait for answer.] When we meet with Terence, we can talk about it some more.

The next example illustrates the mediation process with Kylie, an 8-year-old third grader with Down syndrome who receives special education services, and Felix, another 8-year-old third grader in a general education class. Every day, Kylie and Felix attend the same art class. Lately, Kylie is agitated following the art class and complains about Felix, stating, "I hate that kid!" She then "shuts down" and refuses to do the next set of classroom activities. Recently, it took more than an hour for Kylie to regain her composure. The art teacher has repeatedly asked Felix to leave Kylie alone, but he always seems to whisper, "horsey" or throw small wads of paper at Kylie when nobody is looking.

The principal and both sets of parents are informed about this problem. Instead of continually punishing Felix, the school principal thinks it might be more helpful to teach both students social and advocacy skills through a student mediation. Kylie's parents, in particular, want Kylie to learn to express her feelings and stand up for herself. Felix's parents want him to learn how his actions affect others. Perhaps Felix wants to get Kylie's attention but needs to learn social skills on how to interact with her in a more appropriate way. The mediation may serve to foster understanding and redirect both of their behaviors into a more positive direction. The principal consults with the teachers and parents, and all agree that mediation makes sense. Parents are invited to observe the mediation.

The next morning, the mediator meets separately with Kylie and her mother and Felix and his father for intake meetings. The mediator develops a rapport with everyone, answers questions, explains the mediation format, and identifies each student's needs and feelings. An excerpt from the intake interview looks something like this:

Mediator: Tell me more about how that makes you feel?

Kylie: Mad.

Mediator: Yes, you seem mad. I want to understand your feelings a little better. I have a chart here that has a lot of pictures of feelings. Do you see any pictures of how you feel? [Kylie points to a picture that depicts confusion.]

Mediator: Kylie, thank you for showing me that. That picture shows "confusion." People are confused when they don't know what is happening, or why it is happening. [Mediator uses lots of vocal inflection to emphasize the words *what* and *why*.] Is that the way you feel?

Later, the actual mediation is held. Kylie and Felix's parents and teachers are in attendance, and all adults are asked to be silent observers for the initial stages.

Mediator: Hi Kylie and Felix! Welcome! [Big smile.] Thank you for being here! This morning when we met, I heard about a problem you are having, and now we are going to solve the problem. Does that sound okay? This meeting has some special rules. Here they are:

- Only one person talks at a time.

- When one person talks the other person is quiet and does not make faces or any noises.

- Each of you will get a chance to talk.

- What each of you says is important, so I will listen carefully.

- I want you to speak only to me and tell me your thoughts and feelings. Who would like to go first? [Kylie raises her hand.]

Mediator: Okay, Kylie, please tell me your thoughts and feelings.

Kylie: Felix needs to stop messing with me! [Kylie's fists are balled up and her face is in a tense expression.]

Mediator: You want Felix to stop messing with you. Tell me more.

Kylie: Art class. He says stuff and throws stuff.

Mediator: Okay, Kylie. You are saying that in art class, Felix says stuff and throws stuff. Let's start with what he says. What words does he use?

Kylie: "Horsey." "Nay."

Mediator: So he says "horsey" and "nay?"

Kylie: Yeah. And I don't like it! And he throws papers at me! [Kylie makes a face showing disgust.] I told him to stop! He did not stop!

Mediator: So, Felix says "horsey" and "nay" and throws papers at you. You have told him to stop and he didn't. Kylie, when we looked over the feelings chart, you pointed to some ways you feel about this. Can you tell us about it now?

Kylie: Mad!

Mediator: Yes, you pointed to the face that showed mad.

Kylie: It's not nice.

Mediator: Kylie, you are mad because you think it is not nice of Felix to do those things. You also pointed to another picture. It was the one that showed confusion. Confusion is when you don't know what or why something is happening. [Mediator talks slowly using inflection.]

Kylie: Yeah. What is Felix doing this for??

Mediator: Okay, Kylie. You feel mad and confused because you don't know why this is happening. Now I have a question. Did you ever see Felix in another class?

Kylie: Mrs. B's class.

Mediator: Okay, so you and Felix knew each other from Mrs. B's kindergarten class.

Kylie: Yeah.

Mediator: Did you ever have fun with Felix in Mrs. B's class? [Mining for gold.]

Kylie: Yeah. He played with me. [Kylie starts to smile.]

Mediator: Tell me more.

Kylie: On the playground. The swings.

Mediator: How did you feel when Felix played with you on the swings?

Kylie: Happy.

Mediator: Okay, so you felt happy with Felix on the playground.

Kylie: Yeah.

Mediator: Kylie, is there anything else you would like to tell us?

Kylie: No.

Mediator: Okay, I am going to say what I have heard here so far. Kylie, you said Felix says "horsey" and "nay" and throws paper at you in art class. You have told him to stop and he didn't. This makes you feel mad. Also, you feel confused because you don't know why he does it. Before this art class, you knew Felix in kindergarten. He played next to you on the playground and it made you feel happy. Does that sound right, Kylie? Now, I want to ask Felix to talk to us. Before I do, I want to thank you for being here. You are doing a great job at being brave and telling us how you feel! Talking about a problem is a good way to solve a problem! Now I will ask Felix to talk to us.

Mediator: Felix, thank you again for being here! What are your thoughts and feelings?

Felix: Sorry.

Mediator: Okay, Felix. That is nice of you to apologize. What are you apologizing for?

Felix: I'm sorry I didn't stop when she said to. [Felix looks down.]

Mediator: You are sorry you didn't stop. You are looking down and it does look like you are sorry. Thank you, Felix. [Note: This apology comes early in the mediation, but does not necessarily address the issues. The mediator draws the conversation back to the issues.] We heard from Kylie that hearing you say "horsey" and "nay" made her mad. It also made her confused because she didn't know why. Please talk to us about that.

Felix: Well, in kindergarten, I didn't know anybody. Kylie always smiled at me. I used to like playing with her on the playground. We would swing. She might not remember this, but we played on rocking horses. We called them horseys. When we rode them, we would say "nay." I wasn't saying those words to tease Kylie. I was saying them because we used to say it on the playground.

Mediator: So, Felix, you liked playing with Kylie on the playground. You liked her smiles, going on the swings, and rocking on the horses. [Kylie smiles as she hears this.]

Felix: Yeah, and I'm sorry about throwing paper.

Mediator: Well, that is nice of you to apologize for throwing paper, too, Felix. It seems like you care about Kylie and do not want to hurt her feelings.

Felix: I don't want to hurt her feelings. She is nice.

Mediator: Kids say things or throw stuff at other kids for a lot of different reasons. What was your feeling when you did this?

Felix: I don't know. [Felix pauses and the mediator waits for him to speak.] I guess I just thought it would be fun, like we were playing.

Mediator: So you wanted to play with Kylie, but not in a mean way—more like the way you used to play in kindergarten.

Felix: Yeah.

Mediator: Felix, is there anything else you'd like to tell us?

Felix: No.

Mediator: Well, I want to thank you for your honest words, Felix, and showing care about Kylie's feelings. You told us about playing with Kylie on the playground in kindergarten. In the art class you were trying to be playful—but you heard Kylie say that hearing you say "horsey" and "nay" and throwing paper makes her feel mad and confused. We learned today that you, Felix, wanted to play with Kylie, but Kylie did not understand that you wanted to play with her. I am so glad you are both here because maybe we can find a better way to show friendship.

In the course of the mediation, it becomes clear that Felix wanted to engage Kylie's attention but lacked the social tools to do it appropriately. Due to the children's ages and the impartiality of the mediator, the children's parents decide next steps, for example setting up appropriate play situations outside of school. It is not the role of the mediator to influence those decisions. The mediator will, however, address the in-school situation in the art class and acknowledge the emotions in the mediation. The mediator has observed both students' body language. Kylie's smile and relaxed posture suggests that she felt good hearing Felix's apology and how he enjoyed playing with her in kindergarten. The mediator will give the children an opportunity to speak directly with one another.

Mediator: Well, we have learned a lot by listening to each other today. I'm proud of Kylie for telling us how she felt, and I'm also proud of Felix for saying he was sorry and that he didn't mean to hurt Kylie's feelings. We learned today that Felix actually thinks Kylie is nice. He remembers playing with her in kindergarten on the horses and swings. The reason he said "horsey" and "nay" and even threw paper was that he was trying to be playful. Now I want to return to Kylie to see how she feels. Kylie, how do you feel?

Kylie: Good.

Mediator: Did it help to hear what Felix had to say?

Kylie: Yeah.

Mediator: Well I'm glad this talk helped you feel better. Talks can teach us things we didn't know before! Do you remember playing horsey with Felix on the playground?

Kylie: Yeah. It was fun.

Mediator: Today you learned that Felix thought that was fun too, and that's why he said "horsey" and "nay." He was trying to play again.

Kylie: It's okay. He can say it. [Now that Kylie understands the context of Felix's words, she does not see them as insults.]

Mediator: Oh, you are saying it is okay, now that you know why he says it?

Kylie: Yeah.

Mediator: And the paper throwing?

Kylie: No. Stop that.

Mediator: Okay, the paper throwing needs to stop. Felix, Kylie said your words were okay, but she does not want you to throw paper. Will you stop throwing paper? [Waits for nod.] What do you want to see happen, Felix?

Felix: Could we play on the playground again sometime?

Mediator: Felix, you would like to play with Kylie on the playground sometime.

At this time in the mediation, it is clear that the issues are resolved. The mediator feels that it is appropriate to have the students speak directly to each other:

Mediator: Kylie and Felix, now you can talk to each other. Kylie, tell Felix what you said about throwing paper.

Kylie: Stop. No throwing paper.

Mediator: Felix, it is okay to answer Kylie now.

Felix [looks at Kylie]: Okay, I'll stop.

Mediator: Felix, you mentioned wanting to play with Kylie on the playground. Would you like to invite her to do that now?

Felix [glancing at Kylie]: Do you want to play sometime?

Kylie [looking down, smiling]: Okay. [Note: Students benefit from structure, and the teachers may want to pick specific days and times for this playground activity.]

Mediator: Great. I'll ask the teachers to help make that plan. [If appropriate, the teachers may also wish to schedule collaborative art activities for Kylie and Felix.] Thank you all for being here today. At this time, would any adults like to speak?

When adults are invited speak at the end of a mediation, it is to praise the students and reinforce the lessons learned. This mediation served to stop an upsetting, worsening set of behaviors between Felix and Kylie, and parents will be in a good position to monitor and continue to correct behaviors moving forward. As a student receiving special education, Kylie will have additional resources to help her with the development of her expressive language and social-emotional skills. Felix's teacher or additional school staff will also be in a better position to build his friendship skills.

The following section addresses how to mediate with students when emotions are heightened and there is potential for aggression or outbursts.

MEDIATION WITH AGITATED OR POTENTIALLY VIOLENT STUDENTS

The most important rule is to never begin a mediation unless students are calm. Because mediations are always voluntary, prior to the mediation, the school administrator, parent, and other appropriate adults have spoken to the students to obtain their consent. The students typically agree to mediation as a way to prevent further conflicts and serious disciplinary consequences that would interfere with their education. It is extremely stressful for students to go through their school day in fear of a physical confrontation with other students, and mediation is an efficient way to address the problems.

In cases in which students have fought in the past and may pose a risk for physical confrontation, the mediator may add one or more additional adults to the meeting as a preventive step. The additional adult is ideally an administrator or authority figure who has a positive relationship with the students and whose presence would deter them from engaging in any verbal or physical outbursts. The adult is generally in the role of observer but may speak when appropriate. Students also may be seated so that there is a natural barrier to their access to one another—for example, across from each other at a conference table. As always, the mediator will work to set a positive tone and convey high expectations for a respectful meeting. Consider the following example with Rudy and Zac—two tall, athletic 17-year-old juniors.

Mediator [big smile]: Rudy and Zac—I want to welcome you to this mediation and thank you both for being here. By agreeing to this mediation, you show that you respect yourselves and you respect your education. I admire that. I think you will find that mediation is a great way to learn things you didn't know before. I have been doing this for a long time, and I am always amazed at how a lot of conflicts start because something that started small was misread and became much bigger. I respect that you are both showing maturity by being open to this mediation. In just a second, I'm going to go over the rules of mediation, but before I do—see this outfit I'm wearing [mediator points to clothing]? I kind of like it [smiles]. So you guys have to promise me that you are not going to get physical or start fighting or anything, because then I'd have to jump in and get this outfit all torn and wrinkled [silly attempt to lighten mood]. So you guys are going to help me keep this outfit nice, right? [Boys roll their eyes and nod.] Okay, great! Thanks! And now I'm going to briefly go over the rules and principles of the mediation...

Because voluntariness is one of the principles of mediation, the mediator will once again verify that both students are participating willingly. If either or both students do not agree, the meeting is halted.

Mediator: And you both are here voluntarily, right?

Zac: Not really. I don't want to be here at all. Can I leave?

Mediator: Yes, absolutely, Zac. Just give me a second to call Mr. Hawkes [administrator]. I want to let him know so that he can help figure out our next steps. [Mediator calls administrator and everyone sits quietly and waits for Mr. Hawkes to come to the office. Mr. Hawkes referred the students to mediation and has more familiarity with the background of the conflict. Mr. Hawkes enters, sits down.]

Mr. Hawkes: What's going on?

Mediator: Hi Mr. Hawkes. We're all fine here. I called because when I asked if everyone was here voluntarily, Zac said he didn't want to be here, and that's fine. I gave you a call so that you could discuss next steps with us.

Mr. Hawkes: Zac, you do not have to be in this meeting. I can take you back to my office and we can talk about some other options. I do want to encourage you to give this a try, though. Mediation really helps clear the air. If you like, I can sit here for the remainder of the meeting.

Zac: Okay.

Mediator: Okay, great! It takes courage to participate in a mediation, and I'm so pleased that you are willing to give it a try, Zac. I really think you will find it useful. Rudy, are you also okay with being here?

In this case of Zac and Rudy, inviting an administrator to discuss options and sit in on the meeting was effective in encouraging the students to work on resolving their conflict. Another option for mediating with agitated students involves adding two adults who play active roles in the meeting. This format of mediation is structured like so:

- Prior to the mediation: Adult A is paired with Student A. Adult B is paired with Student B. Each adult holds an intake interview with his or her respective student prior to the mediation. The purposes of the intake session are to build trust and rapport, de-escalate and validate the students' highly charged emotions, and help the students learn additional vocabulary that accurately describes the feelings associated with their conflict. During the intake meeting, the adult representative will take notes and gain a full understanding of their student's perspective.

- During the mediation: The mediator is in a room with Adult A and Student A and Adult B and Student B. The mediator follows the mediation format, yet only speaks to the adults. Thus, Adult A and Adult B represent their students and model appropriate social, communication, and problem-solving skills while the students observe. Once each adult has provided a full story to the mediator and the mediator provides an impartial summary, the mediator asks if the participants wish to continue or if they wish to take a brief break. Both adults may choose to debrief and consult with their respective students (inside or outside of the room) to ascertain the students' willingness to participate in developing a plan or creating and signing a contract. In some situations, the mediation transitions from adult speakers to students speaking for themselves, and the students finalize an appropriate plan and agree on a contract. Otherwise, the adults represent the student for the duration of the meeting, and when the plans are developed, the students sign the contract.

SUMMARY AND NEXT TOPIC

This chapter discussed student conflicts and provided the rationale and data to suggest that student mediation is an effective intervention. Various techniques for mediating with students were discussed depending on the age, skills, and level of emotion of the students involved.

In Chapter 10, I conclude by addressing conflicts between adults in the school community. In today's schools, adult staffs are expected to participate in myriad meetings and activities. However, the trust and teamwork necessary for an optimal work environment does not always exist. I advocate for the use of adult mediations in schools to encourage more respectful, honest, and productive interactions. Additionally, I discuss how difficult it is for some parents to navigate the school systems and show how mediation can be a useful tool to foster trust and understanding in parent–teacher meetings.

10

Mediation with Adults in Schools

The Next Frontier

> Remember that not getting what you want is sometimes a wonderful stroke of luck.
>
> —Dalai Lama

How do adults get along in schools? First, let us discuss how faculty members relate to one another. We differ in age, birthplace, gender, ethnicity, sexual orientation, religion, political viewpoints, and the philosophical leanings and values we obtained in our training. (It is astonishing how many ways there are to argue about reading instruction!) Our socioeconomic backgrounds are diverse, and we each have unique interests, hobbies, and communication styles. Faculty members are also divided based on their subject areas; the ages of their students; whether they focus on general or special education; and whether they are involved in extracurricular activities that include sports, music, service, scholastic organizations, and the arts.

With such diverse backgrounds and daily activities, misunderstandings and resentments can spring up. For example, the structure of a counselor's day looks very different from a teacher's day. ("What do those counselors do all day?") What about the perceptions of who is staying late, who is working the hardest, and who has the most paperwork? ("Gee, it must be nice to roll out of here at 3:00!") Sometimes, conflicts occur when administrators are perceived as having favorites; depending on the administrator, perks can be given out in ways that lack transparency or fairness:

- "Of course Sarah got to go to the conference!"

- "Isn't it interesting to see who gets the classroom with the windows?"

- "Have you noticed who does not serve lunch duty?"

Some schools have strong unions to help balance power, and there is no doubt that contract negotiation time creates tension: "Until we get that contract signed...[fill in the blank]."

In addition to their student-centered duties, educators may also be expected to participate in faculty; staff development; department; IEP; 504 accommodation plan; and Tier I, II, or III team meetings. Also, many educators participate in what DuFour and Eaker (1998) called professional learning communities (PLCs). According to the authors, the characteristics of PLCs include

- A shared mission, vision, and values

- Collective inquiry

- Collaborative teams

- Action orientation and experimentation

- Continuous improvement

- Results orientation (pp. 25–29)

In PLCs, educators engage in structured meetings to collaboratively examine what students are learning, how effectively they are learning, and what changes will improve learning. Ubben, Hughes, and Norris (2011) correctly pointed out, however, that learning communities do not evolve until a strong base of community exists that includes a sense of support, security, and friendship. They note that a "major mistake made in many schools today is attempting to institute learning teams without paying careful attention to the underlying foundation for collaboration" (pp. 25–26).

Over the course of my career in six school districts in two states, I know that many administrators forgo team-building activities and give priority to the more pressing tasks at hand. Some faculty members are reluctant to engage in team-building activities and deride them as being touchy feely or a waste of time. More likely, team-building activities or retreats are bypassed simply due to a lack of time. Most school faculty, department, or team meetings occur on a weekly or monthly basis, and there is insufficient time to fully discuss all agenda items. If a meeting is scheduled after a high-energy day with students (i.e., every day), hunger and fatigue set in, and educators are not always eager to engage in meetings. (Advice for anyone conducting an after-school meeting: Bring snacks!) Many school districts have late start days to provide 1 hour per week for professional learning team meetings. Timing matters, and people are typically fresher in the morning and less likely to be thinking, "Can somebody please just tell us what we need to do so we can get out of here?" Unfortunately, even under the best of conditions, when adults behave in a courteous and professional manner, meetings do not always serve as a forum for productivity, learning, and collaboration. In fact, they may even become a source of further conflict and tension among adults.

Problematic adult relationships can, in some cases, result in aggressive behaviors such as blunt or rude remarks. Most educators know better than to engage in an outright verbal confrontation and would not allow themselves to act unprofessionally. These same educators, however, may not hesitate to use a one-line statement to express their dissatisfaction:

- "I'd like to see that happen."

- "Is that going to change in our lifetimes?"

- "Gee. . .big surprise there. . ."

More often, adults in staff meetings express negative emotion through passive-aggressive behavior. People exhibiting passive-aggressive behavior do not reveal their true feelings or opinions in a direct and understandable way. Instead, they convey dissatisfaction, anger, or resentment through their actions, such as showing up late to meetings or not attending at all. During the meeting, they engage in multitasking, such as grading papers or using cell phones. Despite the invitation to offer their ideas, these individuals withhold their input until the meeting is over, whereupon they freely give their reactions to selected peers in a hallway caucus. Faculty members typically become frustrated when their colleagues employ passive-aggressive tactics:

- "Ms. Lambert just doesn't pull her weight!"

- "Guess who was late again!"

- "Of course Keenan didn't speak. Jeff was in the room!"

Mildly aggressive and passive aggressive behaviors, both those exhibited in occasional meetings and day-to-day in the school building, are rarely challenged or effectively addressed. Grudges may be kept for years, and some educators, even those in the same department, may refuse to speak to each other. Similar to a middle school playground, teams are formed, and loyalties are mapped out.

And in the end, it is the students who lose out: Adults in conflict are not happy people, so school climate is tainted by negativity and cynicism. The lack of teamwork stalls growth as well as the introduction of new initiatives. The business world has, for decades, hired organizational psychologists and other behavioral specialists to promote improved teamwork and enhance productivity among employees. Although public school leaders do their part to address disgruntled employees, I have not observed the formal use of adult mediation in public schools to improve educators' working relationships.

I would like to change this. I believe that adult mediation in schools would be useful, and I speak from personal experience.

TWO EYE-OPENING MEDIATIONS: MR. B AND MR. G

On two occasions, I participated in mediations with another faculty member, and in both cases, the relationships vastly improved. The first mediation took place in a diverse, economically disadvantaged high school in California. By then, I had around 7 years of school psychologist experience and was fairly secure in my skills. Having grown up in Los Angeles in the late 1960s and early 1970s, I had always attended public schools and thought I was an ideal candidate to work in an inner-city school because I had a good heart, an open mind, and "not a bit of prejudice." I now cringe at my naiveté and ignorance.

My conflict was with a young, extremely talented African-American male administrator who handled discipline. Let us call him Mr. B. Mr. B's public speaking at school assemblies was inspirational, and I admired his way of connecting with students. I wanted him to like me and see me as an ally. I wanted him to trust me to do effective work with students because I knew early on that if students were misbehaving, there may be root causes that could be addressed with social-emotional support and counseling. I worked hard at trying to build a rapport with Mr. B, but he remained formal and cold with me. One day, the tension in our relationship came to a head.

An African-American male student was confronted and arrested by a police officer in Mr. B's office. The student was cornered and terrified, and so he resisted arrest. A scuffle ensued as the police officer grabbed and handcuffed the teen. Mr. B came upon the police officer and student during the height of the confrontation. As the student was finally subdued and taken away, Mr. B was deeply shaken and upset.

My office was right next door. I did not know the student or have any background on the situation. I do not recall my involvement outside of a possible bystander role. Did I suggest that it was okay for Mr. B's office to be used? I do not recall. What I do know is that after the arrest of the student, Mr. B's attitude toward me became colder and more hostile.

I regret now reporting what went through my head. "It's discouraging and unfortunate that a student got arrested, but was this not a common occurrence in the life of a high school administrator? Why was Mr. B so shaken? And why was he mad at me? What did I do? Everybody else liked me—why not Mr. B?" As weeks went by, Mr. B's attitude toward me became nearly intolerable. It was as though I was invisible.

Fortunately, the high school had an active peer mediation program run by a talented community trainer. This was my first exposure to mediation, and as the trainer described it to me, it was not about peace and love and making the world a better place. The mediation program was to combat the lethal gang activity and shootings in the neighborhood. It was to save lives.

I discussed my relationship with Mr. B with the mediation trainer and asked if it were possible to hold a mediation between Mr. B and me. This had never been done in the school before, but I thought it could help thaw the now polar freeze between Mr. B and me. My motive in seeking the mediation was for Mr. B to finally learn more about who I was and what I felt and believed. I also hoped to better understand and know Mr. B. The mediator asked Mr. B if he would be willing to participate in a mediation with me, and fortunately, he agreed.

To say the mediation was an eye-opener for me is an understatement. During the meeting, I learned what the arrest of the student meant to Mr. B. In fact, it had traumatic resonance for him. This was the mid-1980s, and although I knew of concepts such as "police brutality," the actual experiences of many black males with police were unimaginable to me, a middle-class white female. Mr. B was courteous and forthcoming in the mediation. He explained that he assumed I was complicit in the arrest of the student in his office. I explained that I did not know what was going on and then expressed my own thoughts and reactions. The mediation served to neutralize the anger, unease, and discomfort in the working relationship and allowed us to move forward in a productive way.

In retrospect, I feel embarrassed by my initial insensitivity, self-focus, and the many ways I misread the situation with Mr. B. At the time, I would have rated pretty low on Bennett's (2004) Developmental Model of Intercultural Sensitivity. Bennett's stages provide a useful way to frame how we communicate and understand each other across cultural lines. There are six stages:

1. Denial: People in this stage do not notice or care to notice cultural differences. They experience their own culture, that is, "the patterns of beliefs, behaviors, and values. . .as unquestionably real or true" (p. 63). As such, members of other groups can be seen as less human, and, in extreme cases, "tolerated, exploited, or eliminated as necessary" (p. 63).

2. Defense: In this stage, people are more aware of cultural differences yet see their own culture as superior and worthy of defense, while using negative stereotypes to describe every other culture. People in this stage may adapt an us versus them mentality and complain about how the other acts. Bennett brings out a key feature: "Defense may be expressed by 'helping' non-dominant group members to succeed by assimilating them into the assumedly superior dominant culture" (p. 65).

3. Minimization: In this stage, people might say, "I don't see color." Or, "We are all humans, with the same wants and needs." People in this stage fail to fully identify their own cultural patterns—food, customs, communication style—or the privileges they may enjoy. "All people are essentially similar in ways that [are] explainable by my own cultural beliefs" (p. 68).

4. Acceptance: In this stage, people experience their culture as "just one of a number" and "equally human" (p. 69) among other cultures. They may have positive attitudes toward other cultures but lack the skills and depth to be culturally effective and appropriate.

5. Adaptation: In this stage, people are able to extend, rather than lose or replace, their own behavior and beliefs to include additional cultural

perspectives. "They are curious about cultural differences and actually eager to experience other cultures" (p. 71). They gain empathy and a broader understanding of others' perspectives.

6. Integration: In this stage, people have internalized multicultural viewpoints leading to presumably greater empathy and may move and live among different cultures.

In reconsidering my relationship with Mr. B, I grew to question my own thoughts and practices. Had I exhibited minimization by not viewing the arrest of the black male teen from any perspective other than my own, which was extremely limited? I was clueless as to how the arrest of the student could be traumatic and upsetting to Mr. B. Had I exhibited acceptance because despite my sincere respect of Mr. B, I had underestimated the differences in our life experiences and cultural perspective? I hope that through the decades, I have moved up the intercultural sensitivity scale. I do know that the mediation was a start and served to broaden my perspective and hopefully Mr. B's as well.

My second mediation was decades later, also in a high school setting. I thought a first-year counselor, who I will call Mr. G, had made a mistake by advising a student, "Troy," to enroll in a newly minted community college program that offered a GED (a high school equivalence certificate) rather than advising Troy to remain in high school to earn his diploma. I had known Troy for years and felt a high school environment was more fitting based on his maturity level. I also felt that a high school diploma would further Troy's goals more than a GED. As the veteran employee, I tried to be diplomatic with Mr. G, but I was intent on stopping Troy from taking Mr. G's advice. I believed that Mr. G did not fully understand what Troy would be forfeiting. Of course, Mr. G was angered by my actions. I could understand why and tried to communicate directly with Mr. G to explain my reasons, but it was clear that our relationship had suffered a major blow. As the weeks went by, the tension remained. I went about my business and largely ignored Mr. G, but things came to a head in a department meeting where he made some angry remarks directed at me.

Our working relationship needed repair, so I asked an assistant principal who had a positive relationship with each of us to allow us to meet in her office for a mediation. This meeting did not have any particular structure, but we each took a turn to tell our story. Mr. G and I could not be more different in every regard: background, interests, hobbies, age, religion, politics, and birthplace. The mediation revealed, however, that we shared a strong work ethic and deep commitment to students and that we meant no harm to each other. In fact, we were equally passionate in wishing to help Troy. The mediation allowed me to explain why I advocated so strongly for Troy to remain in high school and earn his diploma. Once I was able to fully explain myself, Mr. G understood me better as a person and realized the rationale behind my decisions. I also heard more background about his decisions, and they became completely understandable. The mediation allowed us to clear the air and move forward. What a relief to no longer carry the emotional burden of a sour relationship! It takes energy and effort to avoid someone and makes workplace encounters tense and unpleasant.

That mediation was nearly 10 years ago. I am still very different from Mr. G in all ways. However, I have found him to be honest, straightforward, and as caring about our students as he was at the time of the mediation. The mediation built trust between us, and it has allowed our working relationship to grow.

ADULT MEDIATIONS AT CENTENNIAL HIGH SCHOOL

Adult mediations at Centennial High School are uncharted territory and have not been piloted in a systematic way. In April 2014, an instructional coach asked me to attend a meeting of department leaders.

Instructional coach: I was wondering if you could come and give some pointers for handing conflict in the department—maybe how to mediate between two adults.

I was pleased to join the meeting of the nine leaders to explore whether teachers might be open to adult mediation. I started the meeting by asking the leaders to complete an anonymous survey about conflicts within their departments. I purposefully did not define *conflict* or place any positive or negative judgment on whether conflict was good or bad. The results of the survey confirmed some of my suspicions. I was not surprised that the majority of people reported the existence of intradepartmental conflict (Figure 10.1). As shown in Figure 10.2, there appeared to be nearly an even split on the duration of conflicts.

Figure 10.3 indicates that there was a nearly even split on whether the conflicts impeded team productivity. Professionalism often prevails when tasks need to be completed; however, enjoyment from working together can be greatly reduced.

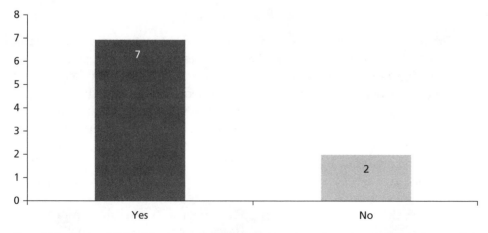

Figure 10.1. Centennial High School survey results: Are there members of your department who have conflicts with each other?

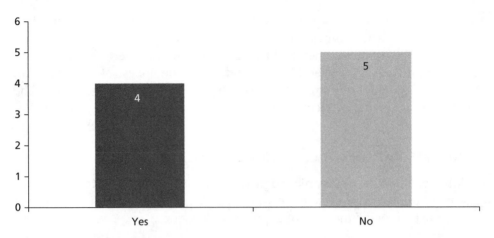

Figure 10.2.   Centennial High School survey results: Are some conflicts long standing?

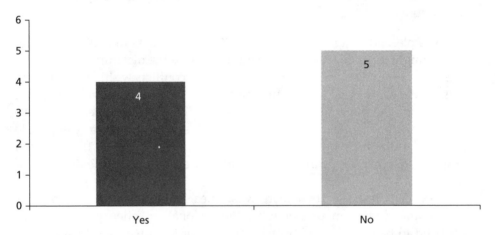

Figure 10.3.   Centennial High School survey results: Do conflicts have an impact on the productivity of your department as a team?

Figure 10.4 also shows a nearly even split on the question of whether or not conflicts had an impact on the mood and climate of department meetings. As shown in Figure 10.5, twice as many leaders reported that the conflicts did not lead to the creation of factions in the department. This, again, showed that a professional demeanor prevails despite the presence of interpersonal conflicts.

I found the unanimity of the response in Figure 10.6 to be very interesting by showing that the leaders did not see intradepartmental conflict as having an impact on students. But might the leaders be underestimating the impact on students? Are any of us at our best when we are upset or stressed by adult workplace relationships?

I spent the remaining portion of the meeting presenting information on the mediation format and enlisted two volunteers to show what an adult mediation entails. The scenario, chosen by the volunteers, was very plausible:

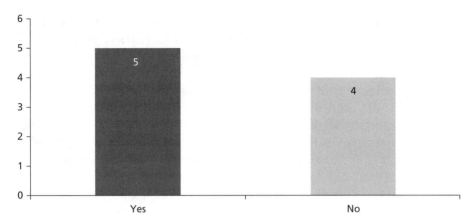

Figure 10.4. Centennial High School survey results: Do conflicts have an impact on the mood/climate of your department meetings?

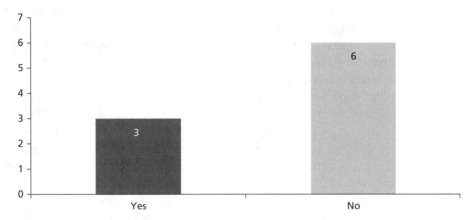

Figure 10.5. Centennial High School survey results: Do conflicts create divisiveness (i.e., alliances or factions) in your department?

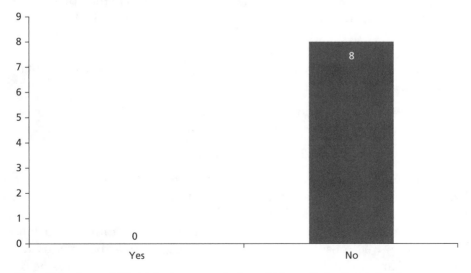

Figure 10.6. Centennial High School survey results: Do conflicts negatively affect students?

Given the space constraints in public schools, many teachers have to share classrooms. Ms. A is a new teacher with less than 3 years of experience. She is assigned to room 14 for several class periods. Ms. B is a veteran teacher who also teaches in room 14 and has a desk there. When Ms. A teaches, Ms. B sometimes remains at her desk in Room 14, speaks to the students in the room, or even disciplines them. Ms. A wonders why Ms. B does not go the department office to do her paperwork. Ms. B knows it is uncomfortable to have another teacher in the room when one is presenting a lesson. She is honestly not trying to meddle. She just cannot pack up fast enough to exit when the next class begins, and most of her grade and attendance data is on the computer screen in the classroom. It is much easier for her to stay there to finish her tasks.

During the mediation demonstration, the two teachers found middle ground and developed a reasonable plan to address the issues. During the debriefing period, we discussed how the teachers saw the wisdom of having an impartial third party in the role of mediator so that each person could adequately air their concerns. The structure of the mediation created a safe, constructive environment for effective problem solving. We also discussed that not all school-based adult conflicts are suitable for mediation, but when the situation involves hurt feelings, a misunderstanding, or a flare-up of angry behavior, a mediation can be worthwhile.

After our meeting and demonstration, I distributed an exit survey to the leaders. All surveys were returned but one. There was clear consensus, as shown in Figure 10.7, that adult mediations could be useful. As shown in Figure 10.8, there was nearly an even split on the leaders' desires to learn more about adult mediation.

As shown in Figure 10.9, there was clear indication that most leaders would not like to receive mediator training. We discussed whether or not it was advisable for department leaders to mediate relationships in their own departments. Many felt it was not an appropriate way to address conflict because:

- Some had a personal level of discomfort with conflict

- Some had friendships with some department members and would not feel impartial

- Some feared others would perceive favoritism because of their personal relationships with other department members

- Some did not want to add to their already busy schedule

Despite their discomfort, the resolution of conflicts between department members is a responsibility that sometimes falls to the department leader. Two leaders shared with the group that they were asked to hold meetings to help resolve department members' differences, and despite their initial reluctance, the outcomes were positive. Participants appreciated that their voices were heard and learned about the other person's perspective. Thus, addressing conflict using a third party to mediate can be effective and restorative.

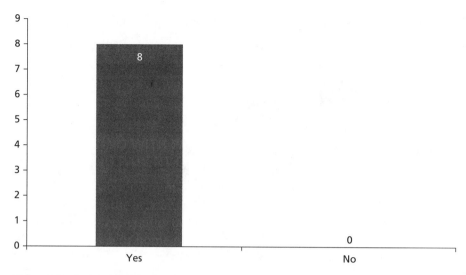

Figure 10.7. Centennial High School survey results: Do you believe that adult mediation could help resolve conflicts?

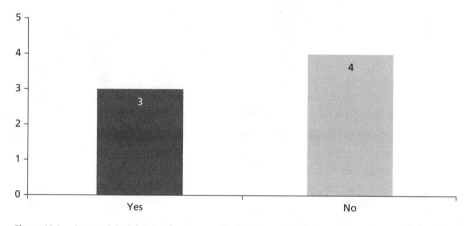

Figure 10.8. Centennial High School survey results: Would you like to learn more about mediation?

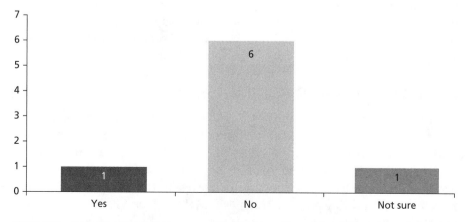

Figure 10.9. Centennial High School survey results: Would you like training to become a mediator?

THE ROLE OF PERSONALITY IN OUR APPROACH TO CONFLICT

There is no doubt that many people avoid conflict, especially in the workplace. We often hear the saying, "Choose your battles!" Others would rather give in or give up rather than stand up for their position: "I'm pretty mad, but what's the point of saying anything? It's just not worth it." Others are at ease with pushing for their position: "I believe too strongly in this to just let it go. I'm going to say something."

Most of us do all of the above depending on the situation. Many of us, however, lean in certain directions based on our personality, family, cultural background, and training. Engaging in a difficult conversation to resolve an adult conflict may feel natural to some and abhorrent to others.

Many educators have attended workshops to gain greater self-awareness about their reactions to situations and people. These workshops range from learning to identify your personality color to generational influences based on your year of birth, to your personality "type" using the Myers Briggs Type Indicator (MBTI; The Myers & Briggs Foundation, 2015). A quote from Isabel Briggs Myers on the website states, "When people differ, a knowledge of type lessens friction and eases strain. In addition, it reveals the value of differences. No one has to be good at everything" (The Myers & Briggs Foundation, 2015).

The aim of all of these instruments and trainings is to teach people to honor the validity and contributions of those who think, work, and feel differently. When considering implementing mediations, for example, many people may respond differently based on their personality types. For example, those who lean in the direction of being open to expressing emotion may be more comfortable with the idea of adult mediations in schools. Others who lean in the direction of avoiding conflict could feel too vulnerable revealing their needs and feelings. Thus, the introduction of adult mediation into schools must be approached gingerly and gradually, but there can be an important place for this technique among willing faculty members.

There is also a place for mediation among additional school staff members, including those who perform classroom aide, clerical, food, maintenance, and bus duties. A professor in my school psychology program taught us that the two most important people in a school are the secretary and the custodian as they are the ones who truly keep the school running.

MEDIATIONS AMONG NONCERTIFIED STAFF

Because of the success of the teacher–student mediation program at Centennial High School, I was asked to help mediate an entire department of noncertified employees: the food services staff. Conflicts had been simmering, and flare-ups had arisen. Some people had become sick from the stress of the workplace. Complaints were moving their way up the administrative hierarchy. When our building administrator, Mr. Maltbia, was asked to intervene, he sought my assistance.

Consider food service employees' demanding work in a public school. It is their job to feed hundreds of children, follow all health and safety guidelines, and have the food ready to serve on a very tight schedule. At a high school, the numbers of students fed could be in the thousands, with multiple lunch periods. Sometimes, the cafeteria at a high school may also cook for other schools, and the food is picked up for delivery. Each day, at a designated time, a bell rings, tables must be wiped down, and serving containers must be replenished. . .within minutes. There is heavy lifting as boxes of produce or frozen food are moved into the kitchen area, and trays of food are placed inside and outside of ovens or refrigerators.

Consider the kitchen area workspaces: There is the constant clanging of pots and pans being moved, dishwashing, and doors shutting and opening. Preparation areas are tight, ovens are hot, cutting areas may be cramped, and people may literally be bumping into each other. The way a kitchen is configured may also create spaces where people's backs are toward each other or small pods of two or three people are grouped together. Once students enter the cafeteria, there is the noise in the lunchroom to contend with, along with an even more hectic pace as workers hurry to feed the hungry children.

Now consider all the differences we discussed previously: age, birthplace, gender, ethnicity, sexual orientation, religion, political viewpoints, socioeconomic backgrounds, interests, hobbies, and communication styles. Layer on the physical demands of kitchen work and the hot, noisy, and cramped spaces within the kitchen. It is not hard to see that all of the misunderstandings and resentments that can be present among faculty members are just as prevalent among food service employees. The following fictitious dialogues serve as generic examples:

- "Wanda is throwing me dirty looks. . .again."

- "Why do we have to listen to Millie's music?"

Similar to faculty departments, some people may be friends outside of school, so cliques and favoritism can be perceived:

- "How come Lenore never has to peel potatoes?"

- "Those three are always on break together. I know they are talking about me."

In a kitchen, it is critical to have reliable teamwork and for all workers to do their part.

- "I almost didn't get the fries out today because Landon was 5 minutes late from break. . .again!"

- "Val is taking too long to wipe those tables. We need her at the register!"

Getting a large group in a room to talk is risky because tempers can flare, and people can walk out of the meeting before anything gets resolved. Prior to the actual mediation meeting, the administrator, Mr. Maltbia, spoke to each individual staff member. This was a critically important preliminary step because the staff members felt their concerns were being taken seriously and that someone in a position of power was listening to them. Mr. Maltbia communicated his support to each person, and this helped develop trust and rapport.

On the day of the mediation, we convened in a large group setting. I reviewed the rules of mediation and Mr. Maltbia's and my role as co-mediators. I then invited the employees to speak to us (in front of the entire group) about their concerns. Once people started relaying their stories, reactions were swift: "I can't believe he just said that. . .that is not what happened!" People who were close friends exchanged glances or words. Some people spoke out: "Oh. . .please!"

It is critical for a mediator to be in control of the meeting, particularly with emotions running high. The mediator must bring calm and slow down the tempo.

Mediator: Remember, each person will have a chance to speak, and right now we want to hear Laura's perspective.

Because there is safety in the structure of a mediation, once people are finally in that safe space, they may wish to speak directly to each other. In this mediation, we made a judgment call to allow each person to speak to one another—if the exchanges were constructive, it made sense. Once people started sharing, it immediately became clear which situations had been misunderstood.

Employee A: When I said "hi" to you, you just turned away.

Employee B: When was that?

Employee A: The Friday before the holiday.

Employee B: When I was at the sink washing carrots? I can't hear anything. I swear I did not hear you say hi to me, and I didn't mean to turn away from you.

This mediation was about people who felt hurt or offended. It was about clearing up misunderstandings. It was emotional. There were some tears.

The group mediation, which took only about 70 minutes, provided a safe venue to clear the air. Things that needed to be said were said. People who had not even looked at each other in months were now speaking. Some people who had been demonized became human again. People spoke honestly and from the heart. Some, who normally remained silent—because communication "just wasn't worth it"—were now speaking openly about their thoughts and feelings. Some even hugged and cried.

Employee A: I was mad at you. . .I had been mad at you all year because of. . . .

Employee B: I'm so glad I understand now. I don't dislike you. . . . We used to get along great. I miss talking with you.

The relief in the room was palpable. Workplace issues such as breaks, music, job responsibilities, and so forth were still to be sorted out, but the kitchen manager would be able to work more productively and collaboratively with the staff on these issues now that the tension had been broken.

Staff members learned a lot as a result of the mediation:

- Before the mediation, Josie might have said, "I can't be in two places at once! I'm tired of covering for Marnie when she gets a phone call."

- During the mediation, Josie learned that Marnie was on the phone because of a terminally ill family member. Now all the kitchen staff members were saying to Marnie, "Now we understand, and we're there for you."

If professional mediators or organizational psychologists are reading this book, they may think that steps were missed in the above process, or that such a meeting does not qualify as a genuine mediation. They may be correct. I do not claim to be an organizational psychologist, and this was my first mediation with such a large school group. What I do know is that public schools, with all the budget constraints, cannot provide funding for professional mediators or organizational psychologists to work with noncertified staff. The meeting just described took place using two personnel who already work in a school: an administrator and myself. That 70-minute meeting was a game changer for that department and completely worth our time and effort.

So far, I have discussed how mediation can be implemented between faculty members and among school support staff. Next, I discuss how to communicate and problem-solve with parents and propose how mediation could be useful in parent meetings.

COMMUNICATING WITH PARENTS
AND RESOLVING PARENT CONCERNS

When we speak about parents of public school students, we must consider their relationship with the academic institution. Some parents appear to "know the ropes" and feel very comfortable when they enter the school. They read all the literature that is sent home or posted online, attend events, and even volunteer. They understand that they have a voice, and that if they have concerns, someone in the school will address them. They function as stakeholders in the school community. These parents are also familiar with the school hierarchy and know that if their concerns are not met, they will be able to move up the chain of command, clear up to the superintendent.

What about parents who are not as comfortable interacting with the school? Perhaps they work during school hours and are unable to volunteer. Perhaps they do not speak English. Perhaps they have had bad experiences with schools, either in their childhood or with their own children. As Shields (2009) pointed out, parents with less clout and know-how (i.e., "social capital"; p. 59), "will experience more difficulty understanding the implicit norms, making sense of the institutional linguistic codes and jargon, and hence participating in the organization's decision making and policy-making processes" (p. 60). Educators often seek improved ways to open the lines of communication with all parents, including those with less know-how so that more voices may be heard. I also suggest that mediation can be an effective means to give voice to parents in a safe way.

Regardless of how involved parents may be in their child's school, all parents may be reluctant to express concerns, particularly about a teacher. They may feel that any complaint will make things harder for their child. These parents may call the principal.

Parent to principal: Please don't tell Ms. Wigg that I'm calling you, but my son reports that she is showing a lot of movies in class. . .I just thought you should know. Maybe you could do something about it in a way that is not traced to my son.

Some teacher unions require administrators to alert teachers of parent complaints and to redirect the parent back to the teacher:

Principal to parent: I know you have a number of concerns, Ms. Bowman, and I know Ms. Rossler will be willing to sit down with you to address them.

The following subsection lists a few simple tips I have garnered from parenting my own children and by observing parent and educator practices that lead to positive and productive involvement.

Tips for Parents

- Read everything that is sent home. It is usually pretty important. If something does not make sense, call the school to ask about it.

- Timing is everything, so address a problem before it gets worse. In a school year, this means in the first few weeks or months of a semester.

- For almost any concern, start with the teacher instead of the principal. It shows the teacher respect. There are always opportunities to add people to the mix.

- Make an appointment. Even though this sounds formal and businesslike, surprise or drop-in conferences may blindside teachers. Appointments allow teachers to gather information, including current attendance, grades, and make-up work, which is useful in the meeting.

- To make an appointment, call the teacher or send an email. Keep the message brief and neutral because the tone of email can often be misconstrued. State your own availability. For example, "Hi, Ms. Egan. I'm Desmond's mother. Could we meet in person or speak on the phone about how Desmond is doing? I'm free on Tuesday and Thursdays after 2:00. Thank you very much."

- Once the conversation has begun, talk about what you would like to see and ask for help. For example, instead of saying, "Desmond hates coming to school" (which could be interpreted by a teacher as "Desmond hates coming to your class"), say, "I'd like to see Desmond happier about coming to school. Could we talk about that?" Or, instead of saying, "Desmond refuses to do any homework," say, "I'd like to see Desmond doing his homework. I was hoping to brainstorm with you about this." These statements might elicit more helpful responses from teachers. Although teachers may not have all the answers, they would be able to direct the parent appropriately.

Teacher: Yes, I'd like to see that, too. Can we put our heads together and come up with a way to help Desmond feel happier in school?

Teacher: Yes, homework completion is hard for students. We have resources that can help students with homework, plus I'm available after school. Do you think that would help?

By using an "I'd like to see" statement, there is no assignment of blame on the teacher. Teachers are human, and anytime any of us are blamed, we naturally come to our own defense, or even counter attack. Following is another example:

Parent: Aliyah says you never call on her.

Teacher: I'd like to call on Aliyah, but she is never in her seat long enough for me to do that. She gets up, wanders the class, and every time I've tried to call home, I can't seem to reach anyone.

Instead, witness how the teacher might respond to an "I'd like to see" statement:

Parent: I'd like to see Aliyah participate more in classroom discussions.

Teacher: Me, too. What are some of Aliyah's interests? I can work those topics into the lessons.

- Offer thanks to the teacher. Teachers are often underappreciated, and an acknowledgment of their hard work goes a long way. Here, I offer a personal example of how thanks and appreciation can be effective in parent–teacher meetings. I am as nervous about expressing a concern to a teacher as anyone. I once had a meeting with my daughter's math teacher. It was her freshman year of high school, and I requested the conference and said I would like to bring my daughter along. (I recommend that practice for secondary students, because the meeting is going to be about the students, and they may as well hear from the teacher firsthand.) I had never met the teacher, but as a good will gesture (and because the meeting was directly after school), I brought her an iced tea and a muffin. She was pleasantly surprised and appreciative, and this small gesture set a happier tone for the entire meeting. The teacher could not have been more accommodating. She turned to my daughter and said, "Tell me how you learn best." This meeting was well worth the time. As simplistic as it sounds, I am convinced that the muffin and iced tea completely changed the climate of that meeting.

In the following subsection, I offer tips for teachers and school staff to help promote positive interactions with parents.

Tips for Teachers and School Staff

- Create a welcoming environment for parents. This requires more than the placement of a welcome sign at the door. Parents deserve our smiles, courtesy, and patience, as they are not as comfortable in schools as educators and may be anxious about the problem their child is experiencing. Provide prompt service, as they may be taking time from their workplace to attend to something at the school.

- Reply to parent phone calls and emails promptly—even if it is to say that you do not have an answer for a question just yet. Follow up on what you say you are going to do.

- Be sure that parents are informed about how the classroom and school operate. It is easy to forget that parents may not know about the school calendar, grading policies, or roles and responsibilities of various staff members. They may be unfamiliar with school rules, regulations, and laws. They may also not know about who has decision-making power and what power they have as parents.

- Many schools have websites or newsletters (including translated material for emerging English speakers), yet written information is not as clear as having a staff member provide additional details. Some schools have parent liaison staff available for this purpose; however, anyone working in a school should be able to say, "Let me see if I can help you with that. If I don't know the answer, I will find someone who does."

- Inform parents about any resources that are available to help their child. For example, show a parent how to obtain services related to health, academic, and/or social-emotional support; after-school tutoring; student vocational opportunities; college planning; extra-curricular opportunities; and community agencies that support youth.

- Provide a direct linkage that connects parents with in- or out-of-school resources whenever possible: "When we are done speaking, I will take you to meet our athletic director, and she will answer your questions about the swimming program." Or, "How about if I send an email to our speech-language pathologist and ask her to contact you? I'll copy you on it as well, so you have her email address. If you have a minute, I can also see if she is available to meet you right now."

- Not all parents are available to attend planned school events, such as a school open house. Do not assume that a parent does not care. Instead, reach out in other ways and personally invite parents to visit the school at a more convenient time. Also schedule events on a flexible schedule (e.g., providing morning and evening options for parent–teacher conferences). A personal outreach phone call, email, or text message is also helpful: "Hi, Mr. Yamamoto. I didn't see you at yesterday's open house but would like the chance to meet you. Is there another time we could meet or speak on the phone about Ryan? I have good news to share!"

- Sometimes during a brief phone call with a parent, it becomes clear that a longer conversation could be helpful. Say, "You have a lot of good questions! Would you like to schedule a time to speak in person?" Even if parents decline, they will appreciate the offer of your time and attention.

PARENT–EDUCATOR MEDIATIONS

Sometimes, conflicts arise in parent–educator conversations, and administrators become involved. Most principals are the ad hoc mediators when a parent and a teacher have a dispute. Principals are experienced in running such meetings, and although they may not follow a structured mediation format, one hopes that such meetings clear the air, clarify perspectives, and help the two parties effectively move forward. Depending on the school district, a teacher may opt to bring a union representative to a parent conference. This could occur in circumstances in which the teacher feels wrongfully accused or mistrustful of the administrator. The union representative witnesses the meeting and provides support and feedback to the teacher. One can hope that these parent–teacher meetings would resolve the conflict, but there is the chance that the tension between the teacher and parent might linger for the remainder of the semester or year. The parents might worry about the impact on their child (e.g.,"Ms. Woo and I are still out of sync. Is she going to take it out on Les?"). Because the teacher has an independent relationship with the student, there would not necessarily be any impact, but there is still that potential. The impact might not be in the form of direct retribution, but the teacher could feel more self-conscious working with the student as a result of the tension and parental mistrust. As such, I propose that schools also consider the use of mediation when there is misunderstanding or conflict in a parent–teacher relationship.

Can an administrator play the role of mediator? My answer is both yes and no. Yes, if the administrator has earned the trust of all parties and is perceived as impartial and willing to give equal attention and validation to each party's perspective. No, if the administrator has exhibited bias toward one side or the other. Another consideration might be to have an outside mediator conduct a parent–teacher mediation.

The following example demonstrates how a mediation format could be applied to a parent–teacher meeting with Ms. Bond, a fourth-grade elementary school teacher who has been teaching for 2 years, and Ms. Diller, a student named Jimmy's mother. It is early November, just 2½ months into the school year.

I. Welcome with a Smile

Mediator: Welcome. I want to thank you both for being here. I think mediation is a great tool to help people communicate and understand each other's perspective, and I'm very pleased that you are willing to give it a try.

II. Review the Rules and Principles of Mediation

Mediator: The format for this mediation is really simple: I am going to ask each of you to tell me what brought us here today. I ask that you speak only to me. When one person is speaking, the other person can sit back and listen. I will take notes and ask clarifying questions. I will then ask the other person the same question. It's amazing how much people learn that they did not know before. I will then summarize everything I've heard and ask what you would like to see happen. Then I invite you to speak directly to each other to develop a plan to move forward. The rules of mediation are that only one person speaks at a time. There are no interruptions, put-downs, or nonverbal reactions such as eye rolling.

There are four principles of mediation:

- I am impartial. I do not take sides.

- What we talk about is confidential.

- We are all here voluntarily, correct?

- And the last principle is called self-determination. That means that what you discuss and plan today is up to you. As a mediator, I am not here to guide you or influence you. Are there any questions?

III. Identify the Issues

The mediator uses the same techniques discussed in Chapters 4–7: reflective, nonjudgmental listening skills, pausing to summarize and ask clarifying questions, and highlighting the feelings and perspectives of each person. What is the story? What are the details? When and how did things go awry? Perhaps a misunderstanding or misstep will be identified. Perhaps explanations (or even apologies) will be offered. Perhaps, the identified problem will not be the issue at all, and the conflict is fueled by something different. Each person's point of view will be fully expressed and validated. The meeting will not be about identifying who was right and who was wrong or about assigning blame. The mediator will infuse the meeting with thanks and praise. The mediator may use humor and brief anecdotes to break the tension. The mediator will also mine for gold to identify any positive regard that exists between the teacher and the parent. If participants take responsibility for any mistakes or offer an apology, the mediator will praise and acknowledge them for doing so.

Ms. Diller: Well, I guess I can go first. I'm here because I really feel like Ms. Bond dislikes my son, Jimmy, and it makes him not want to go to school.

Mediator: Okay, I'm hearing you say that you feel like the teacher, Ms. Bond, dislikes Jimmy, and it has started to make him not want to go to school. When did you start feeling this way?

Ms. Diller: Well, I didn't feel that way at first. Things were going smoothly the first month of school, but soon after, Jimmy started coming home and saying, "My teacher hates me."

Mediator: Okay, so things went smoothly for the first month, and shortly thereafter, Jimmy started coming home saying that the teacher hated him. How did you feel about that?

Ms. Diller: I felt really upset, worried, and confused. I emailed Ms. Bond immediately and wrote, "Something is going on in that class that is harmful to my child!"

Mediator: Okay, so you were very upset, worried, and confused, and you sent a message to the teacher to find out what was going on. Your email said that something was going on in class that is harmful to your child.

Ms. Diller: Well, I can say that my note was written in the heat of the moment, and, to hear you say it now, it does sound accusatory. In any event, I didn't hear back from Ms. Bond that day, and that made me even more upset.

Mediator: Okay. As you are thinking about your note now, you are starting to realize that it had an accusatory tone. It sounds like you did not think about that at the time, though, and you became more upset when Ms. Bond didn't contact you the same day.

Ms. Diller: Yes. And things seemed to go downhill from there. I was called into a parent–teacher conference that included the principal!

Mediator: So you are saying that things went downhill after that, and you had a meeting with Ms. Bond and the principal. Tell me more.

Ms. Diller: Well, basically they reviewed the many ways Jimmy had violated classroom rules. He's always out of seat, he talks to his neighbors, and he doesn't do his work. Frankly, I felt a little beat up in the meeting. . .and overwhelmed. I have taken away Jimmy's privileges at home. What more am I supposed to do?

Mediator: Okay, you are describing the meeting you had with Ms. Bond and the principal, where you were informed of the many things Jimmy was doing in class that were in violation of the classroom rules. That left you feeling beat up and overwhelmed. You said you are already taking away his privileges at home and you don't know what else you can do.

Ms. Diller: Yes. After that meeting, I went home and cried.

Mediator: You have described many strong emotions you have felt: upset, worried, confused, beat up, and overwhelmed. From your tone of voice, I sense that you are still feeling those emotions now.

Ms. Diller: Yes, and I have done a bad job of hiding those feelings from Jimmy. He sees my frustration, and every day when he comes home, I ask him if it was a better day.

Mediator: So Jimmy sees your frustration, and you talk with him every day after school. How do you think Jimmy feels when he sees you upset?

Ms. Diller: Honestly, Jimmy just gets angrier at Ms. Bond, and I'm sorry to say this, but he says he hates her.

Mediator: Okay. Please let me just pause here and summarize what I have heard so far. You said that Jimmy told you that Ms. Bond hated him and he didn't want to go to school. You felt upset, worried, and confused and sent a note to the teacher. You now realize the note sounded accusatory. You didn't hear back from Ms. Bond. Then you attended a conference with Ms. Bond and the principal. They listed the ways Jimmy violates classroom rules. You left the meeting feeling overwhelmed, and when you got home, you just cried. Now, when you and Jimmy talk after school, it is still pretty emotional, and Jimmy says he hates Ms. Bond. You had started this mediation by saying that the first month of school went smoothly. Let's go back to that for a minute. I'd like to understand, in more detail what went well during that month. [Mining for gold.]

Ms. Diller: Jimmy was happy to be in Ms. Bond's class! He came home and told me about the turtles, and the math contests. He was excited.

Mediator: So Jimmy was happy to be in Ms. Bond's class and excited about the turtles and math contests. Does he have special interests in those two things? [The mediator asks about Jimmy's interests in order to shift the tone and climate of the meeting. This allows the mother to relax, elaborate on a more pleasant subject, and share information about her son's interests that the teacher may not know.]

Ms. Diller: Yes, I'm sure he has told Ms. Bond that he has two turtles at home. He has always been a bit of a math nerd. He loves showing off his knowledge of multiplication tables!

Mediator: Oh, great! Anything else that was positive about that first month of school?

Ms. Diller: Well, I felt good about Jimmy being in Ms. Bond's class. I went to the school's open house and saw that her room was cheerful and bright, and she really seems to be organized and caring. It seemed like that first month Jimmy came home proud of his work in the class. I know he raises his hand a lot and loves to be called on, especially when they are doing math, so he was feeling really good because Ms. Bond always called on him. I think he likes that attention and he loves to shine.

Mediator: Wow! It sounds like you had a very positive impression of Ms. Bond. At the open house you found her class to be bright and cheerful, and you liked that Ms. Bond seemed organized and caring about her students. Jimmy, too, was enthusiastic about the turtles and math contests. You mentioned that he has turtles at home and loves to show off his math skills. He seemed really happy that Ms. Bond frequently called on him during math lessons. Now, I'm trying to understand what caused the shift after that first month. . .was there anything that happened that you are aware of that changed Jimmy's feelings about the class or Ms. Bond? [The mediator seeks specific details to understand what happened to shift this relationship in a negative direction.]

Ms. Diller: Well, he was really mad because Ms. Bond stopped calling on him during math lessons, and someone else was assigned the task of feeding the turtles. Of course, I told him that Ms. Bond probably needed to give other students a turn. It seems like he has held a grudge ever since.

Mediator: So you saw a real shift around the time that Ms. Bond stopped calling on Jimmy during the math lessons, and when it was somebody else's turn to feed the turtles?

Ms. Diller: Yes, but I only realized that in retrospect. At the time, I hadn't put two and two together, so I thought something bad had happened, and that's when I sent the email.

Mediator: Oh, so it took a bit of time before you realized that Jimmy's shift in attitude toward Ms. Bond wasn't because of a bad event but because she was no longer calling on him to feed the turtles and to give math answers.

Ms. Diller: Yes, and I just want to say that I'm kind of embarrassed now. I think I really overreacted, and I could see if Ms. Bond thought my email was rude or accusatory. I apologize for that.

Mediator: Well, apologies are never required in mediations, but when people take responsibility and offer an apology, it is often appreciated. And, good grief, when it comes to standing up to protect our children. . .well, I won't tell you the embarrassing things I have done! [Humor to break tension.]

Ms. Diller: Thank you. Jimmy is my only child, so I'm still learning the ropes here.

Mediator: I completely understand! Is there anything else you'd like to say before I ask Ms. Bond to speak?

Ms. Diller: No thanks.

Mediator: Okay, and before I ask Ms. Bond to speak, I just want to thank you both for your willingness to give mediation a try. It takes courage, and I'm so glad you are here! [Thanks and praise.] Okay, Ms. Bond, please tell us your perspective on what brought us here today.

Ms. Bond: Well, I've learned a lot just by listening here. I just want to start by saying that I don't dislike Jimmy. In fact, I like him a lot and enjoy having him in class. He is very bright and full of enthusiasm. I could see, early on, that he likes positive attention and that he wanted to show me and his classmates his impressive math skills. He has also talked, frequently, about his turtles, and has shared with the class lots of information about their care. So, from the first day of school, I assigned Jimmy a special job with the turtles and called on him every day during our math lesson. But, Ms. Diller was absolutely right. I have 26 other students in the class, and I need to encourage everyone to participate. I think Jimmy might have felt the way a king feels who is deposed. I tried to be gradual about it and called on him occasionally in math, but I could see that he was not pleased. I also saw that the only way to bring back his enthusiasm was to give him back the turtle job and call on him to participate in math as much as before, and that just wasn't possible. That was probably around the time when he started violating the classroom rules. I was frustrated, too.

Mediator: Okay, I'd like to summarize here a bit. Ms. Bond, you are saying that you like Jimmy a lot. He is bright and enthusiastic and you spotted early on that he had a lot to contribute to the class. You chose him to feed the turtles, and you also called on him frequently in class during the math lessons. You saw, however, that it was time for other students to participate. Other students were assigned turtle duties and called on during math lessons. You saw that Jimmy was upset and you described it as a king being deposed. You felt frustrated, too, because you knew that you couldn't provide Jimmy with what he had before. Am I getting this right?

Ms. Bond: Yes. And I want to say that I very much appreciate Ms. Diller's apology about the email, and of course, I accept the apology. This is my second year of teaching, and I do try to stay organized, create a cheerful environment, and to be caring and fair to all my students. When I got Ms. Diller's email, it hit me like a brick! I thought, "Wow, where did this come from? Doesn't she know that I care about Jimmy and all my students?" I would never do anything to cause him or any of my students any harm. [Ms. Bond appears emotional and near tears.] When I got that email suggesting that something harmful was happening in my class, I felt attacked and didn't know what to do. I went to the principal, and she suggested that we all meet. That's why the meeting was held. I also want to say that I always do try to respond to parent emails the same day, but I just couldn't for this one.

Mediator: So you are saying that you would never do anything to harm Jimmy or any other student in your class, so receiving the email felt like being hit with a brick. You said you appreciated and accepted Ms. Diller's apology. You also explained that because you felt attacked, you sought out the principal's advice, and that's why the meeting was held. You also said that you typically respond to parent emails the same day, but you couldn't for this one. Tell us more.

Ms. Bond: Well, I agree with Ms. Diller that the meeting with the principal felt tense. I guess I felt defensive, and at that time, I don't think any of us had completely realized what was going on with Jimmy and why his behavior had changed.

Ms. Diller: Can I speak for just a moment?

Mediator: Sure.

Ms. Diller: Well, there were other things going on with Jimmy outside of school. Just some stressors at home. I don't want to go into detail, but we were dealing with some issues that might have also caused Jimmy to act differently at school.

Mediator: Oh, well, thank you for letting us know some new information. I'm sorry to hear that you are having some difficulties at home. Later, in the mediation, when you and Ms. Bond are talking, maybe she can share information about resources that could be helpful. And I just want to take a minute to thank you and praise you both for being here in this meeting today. Your willingness to openly share your thoughts and feelings is really commendable. [Thanks and praise.]

Ms. Bond: I really appreciate that Ms. Diller has shared that with us. I'm so sorry, too, and we can definitely talk about school resources that we offer here.

Mediator: Ms. Bond, it sounded like Ms. Diller had a very positive impression from meeting you at the open house. Do you recall meeting her? [Mining for gold.]

Ms. Bond: Yes. When I met Ms. Diller at the open house, I could see how involved and committed she was in Jimmy's education. Believe me—teachers love it when parents are involved. I was looking forward to a positive relationship. I'm really hoping we can get that trust back.

Mediator: Thank you, Ms. Bond. Is there anything more you'd like to say?

Ms. Bond: No thanks.

IV. Summarize What the Teacher and Parent Have Said

The mediator provides an overall, humanizing summary that presents the teacher's and parent's points of view. The mediator also emphasizes the strengths and positive aspects of the relationship.

Mediator: At this time, I'd like to summarize what has been said. Well, it sounds like the school year got off to a positive start! Jimmy was excited to be in Ms. Bond's class, and when Ms. Diller met Ms. Bond at the open house, she liked the classroom environment and found Ms. Bond to be organized and caring. Ms. Bond quickly realized that Jimmy had two strong interests: turtles and math. He was assigned to care for the turtles and he loved showing his math knowledge during the math lessons. Soon, however, Ms. Bond knew that it was time for some of the other 26 students in the class to participate. She also started to see some classroom violations from Jimmy around that time, but didn't realize why. Meanwhile, Ms. Diller reported that Jimmy started saying that Ms. Bond hated him. Ms. Diller was upset and confused, and in the heat of the moment sent an email to Ms. Bond. Ms. Bond did not respond that day to the email, which upset Ms. Diller even more. Ms. Diller now feels embarrassed by the wording in the email and apologized to Ms. Bond. Ms. Bond said she appreciated the apology because she would never do anything to harm Jimmy or her other students. Ms. Bond explained that when she got the email she was upset, sought the advice of the principal, and a conference with all three was held. Both Ms. Bond and Ms. Diller felt that the meeting with the principal was tense. However, all the information that we now know was not known then. Ms. Diller told us today that her family was facing some difficulties that might have affected Jimmy's behavior in class. Also, we now know that Jimmy's reaction to no longer being. . .let's say. . .the "math king" or "turtle king" [said with affection and humor] affected him more than anyone realized at the time.

We heard many positive statements today. Ms. Bond said she liked Jimmy. He is bright and enthusiastic, and she enjoys having him in the class. Ms. Bond says she sees Ms. Diller as an involved parent, which is something that teachers really appreciate. Ms. Diller said that she was excited at the open house to see that Ms. Bond's class was cheerful and bright and that Ms. Bond was well organized and caring!

V. Identify Next Steps: What Does Each Person Want?

At this point in the mediation, each person will have expressed their full story and will have a better understanding of the other's position. Hopefully, good will, trust, and respect have been rekindled.

Mediator: At this point in the mediation, I would like to ask each of you what you would like to see happen. Anyone can go first.

Ms. Diller: Well, I can go first. I would like to restore the relationship with Jimmy and me and Ms. Bond that we had the first month of class!

Ms. Bond: That's exactly what I was going to say!

VI. Develop a Plan to Move Forward

The mediation principle of self-determination is in full force as the teacher and parent develop their plan. The mediator does not lead the discussion, nor is the mediator responsible for coming up with solutions.

Mediator: Great! It sounds like you each want to restore the positive relationship you had at the beginning of the school year. Now I would like you to speak directly to each other so you can develop a plan to move forward.

By this time in the mediation, an emotional shift has occurred, and participants will likely feel more understanding and compassion toward one another. The mediator listens and takes notes.

Ms. Bond: I would love to see Jimmy as happy and enthusiastic as he was the first month.

Ms. Diller: Me, too. I know he was affected by what was going on at home. Plus, he needs to learn that he doesn't always get to be the center of attention and get everything he wants when he wants it. We are working on that at home, too.

Ms. Bond: Well, we have a really nice school psychologist, and if you would like to talk with her, I could ask her to contact you.

Ms. Diller: Thanks. That would be great.

Ms. Bond: It really sounds like Jimmy feels good when he can sort of be in charge of something. As we were talking, I had an idea. I was thinking of starting a new unit called "Students as Teachers." The class would be divided into five groups of five students, and each day, one of the five students would "teach" a 5-minute lesson. I'm thinking that Jimmy would enjoy that role of teacher. . .particularly when we do math.

Ms. Diller: I think he would like that.

Ms. Bond: Please let me know of any other strong areas of interest for Jimmy. I'll also talk to some other teachers about ideas they have. I want Jimmy to be excited and motivated and to know that I appreciate what he has to offer.

Ms. Diller: Thank you so much. Well, Jimmy has started being interested in racecars. I don't know if you could work that into a science lesson! I will also get some advice on my end on how to show children that they can't always be in the spotlight.

Ms. Bond: I want to ask your advice on the best way for me to move forward with Jimmy. We still have some behavioral areas to address. Do you think he and I should have our own mediation? Or maybe the three of us could sit down?

Ms. Diller: I feel so much better after this meeting today. I will go home and talk to Jimmy, and let him know that you'd like to talk with him. Maybe if the two of you just talk that would be enough to help him believe that you care about him. I really believe that could improve his classroom behavior.

Ms. Bond: That is what I will do. I will talk with him tomorrow.

Ms. Diller: And I just want to say again how sorry I am about that email. I really learned a lesson about firing off an email in the heat of the moment.

Ms. Bond: Trust me, I have learned that lesson myself! And, thanks again.

VII. Conclude the Meeting with Thanks and Praise

Mediator: Thank you both for being here today. I took some notes while you were talking, and I'll write up your plan in an email and send it to you. If I can be of any help to you in the future, please let me know.

Figure 10.10 provides a sample follow-up email to Ms. Diller and Ms. Bond that details the plans made in the mediation.

After the conclusion of the mediation, the teacher and the parent will have exited the meeting with renewed optimism and positive emotions that

---

From: Ellen Braden

Sent: Tuesday, January 8, 4:00 p.m.

To: Amy Diller, Susan Bond

Subject: Follow-Up to Our Parent–Teacher Mediation

Dear Ms. Diller and Ms. Bond,

Thank you again for participating in the mediation. Here are the plans you developed:

1. Ms. Bond will ask the school psychologist to contact Ms. Diller.

2. Ms. Bond will think of ways for Jimmy to be in charge of something. It might be an ongoing student-as-teacher activity. Ms. Bond will consult with other teachers for additional ideas.

3. Ms. Diller said that Jimmy has a growing interest in racecars, and that perhaps Ms. Bond can work that into a science lesson.

4. Ms. Diller said she would seek advice on how to show children that they can't always be in the spotlight.

5. Ms. Diller will talk with Jimmy about the meeting with Ms. Bond. Ms. Bond will follow up with a meeting with Jimmy. There are still some behavioral issues that need to be addressed. Ms. Diller said that if Ms. Bond and Jimmy talk, that could be enough to help him believe he is cared about and that could also improve his classroom behavior.

Please share feedback below and note if you would like additional follow-up:

_____ Meeting to debrief about the mediation or discuss next steps

_____ Follow-up check-in: 1 week   2 weeks   quarterly   (please circle)

_____ Another mediation

Additional comments: _____

_____

_____

Thanks again,

Ms. Braden

Figure 10.10. Mediation Follow-Up Email for Ms. Diller and Ms. Bond.

will have a trickle-down effect on Jimmy. If Jimmy's mother is happy with his teacher, she will smile and ask positive questions about the class, rather than, "What happened in there today?" Jimmy's teacher will no longer be anxious in her dealings with Ms. Diller because they established trust and a caring rapport that will facilitate future communication.

For mediations involving parents and teachers of secondary-age students, once the conflicts are resolved and the slate is clear to make plans to move forward, it may be appropriate to invite the student to join the meeting. The student will see that the adults have worked things out, and the focus will return to how best to support the student's adjustment and achievement in the class.

Could dispute resolution among adults really be as easy and effective as the mediation between Ms. Diller and Ms. Bond? Not always. If disputes are not easily solved by the mediation technique, parents and teachers have recourse and other means at their disposal. However, I have been surprised, over and over, at how efficiently mediation clears up conflicts and reboots relationships like no other intervention that I have used.

SUMMARY

In this chapter, I have proposed that mediation become naturally embedded into the intervention toolbox available to adults in schools. I imagine that as much as schools have employees who serve on crisis teams that are dispatched to buildings when tragedy strikes, school districts could also have teams of impartial mediators to dispatch for mediations among faculty members, non-certified staff, and/or parents on an as-needed basis. Small misunderstandings and conflicts often snowball into bigger problems. Intervening early (and at virtually no cost) using mediation can vastly improve how a school feels and operates and have a positive impact on student behavior and learning.

Whether used to address teacher–student conflicts, conflicts between students, conflicts among school staff members, or conflicts between educators and parents, mediation can truly improve understanding and restore the respect in our schools. Mediation also models effective social, communication, and problem-solving skills so that participants see how to manage difficult conversations on their own. Of course, this intervention is not the end-all be-all solution for improving every relationship in our schools. As with all things human, there are associated challenges and imperfections. However, when mediation works, it is quick, easy, and immensely worthwhile.

Afterword

How wonderful it is that nobody need wait a single moment before starting to improve the world.

—Anne Frank

As I reflect on my nearly 30-year tenure as a school psychologist, my marriage, and my own experience as a parent of now adult children, I believe in some very simple truths:

- Whether you are speaking with a 2-year-old, an 82-year-old, or anyone in between…

- Whether you are speaking with someone who looks and lives like you or someone of a different gender, race, or culture…

- Whether you are speaking with a person challenged with a disability or someone with a genius level of ability…

- Whether you are speaking with a neurotypical individual or someone on the autism spectrum…

- Whether you are speaking with someone destitute or someone living with great wealth…

- Whether you are speaking with a school "drop-out" or someone of high educational achievement…

  - Everybody wants to be heard.
  - Everybody wants to be understood.
  - Everybody wants to be treated with dignity and respect.
  - Everybody wants to believe that someone cares about them.
  - Everybody needs reassurance.

These simple truths were further confirmed to me after watching a 2013 video with Oprah Winfrey. Winfrey shared her observations of the human experience from conducting more than 35,000 interviews with people ranging from convicted criminals to celebrities and world leaders. At the end of each interview she has conducted, Winfrey said that each person she spoke with, in one form or another, whispered or asked: "Did I do okay? How was that?" The interviewees wanted reassurance that what they said mattered. All people, Winfrey (2013) explained, want to be heard, validated, and know that they are making a meaningful difference in the world.

In my work conducting mediations in schools, I have repeatedly witnessed how, in even one meeting, the power of listening, understanding, and showing care bestows dignity and respect to participants and begins a healing process. I have especially seen how mediation fosters effective communication across racial lines. Mediation is a time-honored, internationally practiced process, and by now readers have learned that I deeply believe in its usefulness in schools to improve school climate and promote wellness.

Throughout this book, I have cited principles of mediation that include impartiality, confidentiality, voluntariness, self-determination, and mediator competency. By writing this book, I seek to uphold a final standard: that a mediator advances the practice of mediation by

1. Fostering diversity within the field of mediation

2. Striving to make mediation accessible to those who elect to use it, including providing services at a reduced rate or on a pro bono basis as appropriate

3. Participating in research when given the opportunity, including obtaining participant feedback when appropriate

4. Participating in outreach and education efforts to assist the public in developing an improved understanding of, and appreciation for, mediation

5. Assisting newer mediators through training, mentoring, and networking. (American Arbitration Association, American Bar Association, and Association for Conflict Resolution, 2005, p. 10)

The use of mediation is continuing to grow in our school, in our district, and by the people I have trained at professional conferences. Hopefully this book, and the materials in the Appendices, will provide ample instruction, tools, and forms to assist in making mediation a reality in your school. My plan for the next portion of my life includes spreading the word that mediation in schools is easy, efficient, has measurable benefits, and can be implemented with existing staff. I am available to share my enthusiasm in person—to provide workshops and/or consult with individuals and school districts. I also invite readers to contact me with questions, to continue research into the benefits of mediations in schools, and to share successful mediation strategies online.

Every school is full of students brimming with energy, hopes, and fears. Others have entrusted us with these children and expect the highest level of competency as we impart skills ranging from academics to how to safely navigate conflicts and emotional challenges. As a mother, I, too, entrusted others with my children. Whether dropping our daughters at the door of their preschool or at their universities, my hope was always the same: that someone would show them understanding, encouragement, and care, because even one person can have a huge impact on their emotional well-being. Part of the impetus for this book is to honor and thank the many educators in my own children's lives who showed them that kindness. I am deeply grateful to you.

Children and those who care for them deserve to be heard, validated, and respected. When individuals attend a mediation, they are showing a good faith effort, and that is the first step toward improving any relationship. We know that supportive, trusting educational environments improve student achievement. The heart of this book is that mediation can be one way to help us reach this goal.

A

Your Mediation Toolbox

Teacher–Student Mediation Request Form

Teacher–Student Mediation Invitation Form

Teacher–Student Mediation Follow-Up Email

Teacher–Student Mediation Teacher Feedback Survey

Teacher–Student Mediation Student Feedback Survey

Student Mediation Request Form

Student Mediation Contract #1

Student Mediation Contract #2

Student Mediation Contract #3

Teacher–Student Mediation Request Form

Student name: _____

Date of referral: _____

Teacher name: _____

Referring party: _____

Reason for request: _____

_____

_____

_____

_____

Who is asking for mediation? Please circle and/or provide name: _____

Administrator _____ Teacher _____ Counselor _____

Student _____ Parent _____ Other _____

Teacher is aware of request   Yes   No

Student is aware of request   Yes   No

Parent/guardian is aware of request   Yes   No

- -

The person conducting the mediation will complete this portion and return it to the referring party:

Name of mediator: _____

Date of mediation: _____

Additional information:

_____

_____

_____

_____

_____

Teacher–Student Mediation Invitation Form

Date: _____

Dear: _____ ,
        Teacher's name

I have been asked to do a voluntary teacher-student mediation with you and

_____ .
        Student's Name

Is this okay with you?   Yes   No   Not sure

If yes, please tell me when you are available for this meeting.

Dates: _____ Times: _____

If the answer is *No* or *Not sure*, please let me know if you would like to speak further or if you have questions about mediation.

Comments/questions: _____

_____

_____

_____

_____

_____

_____

_____

Thank you!

_____
        Mediator name

Teacher–Student Mediation Follow-Up Email

Dear:_____ ,
     Teacher's name

Please print this email and provide a copy for _____ .
                                                        Student's name

Thank you again for participating in the mediation. Here are the plans you developed:

1.

2.

3.

4.

Please share feedback below and note if you would like additional follow-up:

_____ Meeting to debrief about the mediation or discuss next steps

_____ Follow-up check-in: 1 week   2 weeks   quarterly   (please circle)

_____ Another mediation

Additional comments: _____

_____

_____

_____

_____

_____

_____

Thanks again,

_____
     Mediator

Teacher–Student Mediation Teacher Feedback Survey

_____
Your name

_____
Name of student

_____   _____
Subject   *Date of mediation*

Was this mediation helpful? _____

How did you feel coming into the mediation? _____

Did you say what you needed to say? _____

Did you feel that you were understood? _____

Did you feel you were treated with respect? _____

Did you learn more about the student's feelings and thoughts? _____

Do you believe the student learned more about your feelings and thoughts? _____

Will this mediation help you and the student? _____

Please explain why _____

_____

On a scale of 1–5, how would you rate this experience?

1	2	3	4	5
Very bad	Bad	Good	Very good	Excellent!

What kind of follow-up would you like to receive after a mediation?

_____ Email from mediator with summary of mediation agreements

_____ Meeting to debrief with mediator

_____ Follow-up email from mediator in: 1 week   2 weeks   quarterly   (please circle)

_____ Offer of additional mediations with the student

Additional comments: _____

_____

_____

Teacher–Student Mediation Student Feedback Survey

_____
Your name

_____
Name of teacher

_____   _____
Subject   Date of mediation

Was this mediation helpful? _____

How did you feel coming into the mediation? _____

Did you say what you needed to say? _____

Did you feel that you were understood? _____

Did you feel you were treated with respect?_____

Did you learn more about the teacher's feelings and thoughts? _____

Do you believe the teacher learned more about your feelings and thoughts? ____

Will this mediation help you and the teacher?_____

Please explain why _____

_____

_____

On a scale of 1–5, how would you rate this experience?

1	2	3	4	5
Very bad	Bad	Good	Very good	Excellent!

Additional comments: _____

_____

_____

_____

_____

_____

Student Mediation Request Form

Student "A" name:_____

                Grade _____ Date of referral: _____

Student "B" name:_____

                Grade _____ Referring party: _____

Reason for referral: _____

_____

_____

_____

_____

_____

Relevant background information:

_____ Student "A" is aware of request   _____ A's parent/guardian is aware of request

_____ Student "B" is aware of request   _____ B's parent/guardian is aware of request

- -

The person conducting the mediation will complete this portion:

Name of mediator: _____

Date of mediation: _____

Students developed and signed a no-harm contract: _____ yes _____ no

(Please attach contract.)

Additional follow-up: _____

Parent contact: _____

Additional contact with student A: _____

Additional contact with student B: _____

Contact with the following staff: _____

Mediator notes: _____

_____

Student Mediation Contract #1

I, _____ ,

and I, _____ ,

participated in a mediation today that resolved our conflict. I promise not to fight. If I become

angry at anything the other does, I will handle it peacefully and/or tell an appropriate adult, such

as _____

or _____ .

Student signature: _____

Student signature: _____

Adult mediator (witness): _____ Date: _____

Student Mediation Contract #2

I, _____ ,

and I, _____ ,

participated in a mediation today that resolved our conflict. I promise that I will not speak to or

about the other, in person or online. I will not ask anyone else to insult or fight the other, in

person or online. I will not touch (shove) or do any nonverbal behaviors (stares, pointing, laughing

at, looks) to the other that are disrespectful or negative. If there are any future conflicts, I will

handle it peacefully and/or tell an appropriate adult such as _____

or _____ .

Student signature: _____

Student signature: _____

Adult mediator (witness): _____ Date: _____

Student Mediation Contract #3

I, _____ ,

promise that I will not fight _____

at school or in the community. If I am physically attacked first, I will defend myself, but I will

not make threats in person, by text message, or on social media. I will also not ask anyone else

to insult or fight _____ in person or online. I will

not touch (shove) _____ or do any nonverbal

behaviors (stares, pointing, laughing at, looks) that are disrespectful or negative. I make this

promise because I care about my education and future and do not want to get suspended or

expelled. If there are any future conflicts, I will handle it peacefully and/or tell an appropriate

adult such as _____

or _____ .

Student signature: _____

Student signature: _____

Adult mediator (witness): _____ Date: _____

B

Tier II Intervention Guide

This appendix provides a comprehensive list of interventions from Centennial High School's Tier II program of supports during the 2011–2014 school years. Recall from Chapter 2 that Tier II interventions are generally intended for the 5%–10% of students that have not successfully responded to Tier I universal interventions and supports. Also included here is a blank Sample Intervention Tracking Tool form that can be modified to track multiple interventions.

Sample Intervention Tracking Tool

School name:

School year:

Months	Intervention 1		Intervention 2		Intervention 3		Intervention 4		Intervention 5		Intervention 6		Total intervention outcomes	
	Number of students participating	Number of students responding	Number of students participating	Number of students responding	Number of students participating	Number of students responding	Number of students participating	Number of students responding	Number of students participating	Number of students responding	Number of students participating	Number of students responding	Total number of participants	Total number of responders
August														
September														
October														
November														
December														
January														
February														
March														
April														
May														
June														
Total sum														
Total %														

From Schoonover, A. (2014). Tier 2 intervention tracking tool. Unpublished form; adapted by permission.
In *Restore the Respect: How to Mediate School Conflicts and Keep Students Learning* by Ondine Gross (2016, Paul H. Brookes Publishing Co., Inc.)

CENTENNIAL HIGH SCHOOL TIER II INTERVENTIONS 2011–2014

Teacher–Student Mediation

Led by: School Psychologist

Description: Mediation helps eliminate problems occurring in a specific classroom with a staff member.

- Mediator serves as a neutral (impartial) party.

- Participation is voluntary.

- Mutually agreed upon plan is created by the teacher and student to help decrease unwanted behavior.

Referral criteria: Three discipline referrals from the same teacher or upon request

Determining response: No disciplinary referrals from the same teacher after the mediation

Check-In/Check-Out (CICO)

Led by: School staff

Description: CICO is designed to help the student "connect" daily for a brief conversation with an adult in the building at the beginning and end of the day. Such conversations are to provide motivation and support by checking on the student's daily progress. Students meet briefly every morning with a staff member and receive a daily progress report that is returned to the same staff member at the end of the school day.

Referral criteria: Students are referred to CICO with:

- Two disciplinary referrals within a 4-week period (not including cell phone infractions)

- One suspension

- A failing grade in one or more classes

- Five or more unexcused absences within a 2-week period

- Two minor infraction referrals within a 4-week period

- Referral from freshman/sophomore team teachers

Exit criteria: Students are moved out of CICO if they do not meet the CICO entrance criteria during the first 4 weeks of participating in CICO.

Skill-Building Groups

Led by: School social worker

Description: There are four skill-building groups: Appropriate Communication, Conflict Resolution, Appropriate Interactions, and Character Counts.

Each skill-building group is 50 minutes long and is led by a social worker. Students develop a written plan to identify ways to improve the targeted behavior. Teachers get an email with a description of the student's plan and language the teacher can employ to reinforce the lessons learned in the skill-building group.

Referral criteria:

- Two disciplinary referrals for the same infraction within a 4-week period
- Three disciplinary referrals total within a 4-week period
- One suspension
- Two minor infraction referrals within a 2-week period

Response criteria: No disciplinary referrals for 4 weeks after the completion of the skill-building group. If the student receives another disciplinary referral for the same infraction, the student moves into an *intensive* skill-building group (discussed next).

Intensive Skill-Building Groups

Led by: School social worker

Description: Designed for students who have not been successful after one skill-building group, this activity provides a student with four 50-minute sessions focused on target behavior. The student develops a written plan that identifies ways to improve the targeted behavior. Teachers get an email with a description of the student's plan and language the teacher can employ to reinforce the lessons learned in the intensive skill-building group.

Referral criteria:

- Four disciplinary referrals within a 4-week period
- Two suspensions for the same infraction within a 4-week period

Response criteria: No disciplinary referrals for the same infraction within 4 weeks after the last session is completed.

Weekly Checkups

Led by: A counselor or an administrator

Description: The counselor or administrator meets with the student weekly to discuss grades in all classes. They discuss appropriate strategies for academic success

Referral criteria:

- Junior or senior student who is failing at least one required course for graduation

- Four or more fails on the weekly Academic Watch List

- Request by parent, administrator, or student services staff

Response criteria: The student is no longer failing any course.

SPARCS: Structured Psychotherapy for Adolescents Responding to Chronic Stress

Led by: Trained SPARCS facilitator (i.e., a community mental health counselor) and a school social worker (see sparcstraining.com)

Description: This is a 16-week small-group intervention for freshmen and sophomores who may have been impacted by past or ongoing trauma. The students meet during their lunch period so as not to disrupt their academic schedules, and lunch is provided. The students learn how to effectively connect with others, cope with life stressors, and develop awareness and meaning from life events. SPARCS was initiated at Centennial High School through a partnership with a community mental health clinic. Parental consents and releases of information forms were obtained to allow the school and mental health clinic to share information. Students and their families can access mental health support within the group and outside of school as needed.

Referral criteria:

- No response to at least two other Tier II interventions

- Freshman or sophomore

- Staff has completed a crisis intervention with this student, such as a threat assessment or a mental health referral for a student in crisis.

Determining response: A student's response to this intervention is determined on an individualized basis according to the student's attendance; disciplinary referrals; and grades prior to the group, midway through the group, and after the group is completed.

References

Adichie, C.N. (2009, October). *The danger of a single story* [video file]. Retrieved from http://www.ted.com/talks/chimamanda_adichie_the_danger_of_a_single_story/transcript?language=en

American Arbitration Association, American Bar Association, & Association for Conflict Resolution. (2005). *Model standards of conduct for mediators.* Retrieved from http://www.americanbar.org/content/dam/aba/migrated/dispute/documents/model_standards_conduct_april2007.authcheckdam.pdf

American Federation of Teachers. (2014). *Reclaiming the promise: A new path forward on school discipline practices.* Retrieved from http://www.aft.org/position/school-discipline

American Psychological Association Zero Tolerance Task Force. (2008). Are zero tolerance policies effective in the schools? An evidentiary review and recommendations. *American Psychologist, 63*(9), 856. Retrieved from http://www.apa.org/pubs/info/reports/zero-tolerance.pdf

Bass, J. (2010, January 12). AFT president unveils new approaches to teacher evaluation and labor-management relationships [Press release]. Retrieved from http://www.aft.org/press-release/aft-president-unveils-new-approaches-teacher-evaluation-and-labor-management

Bennett, M.J. (2004). Becoming interculturally competent. *Toward multiculturalism: A reader in multicultural education, 2,* 62–78. Retrieved from https://workstory.s3.amazonaws.com/assets/541825/DMIS_Model_Reading_original.pdf

Boccanfuso, C., & Kuhfeld, M. (2011). *Multiple responses, promising results: Evidence-based non-punitive alternatives to zero tolerance.* Retrieved from http://dx.doi.org/10.1037/e551982011-002

Bryk, A.S., & Schneider, B. (2002). *Trust in schools: A core resource for improvement.* New York, NY: Russell Sage Foundation.

Carnegie, D. (1981). *How to win friends & influence people.* New York, NY: Gallery Books.

Carr, E.G., Horner, R.H., Turnbull, A.P., McLaughlin, D.M., McAtee, M.L., Smith, C.E., & Doolabh, A. (1999). *Positive behavior support for people with developmental disabilities: A research synthesis.* Washington, DC: American Association on Mental Retardation.

Cates, G.L., Blum, C.H., & Swerdlik, M.E. (2011). *Effective RTI training and practices: Helping school and district teams improve academic performance and social behavior.* Champaign, IL: Research Press.

Center for Appropriate Dispute Resolution in Special Education. http://www.directionservice.org/cadre/DRprocesscomparison.cfm5

Cholewa, B., Goodman, R.D., West-Olatunji, C., & Amatea, E. (2014, February 4). A qualitative examination of the impact of culturally responsive educational practices on the psychological well-being of students of color. *Urban Review.* Retrieved from http://www.researchgate.net/profile/Rachael_Goodman/publication/260527540_A_Qualitative_Examination_of_the_Impact_of_Culturally_Responsive_Educational_Practices_on_the_Psychological_Well-Being_of_Students_of_Color/links/5424770f0cf238c6ea6ecb88.pdf

Coie, J.D., Miller-Johnson, S., & Bagwell, C. (2000). Prevention science. In *Handbook of developmental psychopathology* (pp. 93–112). New York, NY: Springer US.

Cowell, R. Personal communication with the author. 28 September 2014.

Danielson 2013 Rubric—Adapted to New York Department of Education Framework for Teaching Components. (2013). Retrieved from http://schools.nyc.gov/NR/rdonlyres/8A4A25F0-BCEE-4484-9311-B5BB7A51D7F1/0/TeacherEffectivenessProgram1314Rubric201308142.pdf

Danielson, C. (2013). *Framework for teaching.* Retrieved from: www.danielsongroup.org/framework

Danielson, C., & McGreal, T.L. (2000). *Teacher evaluation to enhance professional practice.* Alexandria, VA: Association for Supervision and Curriculum Development.

Dufour, R., & Eaker, R. (1998). *Professional learning communities at work.* Bloomington, IN: National Education Service.

Durlak, J.A., Weissberg, R.P., Dymnicki, A.B., Taylor, R.D., & Schellinger, K.B. (2011). The impact of enhancing students' social and emotional learning: A meta-analysis of school-based universal interventions. *Child Development, 82*(1), 405–432. Retrieved from http://www.wondergrovelearn.com/wp-content/uploads/2014/02/The_impact_of_enhancing_students_social_and_emotional_learning.pdf

Fisher, R., Ury, W., & Patton, B. (2011). *Getting to yes: Negotiating agreement without giving in* (3rd ed.). New York, NY: Penguin Books.

Fixsen, D.L., Naoom, S.F., Blasé, K.A., Friedman, R.M., & Wallace, F. (2005). *Implementation research: A synthesis of the literature.* Tampa, FL: University of South Florida, Louis de la Parte Florida Mental Health Institute, The National Implementation Research Network.

Gehlbach, H., Brinkworth, M.E., & Harris, A.D. (2011, April). *The promise of social perspective taking to facilitate teacher-student relationships.* Paper presented at the American Educational Research Association, New Orleans. Retrieved from http://files.eric.ed.gov/fulltext/ED525283.pdf

Goddard, R.D., Salloum, S.J., & Berebitsky, D. (2009). Trust as a mediator of the relationships between poverty, racial composition, and academic achievement: Evidence from Michigan's public elementary schools. *Educational Administration Quarterly, 45*(2), 292–311.

Goldblum, P., Espelage, D.L., Chu, J., & Bongar, B. (Eds.). (2014). *Youth suicide and bullying: Challenges and strategies for prevention and intervention.* Oxford, United Kingdom: Oxford University Press.

Goleman, D. (1995). *Emotional intelligence.* New York, NY: Random House.

Gottfredson, D.C. (1997). School-based crime prevention. In L.W. Sherman, D. Gottfredson, J. MacKenzie, P. Eck, P. Reuter, & S. Bushway (Eds.), *Preventing crime: What works, what doesn't, what's promising. A report to the United States Congress* (pp. 1–84). Washington, DC: U.S. Department of Justice, Office of Justice Programs. Retrieved from: http://www.rolim.com.br/2002/_pdfs/ing.pdf

Greenberg, M.T., Weissberg, R.P., O'Brien, M.T., Zins, J.E., Fredericks, L., Resnik, H., & Elias, M.J. (2003). Enhancing school-based prevention and youth development through coordinated social, emotional, and academic learning. *American Psychologist, 58,* 466–474.

Hazelden Foundation. (2015). *Recognizing bullying.* Retrieved from http://www.violencepreventionworks.org/public/recognizing_bullying.page.

Hughes, J.N. (2011). Longitudinal effects of teacher and student perceptions of teacher-student relationship qualities on academic adjustment. *The Elementary School Journal, 112*(1), 38.

Illinois Department of Healthcare and Family Services. (2003). Children's Mental Health Public Act 93-0495. Retrieved from https://www2.illinois.gov/hfs/MedicalProvider/sass/Pages/930495.aspx

Illinois State Board of Education. (n.d.). *Illinois Report Card 2013–2014: Centennial High School.* Retrieved from https://illinoisreportcard.com/School.aspx?schoolId=090100040260001

Illinois State Board of Education. (n.d.). *Performance Evaluation Reform Act (PERA) and Senate Bill 7.* Retrieved from: http://www.isbe.net/pera

Illinois State Board of Education. (2002). *2002 Illinois School Report Card: Centennial High School.* Retrieved from http://webprod.isbe.net/ereportcard/publicsite/getReport.aspx?year=2002&code=0901000400001_e.pdf

Individuals with Disabilities Education Improvement Act (IDEA) of 2004, PL 108-446, 20 U.S.C. §§ 1400 *et seq.*

Jensen, F.E., with Nutt, A.E. (2015). *The teenage brain.* New York, NY: HarperCollins.

Khadaroo, S.T. (2013). *Restorative justice: One high school's path to reducing suspensions by half.* Retrieved from: http://www.csmonitor.com/USA/Education/2013/0331/Restorative-justice-One-high-school-s-path-to-reducing-suspensions-by-half

Kirp, D.L. (2014). *Teaching is not a business.* Retrieved from http://www.nytimes.com/2014/08/17/opinion/sunday/teaching-is-not-a-business.html

Klotz, M.B. (2014). IDEA in practice: Federal guidance on school discipline practices: Halting the school-to-prison pipeline. *Communiqué, 42,* (6), 27.

Klotz, M.B., & Canter, A. (2006). *Response to intervention (RtI): A primer for parents.* National Association of School Psychologists. Retrieved from http://www.nasponline.org /resources-and-publications/resources/special-education/response-to-intervention-(rti)-a-primer-for-parents

Koomen, H.M.Y., Verschueren K., & Pianta, R.C. (2007). Assessing aspects of the teacher-child relationship: A critical ingredient of a practice-oriented psycho-diagnostic approach. *Educational and Child Psychology, 23,* 50–60.

Kull, R.M., Kosciw, J.G., & Greytak, E. (2015). *From statehouse to schoolhouse: Anti-bullying policy efforts in U.S. states and school districts. A report from the Gay, Lesbian & Straight Education Network.* Retrieved from http://www.glsen.org/sites/default/files/GLSEN%20-%20 From%20Statehouse%20to%20Schoolhouse%202015_0.pdf

Losen, D. J., & Skiba, R. J. (2010). *Suspended education: Urban middle schools in crisis.* Retrieved from: http://www.saferfoundation.org/files/documents/Suspended_Education.pdf

Maag, J.W. (2001). Rewarded by punishment: Reflections on the disuse of positive reinforcement in schools. *Exceptional Children, 67,* 173–186.

Marzano, R.J., Waters, T., & McNulty, B.A. (2005). *School leadership that works: From research to results.* Alexandria, VA: Association for Supervision and Curriculum Development.

Maslach, C., & Jackson, S.E. (1981). The measurement of experienced burnout. *Journal of Organizational Behavior, 2,* 99–113.

Maslach, C., Jackson, S.E., & Leiter, M.P. (1996). *Maslach burnout inventory manual* (3rd ed.). Palo Alto, CA: Consulting Psychologists Press.

Mayer, J.D., & Salovey, P. (1997). What is emotional intelligence? In P. Salovey & D.J. Sluyter (Eds.), *Emotional development and emotional intelligence* (pp. 3–31). New York, NY: Basic Books. Retrieved from http://www.unh.edu/emotional_intelligence/EI%20Assets /Reprints...EI%20Proper/EI1997MSWhatIsEI.pdf

McIntosh, K., Horner, R.H., & Sugai, G. (2009). Sustainability of systems-level evidence-based practices in schools: Current knowledge and future directions. In W. Sailor, G. Sugai, R.H. Horner, & G. Dunlap (Eds.), *Handbook of positive behavior support* (pp. 327–352). New York, NY: Springer.

Merrell, K.W., & Gueldner, B.A. (2010). *Social emotional learning in the classroom.* New York, NY: Guilford Press.

Miller, C.E., & Meyers, S.A. (2015). Disparities in school discipline practices for students with emotional and learning disabilities and autism. *Journal of Education and Human Development, 4*(1), 255–267.

Montague, M., & Rinaldi, C. (2001). Classroom dynamics and children at risk: Follow-up. *Learning Disability Quarterly, 24,* 75–83.

Murray, C., & Greenberg, M.T. (2001). Relationships with teachers and bonds with school: Social emotional adjustment correlates for children with and without disabilities. *Psychology in the Schools, 38*(1), 25–41.

Murray, C., & Pianta, R.C. (2007). The importance of teacher-student relationships for adolescents with high incidence disabilities. *Theory into Practice, 46*(2), 105–112.

Myers, I.B. (n.d.). The Myers & Briggs Foundation. Retrieved from: http://www.myersbriggs .org/myers-and-briggs-foundation/memorial-research-awards/

National Association of School Psychologists. (2010*). Model for comprehensive and integrated school psychological services.* Retrieved from www.nasponline.org/standards /2010standards/2_practicemodel.pdf

No Child Left Behind Act of 2001, PL 107-110, 115 Stat. 1425, 20 U.S.C. §§ 6301 *et seq.*

Oakland Unified School District. (2015). *Welcome to restorative justice.* Retrieved from http:// www.ousd.org/restorativejustice

Positive Behavioral Interventions & Supports. (n.d.). *PBIS frequently asked questions.* Retrieved from https://www.pbis.org/school/swpbis-for-beginners/pbis-faqs

Reducing Stereotype Threat. http://www.ReducingStereotypeThreat.Org

Rogers, C. (1980). *A way of being.* Boston, MA: Houghton Mifflin Company.

Rogers, C.A., & Roethlisberger, F.J. (1991). Barriers and gateways to communication. *Harvard Business Review.* Retrieved from https://hbr.org/1991/11/barriers-and-gateways-to-communication

Schoonover, A. (2014). Tier 2 tracking tool for Centennial High School. Unpublished form.

Shellenbarger, S. (2013, May 28). Just look me in the eye already. *The Wall Street Journal.* Retrieved from http://www.wsj.com/articles/SB10001424127887324809804578511290822228174

Shenfield, T. (2014). *How to react when your child is lying?* Retrieved from http://www.psy-ed.com/wpblog/how-to-react-when-your-child-is-lying/

Shields, C.M. (2009). *Courageous leadership for transforming schools: Democratizing practice.* Norwood, MA: Christopher-Gordon Publishers.

Skiba, R.J. (2000). *Zero tolerance, zero evidence: An analysis of school disciplinary practice.* (Report No. SRS2). Bloomington, IN: Indiana Education Policy Center. Retrieved from http://indiana.edu/~safeschl/ztze.pdf

Skiba, R.J., Michael, R.S., Nardo, A.C., & Peterson, R.L. (2002). The color of discipline: Sources of racial and gender disproportionality in school punishment. *The Urban Review, 34*(4), 317–342.

Skiba R.J., & Peterson, R. (1999). The dark side of zero tolerance: Can punishment lead to safe schools? *Phi Delta Kappan, 80,* 372–382.

Steele, C.M., & Aronson, J. (1995). Stereotype threat and the intellectual test performance of African Americans. *Journal of Personality and Social Psychology, 69*(5), 797.

Sugai, G., & Horner, R.H. (2009). Responsiveness-to-intervention and school-wide positive behavior supports: Integration of multi-tiered system approaches. *Exceptionality, 17,* 223–237. Retrieved from http://rtiandbehaviorprocessimprovementgroup.wikispaces.com/file/view/RTI+SWPBS+Sugai+Horner.pdf

Sugai, G., Horner, R.H., & McIntosh, K. (2008). Best practices in developing a broad-scale system of support for school-wide positive behavior support. In A. Thomas & J.P. Grimes (Eds.), *Best practices in school psychology V* (Vol. 3, pp. 765–780). Bethesda, MD: National Association of School Psychologists.

Sugai, G., & Simonsen, B. (2012). *Positive behavioral interventions and supports: History, defining features, and misconceptions.* Retrieved from http://www.pbis.org/common/cms/files/pbisresources/PBIS_revisited_June19r_2012.pdf

Ubben, G.C., Hughes, L.W., & Norris, C.J. (2011). *The principal: Creative leadership for excellence in schools.* New York, NY: Pearson.

U.S. Department of Education. (2014). *Guiding principles: A resource guide for improving school climate and discipline.* Retrieved from http://www2.ed.gov/policy/gen/guid/school-discipline/guiding-principles.pdf

U.S. Department of Education, Institute of Education Sciences. (n.d.). *What works clearinghouse.* Retrieved from http://ies.ed.gov/ncee/wwc/

Wang, M.T., Brinkworth, M.E., & Eccles, J.S. (2013). The moderation effect of teacher-student relationship on the association between adolescents' self-regulation ability, family conflict, and developmental problems. *Developmental Psychology, 49,* 690–705.

Weingarten, R. (2010). *A new path forward: Four approaches to quality teaching and better schools.* Retrieved from http://aft.3cdn.net/227d12e668432ca48e_twm6b90k1.pdf

Winfrey, O. (2013). *What Oprah has learned from her 25 years of interviews.* Retrieved from http://www.forbes.com/video/3122778163001/

Index

Page numbers followed by *f* and *t* indicate figures and tables, respectively.